Women
100 [illegible]

HARRIET MARTINEAU
ON WOMEN

Harriet Martineau in 1833
Reprinted from Martineau, *Autobiography*

HARRIET MARTINEAU
ON WOMEN

EDITED BY GAYLE GRAHAM YATES

Rutgers University Press
New Brunswick, New Jersey

The Douglass Series

On Women's Lives And The Meaning Of
Gender

LIBRARY OF CONGRESS CATALOGING IN PUBLICATION DATA

Martineau, Harriet, 1802–1876.
    Harriet Martineau on women.

    Bibliography: p.
    Includes index.
    1. Feminism—Great Britain—Addresses, essays, lec-
tures. 2. Feminism—Addresses, essays, lectures. I. Yates, Gayle
Graham, 1940–   . II. Title.
HQ1597.M375 1984   305.4′2   84′-4827
ISBN 0–8135–1057–0
ISBN 0–8135–1058–9 (pbk.)

To
Natasha and Stiles,
my daughter and son

I cannot enter upon the commonest order of pleas of all;—those which relate to the virtual influence of woman; her swaying the judgment and will of man through the heart; and so forth. One might as well try to dissect the morning mist.

—*Harriet Martineau*
SOCIETY IN AMERICA

CONTENTS

vii

CONTENTS

ILLUSTRATIONS

A Contemporary Opinion

Here is Miss Harriet in the full enjoyment of economical philosophy: her tea-things, her ink-bottle, her skillet, her scuttle, her chair, are all of the Utilitarian model; and the cat, on whom she bestows her kindest caresses, is a cat who has been trained to the utmost propriety of manners by that process of instructions which we should think the most efficient on all such occasions. There she sits cooking

". . . rows
Of chubby duodecimos;"

certain of applause from those whose praise is ruin, and of the regret of all who feel respect for the female sex, and sorrow for perverted talent, or, at least, industry; doomed to wither in the cold approbation of the political economists; and, after ghosting it about for their hour,

. . . thence
Be buried at the Row's expense."

Sketch of Martineau from *Fraser's Magazine*, November 1833
Reprinted from Webb, *Harriet Martineau*

PREFACE

This volume is the intellectual harvest of an idea planted in 1973. Having just finished my Ph.D. in American Studies, which involved analyzing the ideas of contemporary American feminism, I wanted my next project to be historical, to be about women, and to be suitable for an Americanist working in England. Professor Chadwich Hansen, then at the University of Minnesota, proposed that I study Harriet Martineau. When I left for England that summer, all I knew about Harriet Martineau's work on women came from *Society in America*, in which she wrote a chapter entitled "The Political Non-Existence of Women." Now a decade later I know a great deal more, have read massive amounts of what she wrote and what has been thought and written about her, and have lived with her hovering presence for months on end. Feminist scholarship has come of age in those years, a new biography of Martineau has been published, her autobiography and her novel *Deerbrook* have been reissued, a volume of her letters has been brought out, and I have changed, too, in what I wanted to know and do about Harriet Martineau. At first expecting merely to do a study of what Martineau wrote on women, I now feel compelled by what I found in her work to present her as an important antecedent to contemporary feminism through the publication of a collection of her own writings about women. This is a small collection; I could have filled three volumes and not have presented all that she wrote on women.

I owe a lot to many people for support, criticism, advice, and information that helped this book to be realized. My family (Wilson, Natasha, and Stiles) and I spent two of the happiest periods of our lives together in England when I was doing my research. We went to the Lake District as a family on the children's school holiday "to see where Harriet Martineau lived." (We recommend the lodging and food at the Rydal Lodge.) I jiggled alone over to Norwich on the pay train "to see Harriet Martineau's birthplace." (I went to the library instead of her house. I'll have to go back.) Wilson's very best Christmas gift to his wife was a 35-pence purchase from a London bookseller, a portrait of Harriet Martineau. With the English friends we made in Cambridge, we learned how to "muddle through" as a family in a foreign culture with both parents at work. Natasha and Stiles survived as wonderful teenagers who sometimes feel they gave their all for their mother's work and would do it again. Wilson is my best critic and best friend. I probably could have finished this book more quickly without them. I'm glad I didn't.

I have a long train of mentors who fed me intellectually over the years: Bond Fleming and Robert E. Bergmark, who taught me to think philosophically at Millsaps College; Ruth Winfield Love, who, although I dropped out of the seminary where she was the first woman professor, taught me that feeling and intellect need not be separate and insisted that I go on for a Ph.D.; David W. Noble, Mary Turpie, Clarke Chambers, and Mulford Q. Sibley, who transformed my tentative questions into scholarly commitment and who made a sport of getting my unorthodox dissertation on feminism, which they had encouraged me to undertake, through the graduate school. Noble, Chambers, and Sibley, after having been my teachers, gracefully became my colleagues when I was brought onto the faculty of the University of Minnesota, and they remain among the best support system a person can have.

Several proper Victorianists, historians and English professors have read parts of my material and given me helpful criticism and encouragement. I want to thank Florence Boos of the University of Iowa and Joseph Altholz and William Madden of the University of Minnesota for contributing their expertise in aid of this Americanist stepping into their field. Some of my Minnesota colleagues from American studies, history, and women's studies have read my material critically from their own special angles. I am grateful for hearings before the history department's Monday Club and before the Feminist Scholars' Colloquium. I wish especially to thank Margot Kriel, Jean Ward, Cheri Register, John Modell, John Howe, Edward M. Griffin, Paul Murphy, and Ann Pflaum for their critical reading of an earlier essay from this research.

The Graduate School of the University of Minnesota provided funds for a research fellowship in the summer of

1978 and for a research assistant in the summer of 1982. The
College of Liberal Arts provided money for typing. Librarians
at the University of Minnesota libraries have helped, particularly Sandra Allen, Shirley Stanley, and Marcia Pankake. Our
secretary in women's studies, Judy Treise, has often been
as much an editor as a typist, and I am deeply appreciative of
her conscientious and thorough help. My research assistant
in 1982, without whom I truly could not have done it, was
Rosalind Urbach Moss. Because of her, many a fact here is
more factual, many a sentence clearer, several items discovered and questions raised in time. Her well-ordered and quick
intelligence doubled my ability to meet my deadline.

At Cambridge University with which I was affiliated
while I did this research, I wish to thank the members of
my host college, Lucy Cavendish College, particularly Hilda
Davidson, who was my especial host as college vice-president.
The staff of the Cambridge University Library was greatly
helpful.

Editors at Rutgers University Press have been generous
and thorough. I thank Kenneth Arnold, Leslie Mitchner, and
Barbara Westergaard for their considerable investment of time,
resources, and painstaking care in seeing this book through to
its finish.

For use of materials in their libraries and their helpful-
ness, I thank the following: the Fawcett Library, City of London Polytechnic, especially librarian David Doughan; the
Colman and Rye Libraries of Local History in Norwich; the
library of Manchester College, Oxford University; the Rare
Books Library of Cornell University and its librarian Joan H.
Winterkorn; the National Library of Scotland, Edinburgh;
and the library of the Fitzwilliam Museum, Cambridge. For
permission to reproduce photographs and cartoons in their
possession, I thank R. W. Webb, the Boston Public Library,
the National Portrait Gallery in London, *Punch*, and the *Daily
News* Trust.

Sometimes this book has been a joy. Sometimes it has
been a chore. Responsibility for it is finally my own, but the
graciousness and help of these persons and institutions have
made it worthwhile.

CHRONOLOGY

1802	Harriet Martineau born at Norwich
1806	James Martineau born
1818	Sent to school in Bristol with Aunt Kentish, studied with Lant Carpenter, deafness appeared
1821	Published "Female Writers of Practical Divinity" in *Monthly Repository*
1829	Experienced family financial failure
1832–1833	Published and became famous for serial *Illustrations of Political Economy*
1832	Moved to London from Norwich
1834–1836	Traveled in America
1837	Published *Society in America*
1838	Published *Retrospect of Western Travel* and *How to Observe Morals and Manners*
1839	Published *The Guide to Service* and novel *Deerbrook*, traveled to Europe, became ill in Venice
1839–1844	Ill at Tynemouth
1841	Published *The Hour and the Man*
1844	Published *Life in the Sick-Room*, introduced to mesmerism, wrote "Letter on Mesmerism" for *Athenaeum*
1844–1846	Recovered, bought land and built house, The Knoll, near Ambleside
1845	Met Henry G. Atkinson
1846	Traveled in Egypt and Palestine

1848   Published *Eastern Life, Present and Past*

1849–1850   Published *A History of England during the Thirty Years' Peace*

1851   Translated Comte's *Positive Philosophy*, published with Atkinson *Letters on the Laws of Man's Nature and Development*

1852   Published *Letters from Ireland*, first work for the *Daily News*

1852–1869   Wrote for the *Daily News*

1855   Again became ill, believed herself dying, wrote autobiography and her obituary

1853–1857   Wrote editorials dealing with the Divorce and Matrimonial Causes Acts

1863   Wrote *Daily News* editorials opposing the Contagious Diseases Acts

1866   Signed petition to Parliament on woman's suffrage

1869–1871   Wrote actively for the ladies' campaign against the Contagious Diseases Acts

1876   Died at Ambleside

HARRIET MARTINEAU
ON WOMEN

Martineau's birthplace
Reprinted from Martineau, *Autobiography*

INTRODUCTION

Harriet Martineau was the most astute female politician in England through almost four decades of the mid-nineteenth century. She did her work as a writer, an investigative traveler, a correspondent, and an interpreter of a multitude of intellectual trends. In all the vast number of her works and interests she was ever conscious of being female. She knew that being a woman meant that she had to do whatever she did differently from a man. Early in 1832 she wrote in a letter to Francis Place from her native Norwich, "I wish I were in London, . . . I want to be doing something with the pen, since no other means of action in politics are in a woman's power."[1]

She was able to move to London within the year, for her monthly series of didactic fictional accounts of the ideas of the new economics, *Illustrations of Political Economy*, had made her instantly famous, and the income from the series made her self-supporting. She was to earn her living as a writer, her reputation as a radical economic, political, and social commentator, and her historical mark as a social scientist, current historian, and feminist. She is known today by scholars of American society through her keenly analytic work, *Society in America*, published in 1837 after a two-year journey in Jacksonian America. She is known by English people as the renowned progressive journalist and leader writer (editorialist) for the London *Daily News*, author of a history of a period through which she lived, *The History of England during the Thirty Years' Peace, 1816–1846*, translator into English of Auguste Comte's *Positive Philosophy*, and proponent of positivism and the social scientific method. In England she is even remembered locally as an amiable resident-householder of Ambleside in the Lake District, the informal educator of local workers through her winter series of instructive evening lectures and her personal lending

[1] Quoted in R. K. Webb, *Harriet Martineau* (New York: Columbia University Press, 1960), p. 114.

library. In this, as in all her work, she was the progressive, enlightening reformer, perpetually confident in the rightness of her truth. Her feminism, perhaps because it was part and parcel of the whole of her political philosophy, is not as well known as her other ideas. Yet she took a stand and commented on virtually every campaign regarding women in England and America of her day and addressed some women's issues that were not identified so clearly as such until the women's movements of the 1960s and 1970s.

Martineau's politics included a thoroughgoing attention to women. It was an essential part of her blend of radicalism, and it had emerged well before her declaration to Place a month before her thirtieth birthday in 1832 that she must act with her pen, as that was the only access to politics a woman had. Her feminist politics was to continue strong throughout her life. Sensitive to her own womanhood and the limitations it imposed on her, the entry to feminism for many a woman through several feminist generations, Martineau gradually turned this personal sensitivity to social ends until the rights of women and advocacy of women's causes became one of her lifelong major efforts. The first piece she ever published—at age nineteen—was on women: "Female Writers of Practical Divinity." In 1869, while an invalid confined to her home The Knoll at Ambleside, as her last public work she applied her mighty pen in support of the campaign by the Ladies' National Association for the Repeal of the Contagious Diseases Acts. This campaign was an organized effort by women to get Parliament to repeal a group of laws that they believed incriminated women indiscriminately. Euphemistically named, the laws purported to control syphilis and gonorrhea through controlling prostitution, while giving sweeping authority to police in garrison towns to detain and examine women on mere suspicion of prostitution. Englishwomen made the repeal of these laws a rallying focus for their first fully organized feminist operation. In her sixties Harriet Martineau wrote the drafts for their petitions, wrote speeches for the campaign leader, Josephine Butler, wrote the newspaper letters that launched the effort.

A London female journalist, Sarah Curtis, standing for Parliament in 1974 at the peak of the contemporary women's movement in Great Britain, called Harriet Martineau "the woman journalist of *our* time, then."[2] Curtis encapsulated in that statement the reason we need a fresh look at Martineau's feminism. I think this can best be accomplished through reading her own words on the subject, and to that end I present these selections of her works on women.

Harriet Martineau was a complicated female intellectual at a time when often the most a bookish middle-class woman in need of employment could aspire to was a position as a governess. She was full of contradictions, at times the advance messenger of a new movement, at times a reflector of Victorian eccentric views and narrow morality, sometimes farsighted, other times petty, sometimes mean, other times generous and wise, occasionally brilliant, but often verbose, repetitious, and tedious. Yet she was surely what we called in the early days of the recent women's movement "a role model from history," a woman of achievement, independence, and autonomy, whose hard-won gains resulted from her own effort. For Victorian England the magnitude of her accomplishment is astounding. She wrote without a significant break from early adulthood into her late sixties, despite health obstacles, supporting herself all her life by writing, and publishing well over 100 separately printed titles, scores of periodical articles, and some 1,642 newspaper editorials. The content of all that she wrote was wide-ranging, substantial, and serious.

As we reconsider her influence, we realize that we are not recovering a "lost woman writer" whose few small gems have been lost to the public for many years. Rather, hers is an enormous output. She never revised, and although some of her writing is lively and brilliant, some of it is very dull. She can be credited with neither painstaking attention to craft nor stylistic grace. Some of her vast outpouring has remained in print, and she has continued to hold a small place of historical recognition. Thus, it is neither because of neglect nor because of her virtuosity as a writer that we should again turn our attention to her.

As she was not entirely lost to history, so she was not a typical woman of her time, either. Harriet Martineau cannot be used as a case study of a nineteenth-century woman. She was not inarticulate or limited in public expression as most

[2] Sarah Curtis, quoted in *Observer*, February 17, 1974, p. 26.

3

women were. She was not even a typical woman writer, for there were few women journalists, women writers tending to concentrate more on fiction and poetry. As a single woman, she was not dependent on an individual man for her economic or emotional well-being as the vast majority of women were.[3] No one thing that she did, no one aspect of her life makes her in any way a representative nineteenth-century woman.

On the other hand, even though she more often expressed new trends than typified currents, she was not an original thinker. Her genius lay in her ability to discern new ideas with quick intelligence, to communicate them clearly to the popular mind, and thus to rally, time and again, supporters and advocates of the new viewpoints and causes. Adam Smith, Thomas Malthus, David Ricardo, James Mill, Joseph Priestley, Jeremy Bentham thought up the doctrines of political economy, necessarian philosophy, and utilitarianism that she taught in the early years of her adulthood. Mrs. Jane Marcet in *Conversations on Political Economy* even invented the format she first used, the simplified lesson in print aimed at educating common people. Martineau took the ideas and perfected the form—the primer textbook in a sophisticated field, the how-to manual—at a time when the desire for general education was highly developed, but the instructional materials for it were not. Similarly, her account of her travels in the United States helped change the shape of the travel book. Although it was in vogue for Europeans to travel in the new republic and write

[3] Though, like other women writers, she was indebted for encouragement and opportunity to many men. W. J. Fox of the *Monthly Repository* first paid her for her writing, trained her in his study, and with his publisher brother Charles was responsible for putting her political economy tales into print. Her beloved older brother Thomas, who died young, on discovering that she was the anonymous Discipulus in the *Repository*, encouraged her to write seriously. To her even more adored younger brother James, she owed early companionship, affection, and advice that led to the establishment of her career. After she was established, many men, members of Parliament, various government commissioners, and celebrated male literary figures, contributed to the stream of information that allowed her to keep informed and to write intelligently. It was men, too, who hurt her most, James the foremost of them when he, by then an eminent member of the Unitarian clergy, wrote a scathing review of a book on which she collaborated and which disavowed Christianity. That exchange caused a permanent rupture between them.

about it, Martineau did more than simply describe her journey. She formulated a comparative method for studying societies and analyzed the new American culture by measuring it against carefully stated principles. Quite possibly, she wrote the first "methodological essay" ever published, *How to Observe Morals and Manners*. Her greatest originality was in her method. Significantly, she translated and abbreviated Comte's *Positive Philosophy*, the wellspring of social scientific thought, so effectively that it spread the Comtean word far and wide and gave Martineau herself a new systematic framework in positivism. Comte himself believed it was so good that he had it retranslated into French for his French disciples, and her translation and abridgment are still the standard edition of Comte's work used in English sociology textbooks today.

It was the same with political issues. She did not begin a single campaign, but whether it was British reform politics, American abolitionism, nursing in the Crimean War, or feminism, she was in the forefront, interpreting and fighting for the cause. John Stuart Mill took the first petition for woman's suffrage to Parliament in 1866, but Harriet Martineau signed it and had long worked for it. American abolitionist William Lloyd Garrison was her hero, and no other English writer wrote so much in the cause of American abolition of slavery as she. Florence Nightingale was on the battlefield, organizing and professionalizing nursing in the Crimea, and then back home organizing nursing education and the War Office in England, but Martineau was her champion in the press. It is the cumulative effect of Martineau's numerous contributions that forms a part of her lasting contribution.

Although in some ways Martineau was very much a woman of her time and a Victorian intellectual, she was also, along with a group of her contemporaries, a true progenitor of the intellectual mode that reigns in Anglo-American liberalism today and provides the dominant informing paradigm of mainstream Western feminism. It is this intellectual influence that constitutes her greatest contribution. Her radicalism was the consistent strand in all her far-flung efforts. Its tenets were rationalism, progressivism, organizational order, voice for the inarticulate, respect for the individual, and faith in science, all of which determined right thinking. Hers was a singularly principled posture. She held the position that human free will is limited. What free will there is rests on the ability of the human to uncover the immutable laws of nature, physical, economic, and social. This radicalism of the Victorian era became the twentieth century's liberalism, and liberalism became the idea that did more than any other conceptual nucleus to make room for twentieth-century feminism clear into the 1980s. Harriet Martineau, I think, spelled out a feminist overview in the nineteenth century in terms that were radical then, and did it better, more consistently, and more often than most other feminists. I do not think she knew what she was doing, and I think she was often "wrong." I find some of her conclusions inadequate and even bigoted for my time and place. As an English-language feminist intellectual, I think I would recognize her as my forebear and the ancestor of my culture more readily than I would identify my illiterate Irish American great-grandmother who came to America in 1850 to escape the potato famine—or Emma Goldman, the Russian American anarchist feminist whom I would like a great deal, and whose radical twentieth-century ideas I enjoy exploring. But Goldman and our great-grandmothers have had minimal influence on what most American and English women think, and what we socially assume even outside the range of our conscious deliberations, whereas Martineau spelled out a century ahead of us these thoughts and deliberations. Harriet Martineau's radicalism led her to make a cogent, rational economic argument about conditions in Ireland in 1843 that included specific consideration of the special poverty of women in the same decade that my great-grandmother Graham was preparing for her boat trip to New Orleans to avoid starvation near Dublin. Martineau's kind of radicalism rattled the whole Anglo-American cognitive universe as well as the political one. Unlike the radicalism of the Emma Goldmans, it set in place the cognitive assumptions the majority of us, whether socialist, radical, or liberal feminists, operate under today, whether fully consciously or vaguely from within our culture's orientation to the world. These assumptions are the belief in order, the belief that change will bring about betterment, the belief that knowledge is power, the belief that the individual will do good if she or he is taught the good, and, above all, the substitution of a science of society for a theological or speculative base, as the first premise for other individual and collective ideas.

6

For the contemporary British journalist Sarah Curtis and me, and, I believe, the majority of the world that looks to concepts originating in English, Harriet Martineau articulated the world view that was formative, comprehensible, palatable for our feminism. For Martineau, it was very much a part of a whole, of politics, of economics, of life-style, of philosophy, of a belief system. Being inside the paradigm, she did not know this was so. She gave us our liberal faith in progress, science, and order, a faith that included feminism, what she and her contemporaries called the woman question, which would have as its "natural," inevitable outcome rights of women corresponding to those of men.

Although in our day challenges to the paradigm, both the undergirding philosophic one and the feminist one, have arisen, making us conscious of the characteristics of that world view and challenges to it, I believe that what Martineau gave us is an expalanation of the fundamental intellectual precepts on which most of our feminism is posited. A retrospective look at some of her works on the subject of women and some of her advocacy of women's causes will help us, I believe, explain to ourselves where we have come from.

MARTINEAU'S LIFE AND BACKGROUND

Born into a middle-class manufacturer's family in Norwich at the beginning of the nineteenth century, Harriet Martineau found in her personal and social circumstances factors that helped her—albeit sometimes because she reacted against them—to become an independent woman and a thoughtful social critic. Norwich was a provincial cathedral city, but the Martineau family went to chapel as Unitarians. In region-, religion-, and class-conscious England, Martineau started as an outsider. Norwich was not London, the political and cultural center and the birthplace of new trends and ideas. Unitarians were not members of the Church of England, but Dissenters, as chapelgoers were called in England, which placed the Martineaus outside the religious Establishment as well. And Unitarians were as a group left-wing politically and intellectually, as well as religiously, which placed them outside popular conventions. In fact, being social and intellectual frontrunners was at that time already the mark of Unitarians, although their views were often considered deviant by the mainstream.

Martineau's family was in many respects typically middle class, and she described these aspects matter-of-factly in her *Autobiography*. "My grandfather, who was one of the honorable series [of surgeons], died at the age of forty-two, of a fever caught among his poor patients. He left a large family, of whom my father was the youngest. When established as a Norwich manufacturer, my father married Elizabeth Rankin, the eldest daughter of a sugar refiner at Newcastle upon Tyne. My father and mother had eight children, of whom I was the sixth: and I was born on the 12th of June, 1802."[4] She experienced neither the privilege of aristocracy nor the oppression of the working classes, but had a consciousness of the meaning of both privilege and deprivation from her vantage point as a member of her particular family, and then as an individual subject to the vicissitudes of earning her living by selling her product. Although she was sometimes patronizing of the poor and solicitous of the wealthy, she was often able to be clear-sighted about social realities through the lens of her middle-class origins.

Along with her middle-class and outsider status, her psychological estrangement as a child gives another, at least equally important, clue to her adult perceptivity, which was both socially profound and personally eccentric. In her memoir she describes without comment her troubled childhood. As a child she was often terribly unhappy, morose, and distressed, though she was very pious and received an uncommonly good education for a girl of her time. Offering no suggestion of its meaning, she recounts an anxiety dream she had when she was four years old. Out for a walk with her nursemaid and the other children, she was beckoned into a public house by a stag with high antlers. Frightened, she returned home in the dusk to be welcomed into a sunlit kitchen where she was lifted up into the sunlight by her mother and given sugar to eat. In waking life her mother was cold to her and she had frequent indigestion, so the dream readily admits to a post-Freudian interpretation as a cry for attention and protection from the threats and discomforts in her troubled small-child's universe.

[4] Harriet Martineau, *Autobiography*. With Memorials by Maria Weston Chapman, 4th ed. (Boston: Houghton, Osgood and Co.), vol. 1, p. 6. All references to the *Autobiography* are from this edition.

One of the pleasures of her early memories was expounding her religious views to "the baby," her favorite brother James, in his crib. Her anxiety and morbidity were at times acute and her health delicate, and these difficulties were linked by her to her childhood religion which was, however, her chief pleasure. She wrote, "While I was afraid of everybody I saw, I was not in the least afraid of God. Being usually very unhappy, I was constantly longing for heaven, and seriously, and very frequently planning suicide in order to get there."[5]

A favorite childhood fantasy would take place in the Octagon Chapel, their Unitarian meeting place in Norwich, which had unusual windows in the roof. Young Harriet would stare up at the high windows and imagine angels coming to get her and taking her away in full view of the congregation.

It was in the emotional context of infantile hunger for attention, anxiety, and morbid comfort in religion that Martineau was educated alongside James. They first studied at home, learning reading and numbers, Latin and music. Her older brother Thomas was their Latin teacher. Then in 1813, she and her sister Rachel were sent to a new Unitarian girls' school in Norwich headed by the Reverend Isaac Perry. During their two years there she added French to her studies. Upon the closing of the school, she again studied a classical course at home, although she and her sisters were also taught domestic skills, particularly sewing. It was during the time that she was in Perry's school that she began to lose her hearing. The deafness worsened when she was sixteen, and she became almost entirely deaf, though she used an ear trumpet and overcame the disabling effects of deafness as an adult.

In 1818 she was sent to Bristol to a school run by the wife of her mother's brother. There she found in her Aunt Kentish a compassionate human influence and in the Reverend Lant Carpenter, the Bristol Unitarian minister, a mentor she idolized. The fifteen months spent in Bristol provided both personal and intellectual release for her. She returned to Norwich suffering deafness, but somewhat liberated from mental and emotional stress.

Carpenter introduced her to the ideas of David Hartley and Joseph Priestley, and their philosophy of necessity held

[5] Ibid., p. 14.

9

her attention for some years to come. Only a step to the side of Calvinist predestination, but couched in the language of philosophy, necessarianism was a doctrine of causation that held that everything was a consequence of what had preceded it, that there is no free human action, no free will, but a necessary sequence of effects brought about unavoidably by what had gone before them.[6] The other central philosophical influence she felt was utilitarianism. First studying such radical philosophers as Jeremy Bentham and James Mill on her own, she was later to meet Mill in London.

By the late 1820s, Martineau, herself in her twenties, was a serious but little-known writer, whose boundaries were the Unitarian religion, its propagation and interpretation. She was, however, a quick and searching student, if a solitary one, open to new ideas. Her brother James had by then been sent off for formal education at the Unitarian college at York, later to become Manchester College, Oxford, which he was one day to head as principal, but Harriet remained at home, as women did.

Her older brother Thomas died; her father's business failed; and he, too, died. His investments on behalf of his family failed, and Martineau was left to find ways to support herself. Earning some money from her needlework, at which she was very skillful all her life, and fifteen pounds a year from the *Monthly Repository*, for which she had written without pay until her time of financial need, she decided that she must earn her livelihood from her writing.

Visiting James in his parish in Dublin she hit upon the idea of a series of tales to illustrate the concepts of political economy in which she had newly become interested. She determined with James's advice that she would publish a monthly series over two years. Discouraged by several publishers, she finally was helped by W. J. Fox, her editor at the *Monthly Repository*, to persuade his brother, Charles Fox, to bring out the tales. The terms were very unfavorable to her, and he made

---

[6] For a clear explanation of Martineau's necessarian views, see the excellent biography by Valerie Kossew Pichanick, *Harriet Martineau: The Woman and Her Work, 1802–76* (Ann Arbor: University of Michigan Press, 1980).

more money from her work than she ever did, but the first number of the *Illustrations of Political Economy* was an instant success, and her reputation was made. She worked feverishly for two years to keep to her tight schedule. She moved to London, was celebrated in London society, and her thought, as well as her life, moved permanently into another realm.

Whigs and Tories alike asked her to write on their causes. Although she was not partisan, she found the Whigs' views more compatible. She formed friendships with such political and intellectual notables as Richard Monckton Milnes, Charles Buller, and Thomas Malthus. Lord Brougham, the Scottish political leader, was quite taken with her and enlisted her to write on behalf of poor law reform. She visited with Thomas and Jane Carlyle. She was approached by Robert Owen to endorse his socialism, but she resisted. She was "in" as a literary figure in London.

After the strenuous labors of these two years, she was exhausted. On the suggestion of Lord Henley,[7] who told her that she would enjoy seeing the United States where justice and liberty flourished, she traveled in the United States from 1834 to 1836. Vowing that she had no intention of writing about her travels, she nevertheless kept a journal. Her lassitude was too great, she insisted, to write profitably. However, on board ship, she wrote a chapter entitled "How to Observe Morals and Manners" for a work that had been requested by a publisher.

Her American journey was quite splendid. She was entertained by leading people of politics and letters and by fashionable society throughout the country. She also talked to scores of common folk and had varied experiences from chopping wood on the frontier, to visiting prisons, to being a guest at the White House. Near the end of her stay she spoke up in a public meeting for the abolitionists of William Lloyd Garrison's

---

[7] A wealthy philanthropist, relative of Lord Brougham, with whom Martineau apparently had only one meeting. According to her *Autobiography* (vol. 1, pp. 203–204), he was introduced to her by members of his family with the hope that she would be a good influence on him and help counteract his tendency to give away money foolishly. Mentally ill, he "disappeared from society" before she returned from the United States and soon died, giving her no opportunity to report to him on the travels he had suggested.

circle and lost much of her welcome in the United States, since the abolitionists were thought wildly fanatical by many Americans at the time.

Upon her return she published *Society in America*, in which she measured American society against its own principle of democracy. She cringed over the publisher's title; "Theory and Practice of Society in America" was what she wanted to call it. It was followed by the more anecdotal *Retrospect of Western Travel*, and only after that, the methodological book *How to Observe Morals and Manners*. During this period she also published in several periodicals, and her novel *Deerbrook* appeared.

In the spring of 1839, again overtired, she took a trip to the Continent, but while in Venice illness forced her to return home. For nearly five years she lay ill at Tynemouth under the care of her physician brother-in-law, Thomas Greenhow. Lord Melbourne, then prime minister, offered her a public pension, but she declined on the grounds of not wanting to be in the pay of one party or another in government, a personal action reflecting her deep-seated economic philosophy combined with what we would now call a sense of professionalism as a journalist. Her friends raised money privately to invest for her in long-term annuities. Though an invalid, she published during the Tynemouth years a novel, *The Hour and the Man*, based on the life of Toussaint L'Ouverture, black political liberator of Haiti; a series of children's books; and a practical manual, *Life in the Sick-Room*. In 1844, she was introduced to mesmerism, an early and controversial form of hypnotism, was mesmerised, and soon got well. She believed she was cured by mesmerism, and, insulting her physician, published "Letters on Mesmerism" in the *Athenaeum*. It was not until a coroner's post mortem examination showed that she had had an ovarian tumor that her doctor was vindicated; but in 1844 personal and professional hostility swirled, and some members of her family stopped talking to her for a while. Greenhow wrote an angry rebuttal in the press, and Martineau became known to the general public as one of the people involved in the mesmerism debate.

I think her dogmatic approval of mesmerism is one piece in the puzzle of her emotional and rational contradictions. For so logical and analytic a writer to participate in such a mysterious and controversial medical process might seem bewildering. However, I think it makes sense as a link between the religious faith she was leaving behind and her need for something other than sheer theory and argument as a stabilizer for personal meaning in her life. She never overcame her personal rigidity, which sometimes led to her ideas being unnecessarily cast in concrete. Otherwise, she might not have needed any authoritative system, or she might have found flexibility for change within her original philosophical and religious framework. Her exhaustion and her volatile behavior in the publication of the mesmerism letters suggest that emotional distress was at least a part of her illness. The comfort of mesmerism may well have relieved her, since it gave her something new to believe in, something that purported to be "scientific," yet came from a nonphysical power similar to the power she had hoped for in her abandoned childhood God. But, also, if one is willing to consider the evidence of Greenhow's interpretation of the post mortem in 1876, the tumor in her abdomen might have moved in fortuitous concert with the mesmerist's acts.

One of her acquaintances among the advocates of mesmerism invited her to the Lake District after she recovered, and she so enjoyed the area that she decided to buy a small plot of land and build a house there. Her house, The Knoll, at Ambleside, was finished in 1846. Loving her new home and relishing her renewed health, she went about her work with fresh vigor.

A trip and a new acquaintance during the first Ambleside years provided another step in her changed intellectual direction. Mr. and Mrs. Richard V. Yates invited her to go with them to Egypt and Palestine; and on her return in 1847, she wrote *Eastern Life, Present and Past*.[8] The book focused on those lands as the cradle of four great religions. She presented a not entirely developed thesis that those religions were founded by human beings, not divinely revealed, as their practitioners usually believed.

Her new acquaintance, Henry G. Atkinson, fueled with his skepticism her movement out of Christianity into atheism.

---

[8] She refers to her hostess as "Mrs. Yates," or "Mrs. Richard V. Yates," but does not give her first name either in the account of the journey in her *Autobiography* (vol. 1, pp. 531–552) or in *Eastern Life, Present and Past* (Philadelphia: Lea and Blanchard, 1848).

She met Atkinson in 1845 and became greatly attached to him. In 1851 they published together *Letters on the Laws of Man's Nature and Development*, largely Atkinson's work, discrediting all theological explanations of intellectual problems. James Martineau's antagonistic review of this book was the source of the permanent breach between them.

Meanwhile, her political journalism had gone on apace. She wrote *Forest and Game-Law Tales* and was asked by Charles Knight in 1848 to finish a "History of the Thirty Years' Peace" that he had begun. Not having written history before and cautious about writing current history, she nevertheless wrote a work that has received good marks from professional historians of several generations.

Early in the 1850s Martineau took two steps that stretched her intellectually and established her in the final professional capacity of her career. She began writing as a kind of foreign correspondent and then political commentator for the *Daily News*, a remarkable and unusual position for a woman, which eventuated in her writing several editorials a week for over fifteen years. Simultaneously, as she was finishing the *History of the Peace*, she read and then translated and abridged Auguste Comte's *Positive Philosophy*. Comte was to articulate for her the philosophical position she needed to unify her own thought, the social scientific method.

In the preface of her abridgment and translation of Comte's *Positive Philosophy*, Harriet Martineau wrote:

> Whatever else may be thought of the work, it will not be denied that it ascertains with singular sagacity and soundness the foundations of human knowledge, . . . and that it establishes the true filiation of the sciences within the boundaries of its own principle. Some may wish to interpolate this or that; some to amplify, . . . but any who question the general soundness of the exposition, . . . are of another school, and will simply neglect the book. It is not for such that I have been working, but for students who are not schoolmen; who need conviction, and must best know when their need is satisfied. When this exposition of Positive Philosophy unfolds itself in

order before their eyes, they will, I am persuaded, find there at least a resting-place for their thought,— a rallying-point of their scattered speculations,—and possibly an immoveable basis for their intellectual and moral convictions.[9]

In the work that follows this introduction, Martineau turned six volumes of difficult and wordy French philosophy into two volumes of clear English for the general reader.[10] The passage quoted above, written at the peak of her adult powers in 1852, echoes "the greatest good for the greatest number," "the free marketplace of ideas," the importance of first principles, the need to appeal to the common person, the framework of morality, and the sure triumph of good, all of which were cornerstone doctrines of Martineau's earlier intellectual circles, the utilitarian or radical philosophers, the political economists, the Unitarians, and the necessarians. Also, these beliefs are rooted here in a verbalization of faith that sprang from a once-religious soil. The new faith that Comte's philosophy gave her as she neared fifty years of age was continuous in many ways with her old one. She found better expression for what she already believed in the way Comte said it. Comte had developed a view of a hierarchy of fundamental intellectual postures: the theological, which was founded on revealed religion, superseded by the metaphysical, which was posited on speculative reasoning and which was to be superseded by the positive sciences, founded on experiment and observation. Further, in the hierarchy of sciences, sociology would be the highest. Thus a science of society would be the zenith of sciences.

[9] "Preface," *The Positive Philosophy of Auguste Comte*, freely translated and condensed by Harriet Martineau (New York: D. Appleton and Co., 1853), vol. 1, p. ix.

[10] It is interesting to note that Seymour Martin Lipset said he was doing the same thing to Harriet Martineau's work when he abridged and brought out a paperback edition of *Society in America* for American readers in 1962 (Garden City, N.Y.: Doubleday). My motivation in condensing Martineau's huge quantity of extravagant Victorian prose about women to achieve greater sharpness for 1980s readers was at least partially the same. (The Lipset edition has been reprinted by Peter Smith.)

For Martineau, if not for modern readers, this resolved the contradiction between authority and investigation. She could retain an absolute posture in method, and thus not have to abandon the traces of her necessarianism and her need for commitment, and yet allow for flexibility in the outcome, in results. She could then subscribe to a First Cause and rest easy that people misunderstood her viewpoint when they called her an atheist. The First Cause would eventually yield knowledge of itself to the highest science, sociology. It could be safely predicted that a fully scientific explanation of human beings was possible. Knowing human societies in their variations is all one needs to know, all there is "above" the physical world. This belief was for Martineau progressive, enlightening, practical, and satisfying, and provided the equivalent of religious fulfillment, although she did not literally see it as a religion as Comte eventually did.

A few years after her move to Ambleside, Martineau again became seriously ill. On going down to London to be examined for what she thought was heart disease, she again came to the conclusion that she was fatally ill, even though her physicians seem to have told her otherwise. In 1855, she put her life in order for her death, including writing her *Autobiography*. Though largely confined to her home after that, she had many more productive years of writing for the *Daily News* and staying in the thick of things political through the mail. She was to make some of her best contributions to women's causes during those last invalid years. She died in 1876, having been inactive for only a very few years.[11]

HARRIET MARTINEAU'S FEMINISM

It is tempting to follow Martineau's own method and measure her feminism against specific principles. For historical fairness, they should be principles that she herself endorsed. Yet that would not yield a full enough picture, for it is my intent to show her contribution to later feminism, including that of our time, as well as to the efforts of her time. Thus, the criteria must be both her own and ones that we still consider important today, though we must be aware of the difference be-

[11] The obituary she wrote for herself, which appeared in the *Daily News*, is the second selection in Section I.

tween those ideas that were deliberately feminist on her part and the ones to which we in a later age have assigned feminist significance.

Martineau, herself a model of women's accomplishment for later feminists, was often a genuine promoter of other women. She was sensitive and conscious of efforts made by women on women's behalf, even though her tongue could sometimes be acid in gossip about some women. Contemporary feminist scholars can note with appreciation that in her *Illustrations of Political Economy* she repeatedly gave Mrs. Jane Marcet credit for the idea of her own work. Though she raised her eyebrows at Mary Wollstonecraft's personal sexual behavior and what she regarded as her romantic excesses, she fully acknowledged Wollstonecraft as the first English public advocate of women's rights. Present at the dinner at which John Stuart Mill and Harriet Taylor met, she is reputed to have been one of the worst gossips about the long, devoted relationship Taylor and Mill maintained while Taylor was married to someone else. Yet she was supportive of their feminism. Although she was not very tolerant of or informed about sexuality and unorthodox relationships, she was very supportive of work, education, political rights, and personal dignity for women; and she went a long way in supporting all manner of their manifestations. She came to be able to do this by objectifying the actual women involved as she led their causes.

In a leader in the London *Daily News* published June 28, 1854, Harriet Martineau wrote that "the wife-beating which has excited so much attention for the last two or three years, and which we have endeavored to meet by express legislation, has revealed to alarmed thousands of us that the mistresses of tyrannical men have a great advantage over the wives in being able to free themselves from their tyrant when they please. They can tell the truth in court about the treatment they have undergone; for they have nothing to fear from the vindictiveness of the brute when he comes out of gaol again."[12] This observation came in response to a report of a parliamentary Commission on Divorce. A Divorce and Matrimonial Causes Act was to pass in 1857, and Martineau's support of it in the newspaper and her expression of that support in terms of the

---

[12] Leader 2 beginning "Divorce and Matrimonial Causes," p. 4.

easing of brutality against poor women are indications of her surprisingly foresighted feminist outlook. The new law only established a single court where there had previously been three different jurisdictions to handle divorce cases and did not actually give women much relief, but Martineau's argument is immensely important as an early feminist framework for later criticism and campaigns. Long before the coining of the word "feminist" and thirty years before the beginning of an organized women's rights campaign in England, Harriet Martineau was a wide-ranging, progressive, and thoroughgoing feminist in nearly every sense in which that word is used today.[13] Embracing practically every cause clearly in favor of women's advancement in her lifetime and taking up certain issues that were not so definitely identified as parts of the feminist fabric until the 1960s and 1970s, Martineau was a giant among early feminists. An overview of Martineau's writings and the issues and campaigns she fought for with her pen gives a contemporary reader both a profile of the emergence of feminism in nineteenth-century England and America and a theoretical foundation for the feminist social philosophy still dominant today.

She was the first Englishwoman to make the analogy between the American woman's lot and the slave's.[14] Publishing that claim in *Society in America* in the context of a full analysis of the situation of American women, she and her book received far more attention, both positive and negative, for her abolitionist views than for her feminism. Yet the book included a very astute chapter entitled "The Political Non-Existence of

---

[13] Alice S. Rossi, in *The Feminist Papers* (New York: Columbia University Press, 1973), p. xiii, says that the word "feminism" was first used in print in a book review in the *Athenaeum* on April 27, 1895.

[14] Martineau, *Society in America*, Lipset ed., pp. 126, 292. Sarah Grimké made the same analogy the same year, in her *Letters to the Congregational Clergy*, which shows that the analogy was being made in the abolitionist circles in which they both moved in the United States. Although Grimké and Martineau did not meet, the Grimké sisters, like Martineau, were welcomed and sponsored by Maria Weston Chapman when they first went to Boston, the year after Martineau's departure. Most of the chapter "Political Non-Existence of Women" as it originally appeared in *Society in America* (London: Saunders & Otley, 1837, vol. 1, pp. 148–154) is reprinted as the first selection in Section IV.

Women," in which she claimed that the democratic principle was violated by the denial of political participation to women. It was from women that she had learned much that she knew about the United States, and she gave credit to these women for their achievements and talents. At the same time she criticized the lack of authority and choice for American women and the resulting servitude for many of them.

Martineau's position as a model for today's feminists or as an inspiration for female achievers is important. Alice S. Rossi's inclusion of Martineau's chapter on women from *Society in America* in her selection of classic feminist statements, *The Feminist Papers* (1973), indicates the current value of Martineau's thought. In presenting her chapter from Martineau, Rossi especially represents Martineau as a forerunner of the discipline of sociology.

Others could make such a claim for her relation to economics, though Martineau was a popularizer in that field, not an original thinker. Although it would be much too extravagant to claim a significant place for her as a fiction writer—her didactic tales, children's stories, and novel *Deerbrook* having small current readership—it is, nevertheless, important to note that she wrote a considerable amount of fiction. The most comprehensive "first" that Martineau accomplished as a woman was as a journalist, for besides earning her living from her early thirties by writing numerous popular books and many articles for major journals, she contributed, as mentioned, over 1,600 editorials to the London *Daily News* on an enormous range of political and social topics during the 1850s and 1860s.

The historian Janet Courtney, writing in the 1930s about the British women's movement in the 1830s, believed Harriet Martineau to be the leading feminist of the period. Courtney wrote, "And when I found Harriet Martineau, the ablest of them all, announcing that the best advocates of women's rights would be the successful professional women and the 'substantially successful authoresses,' I recognized that she had put in a nutshell the whole truth about the women's movement." [15]

Courtney believed that in the 1830s women and women's

---

[15] *The Adventurous Thirties: A Chapter in the Women's Movement* (London: Oxford University Press, Humphrey Milford, 1933), p. 1.

rights made great advances only to fall back under the influence of Queen Victoria and the Victorians. Though Martineau did not write the passage Courtney selected until she wrote her *Autobiography* in 1855, faith in individual women's accomplishments was a central point of Martineau's feminism from the beginning.

The female role model idea is significant in Martineau's first published piece, "Female Writers of Practical Divinity," published in the Unitarian journal *Monthly Repository* in 1822. The article opens,

> I do not know whether it has been remarked by others as well as myself, that some of the finest and most useful English works on the subject of Practical Divinity are by female authors. I suppose it is owing to the peculiar susceptibility of the female mind, and its consequent warmth of feeling, that its productions, when they are really valuable, find a more ready way to the heart than those of the other sex; and it gives me great pleasure to see women gifted with superior talents, applying those talents to promote the cause of religion and virtue.[16]

In contradiction to her theme, however, she signed the article, "Discipulus," implying a male author, a practice she followed in pseudonym or textual voice off and on throughout her career in spite of the fame she gained in the 1830s writing in her own name.

She was to echo her first printed sentiment about women achievers as models in a piece written as an obituary for Florence Nightingale when Nightingale was believed to be dying after the Crimean War, but not published until 1910 when Nightingale actually died. Florence Nightingale was the woman of her time whom Martineau perhaps most greatly admired, and she wrote,

> Florence Nightingale encountered opposition—from her own sex as much as the other; and she achieved, as the most natural thing in the world, and without

[16] *Monthly Repository* 17 (October 1822): 593.

the smallest sacrifice of her womanly quality, what would beforehand have been declared a deed for a future age.

She was no declaimer, but a housewifely woman; she talked little, and did great things. When other women see that there are things for them to do, and train themselves to the work, they will get it done easily enough. There can never be a more unthought-of and marvellous career before any working woman than Florence Nightingale has achieved; and her success has opened a way to all others easier than anyone had prepared for her.[17]

Education for women was another theme Martineau pursued all her life. Her second published piece was on that topic. She was well aware early that intellectual occupation was not considered fitting for a girl, writing that "when I was young, it was not thought proper for young ladies to study very conspicuously; and especially with pen in hand. . . . and thus my first studies in philosophy were carried on with great care and reserve."[18] Martineau's youthful writings suggested that women should be educated in order to enhance their companionship with men and improve their teaching of their own children, although she always advocated a rigorous course of study for girls, physical exercise for girls as well as boys, and domestic arts for women in addition to the program followed by males. Her feminist consciousness grew, and in later life, she encouraged the idea of education of women for its own sake and recommended a full program of advanced subjects. As a public figure and in the press, she supported the establishment of the colleges for women in London, Queens College in Harley Street and the Ladies College in Bedford Square, of the first professional school of nursing at St. Thomas' Hospital in London, and of women's medical education.

Work for women was also a frequent theme. Martineau made a strong argument—amazing for the time—in favor of equal pay for equal work. Hers was not the literal argument

[17] The obituary from which this passage is taken forms the closing selection of Section V.

[18] *Autobiography*, vol. 1, pp. 77–78.

still heard today that women should be paid the same amount of money for exactly the same jobs as men but was much stronger, insisting that equivalent labor deserves equal pay. She made it most forcefully, in fact, on behalf of the dairymaids whose job of milking the cows twice daily, straining the milk, preparing cheese, and churning butter had formerly been exclusively a female occupation. She wrote that "such work as this ought at least to be paid as well as the equivalent work of men; indeed, in the dairy farms of the west of England the same labour of milking the kine is now very generally performed by men, and the Dorset milkmaid, tripping along with her pail, is, we fear, becoming a myth."[19]

In her writings on women's work Martineau repeatedly expressed a concern for health as well as pay. She wrote in several pieces of the degeneration of stamina and mental well-being experienced by governesses and servant women because of the crushing demands of their employers: "The physician says that, on the female side of the lunatic asylums, the largest class, but one, of the insane are maids of all work (the other being governesses). The causes are obvious enough: want of sufficient sleep from late and early hours, unremitting fatigue and hurry, and, even more than these, anxiety about the future from the smallness of the wages."[20] If not the insane asylum, then the workhouse followed for many of these women, for they did not earn enough to save for their old age. But it was better wages and the obligation of good advice from their employers on savings pensions for themselves that Martineau advocated. Ever the laissez-faire economist, she did not envision a social scheme for retirement benefits.

For middle-class married women, Martineau advocated improved household management skills exemplified in learning expert cookery. The teaching of such skills as cookery could also become an occupation. These women need not be housebound, though, for many of them were already engaged alongside their husbands, brothers, and fathers in shopkeeping, crafts, small manufacturing, and the deskwork, especially accounting, that went with such employment. Martineau

---

[19] "Female Industry," *Edinburgh Review* 222 (April 1859): 300.
[20] Ibid., p. 307.

believed that such women should be encouraged to be more active in these pursuits, but that they would be much more useful if they were taught sufficient arithmetic to manage sales and accounting effectively. Though she did not propose wide-scale female ownership of businesses in preference to men and typically discussed female shopkeeping as though husbands were in charge, she did encourage single women to learn business skills and widows to learn to manage their inherited shops to avoid having to remarry so quickly. She spoke of nursing and medicine as newly opened occupations that should be attractive to middle-class women and predicted that scientists, artists, and writers would emerge from among educated women.

When Harriet Martineau was fifty-two, she wrote to all her correspondents asking them to address her henceforth as "Mrs.," but her request had nothing to do with marriage. It was an acknowledgment that greater respect was carried by the title "Mrs." than "Miss" and an assertion that she was entitled to such respect. This was resonant with the original meaning of the word "mistress," of which "Mrs." was first an abbreviation, a word that meant female authority in the household and had nothing to do with marital status. That meaning was largely gone by the end of the eighteenth century, but a few distinguished nineteenth-century single women like Martineau attempted to renew it, showing a sensitivity to the dignity conveyed by a title. Their attempts came from the same impulse that pressed feminists of the 1970s to introduce "Ms." as a general title by which a woman might be addressed whatever her marital status.

Martineau was outspoken about the degradation and limits imposed on women by marriage, but she was understandably ambivalent in some of her statements and contradictory in some of her behavior having to do with marriage. In her time and place where marriage was so definitively normative for women, the wonder is that she was at times so piercingly critical of marriage in general, not that most of the time she fostered and approved of specific marriages between people she knew. This too is more consistent with contemporary feminists' views of the disabilities of marriage than with those of Martineau's own time.

This contradiction is vividly seen in two illustrations. In the "Memorials," Maria Weston Chapman reports the memory one of Harriet Martineau's oldest friends had of Martineau's deep regret at the marriage of a young lady friend. She related that Martineau said that marriage "would deprive her of larger opportunities of usefulness to the world."[21] Yet in 1854 she was apparently very happy to sponsor the wedding for her maid from her house at Ambleside. She wrote, refusing an invitation received from a Mrs. Barkworth: "Many thanks for your invitation; but the intended bridegroom will be here on Sunday, and I am engaged every day till after the wedding. My house, hands, heart and time will be very full till it is over."[22]

More enigmatic is her approval of Margaret Fuller's marriage to Count Ossoli during the last years of Fuller's life. Given her opinion that marriage would "deprive [one young woman] of larger opportunities of usefulness," it is striking to find Martineau writing of "that remarkable regeneration which transformed her [Fuller] from the dreaming and haughty pedant into the true woman. In a few months more she had loved and married; and how interesting and beautiful was the closing period of her life, when husband and child concentrated the power and affections which had so long run to waste in intellectual and moral eccentricity."[23] This is a rather severe judgment of Fuller, for although Martineau claims to have been her friend, twice in the *Autobiography* she sharply criticizes the American woman. She is resentful that Fuller negatively criticized *Society in America* for its emphasis on the abolition of American slavery.[24] She was also stung by a report from London that Fuller had called her "commonplace" after a visit as her houseguest at The Knoll.[25] Though near in age and occupation, and even in high-strung temperament, Martineau and Fuller were opposites philosophically, Martineau the rationalist, Fuller the romantic, Martineau the positivist, Fuller

[21] *Autobiography*, vol. 2, p. 157.
[22] Harriet Martineau, manuscript letter to Mrs. Barkworth, n.d., n.p. Ashcombe Collection, 1917, Fitzwilliam Museum Library, Cambridge, England.
[23] *Autobiography*, vol. 1, p. 518.
[24] Ibid., pp. 380–381.
[25] Ibid., p. 518.

the transcendentalist. It is no wonder that they finally did not get along with each other. This evidence makes me wonder if Martineau was not being spiteful rather than truthful about the value of marriage for Margaret Fuller.

On marriage in theory, Martineau wrote in *How to Observe Morals and Manners*: "The traveller everywhere finds women treated as the inferior party in a compact in which both parties have an equal interest. Any agreement thus formed is imperfect, and is liable to disturbance; and the danger is great in proportion to the degradation of the supposed weaker party. The degree of the degradation of woman is as good a test as the moralist can adopt for ascertaining the state of domestic morals in any country." And "It is a matter of course that women who are furnished with but one object,—marriage—must be as unfit for anything when their aim is accomplished as if they had never any object at all. They are no more equal to the task of education than to that of governing the state; and, if any unexpected turn of adversity befals them, they have no resource but a convent, or some other charitable provision."[26] Her observations of marriage were confirmed by letters she received from Englishwomen describing the "intolerable oppression" of women under law and custom in England.[27]

Martineau published theoretical considerations of political equality for women several times between 1837 and 1851. All were about women in American society; and all were very positive. But only once, in a passage in her *Autobiography*, did she address at its most abstract level what was typically called in her day the woman question, and on that occasion she is atypically negative. The tone of that piece suggests that women will come to have political rights if women will be worthy of them. Most other times she was far more willing to indict the political system for excluding women.

The woman's suffrage campaign did not really get under way until the late 1860s when Martineau's health was failing. However, she had written in 1855, "I have no vote at elections, though I am a tax-paying housekeeper and responsible citizen; and I regard the disability as an absurdity, seeing that

---

[26] For more from this passage, see the first selection in Section II.
[27] *Autobiography*, vol. 1, p. 406.

I have for a long course of years influenced public affairs to an extent not professed or attempted by many men." [28]

She went on in that passage, however, to disclaim any intention of agitating over suffrage, believing that women would have a vote in time. The vote was clearly simply one among many women's issues for her, not the central, singular driving focus for women's rights that it came to be in both England and America after her death. Nevertheless, she readily signed the petition for women's suffrage that John Stuart Mill presented to Parliament in 1866. She admired Mill and believed him to be an effective supporter of women's rights, but adding her name to those of the 1,498 other women on the petition was not a strong gesture. Her conviction of the rightness of the principle of the vote for women, incidentally, was not shared by the ruling Queen Victoria, still mourning deeply for her husband, then dead for five years, nor by the most admired woman in England at the time and Martineau's friend, Florence Nightingale. [29]

Martineau's final act of political activism in her old age was on behalf of women and again in the service of a campaign led by another, the campaign of the Ladies' National Association for the Repeal of the Contagious Diseases Acts led by Josephine Butler. This time a thoroughly feminist organization was launched. It was liberal and even patronizing in the sense that it consisted of "respectable" women working for "fallen" women. Nevertheless, this movement was radical in the sense that the women involved realized that all women were potentially incriminated by laws that identified prostitutes too vaguely and punished women but not men for acts of prostitution.

Martineau was invigorated by writing publicly for this campaign, which provided an appropriate finale for a distinguished career as journalist, thinker, and feminist.

A NOTE ON METHOD

The selections in this book were chosen to give a full view of the ways in which Harriet Martineau wrote about women and

[28] Ibid., p. 303.
[29] Doris Mary Stenton, *The English Woman in History* (London: George Allen and Unwin, 1957), p. 344.

about those feminist issues, both historical and contemporary, that she addressed. Often she wrote several pieces on the same topic, and I usually picked the shortest one if it gave the complete scope of her argument. To choose from her many biographical works on women, I used two criteria: that a particularly feminist point was made and that the biographee was herself notable. To my knowledge, the pieces on American women, Irish women, and the women in the harems in Cairo and Damascus are the only ones she wrote in a deliberately social mode about women in groups. I wanted to show how she attended to feminist material and developed feminist theory throughout her lifetime, so I chose material from different periods of her writing. Since my purpose was solely to develop the idea that over forty years Martineau fostered feminist causes and structured feminist theory in a great many works, I excluded from the selections printed here passages that were not directly about women. I have left nearly all of Martineau's spelling, punctuation, and phrasing as they were in the original source, even though occasionally one looks like a printer's error or a grammatical oversight. I have assumed that the reader's interest will be primarily on the topic of women, so I have kept to a minimum, interesting though it is, commentary or notes on the surrounding historical background or incidental figures in Martineau's texts.

Notes appearing in Martineau's original texts are indicated by an asterisk (*); the numbered footnotes are the editor's.

I

SELF-ESTIMATE

Simply the need of utterance.

—*Harriet Martineau*
self-obituary

Harriet Martineau in 1849
From the drawing by George Richmond
National Portrait Gallery, London

Exhibiting her self-reliant spirit, and perhaps a bit of egoism, Harriet Martineau the journalist wrote her own obituary for her newspaper, the London *Daily News*. The fact that she did it at all is striking, but the fact that she wrote it in 1855 and it was published in 1876 is even more remarkable.

Martineau began writing for the *Daily News* with a series of letters from Ireland in 1852. By then she was long established as an accomplished travel commentator from journal, pamphlet, book, and serial writing on the conditions and politics of people she met abroad. Her editorials for the new Liberal newspaper covered the widest possible range of subjects from foreign affairs to agriculture, from opposition to marriages between cousins (in spite of her monarch's interest in that subject, Prince Albert being Queen Victoria's cousin) to education. She sometimes sent as many as six editorials a week down to London from Ambleside. She wrote special articles, book reviews, and many fine obituaries regularly until 1869. Thus, it is particularly fitting that her own account of her life should be published at her death in the newspaper that had been her employer in the last period of her career.

When in 1855 Harriet Martineau became seriously ill and believed that she was about to die, she decided to interpret her own life for her public. She wrote her *Autobiography* and entrusted its publication to Maria Weston Chapman, her American friend, whom she had met on her visit to the United States. The two had corresponded constantly, pursuing together the issue both saw as urgently pressing, abolition of American slavery. Martineau had the plates for the book prepared for printing in both London and Boston to save her friend that effort. The *Autobiography* was dutifully brought out in three volumes in 1877.[1] It was in this same push of eval-

---

[1] The autobiography was printed by different publishers in both Boston and London in 1877, and by 1879 had gone to a fourth edition in Boston. A facsimile edition was published in the 1970s (Farnborough; Gregg International, 1972, 2 vols., illustrated), but it is no longer in print. In 1983 the two volumes of autobiography itself as they had originally appeared in the London version minus the letters, clippings, and commentary from Chapman's "Memorials," were published in paperback (*Harriet Martineau's Autobiography*, 2 vols., with a new introduction by Gaby Weiner [London: Virago, 1983]). The claim is occasionally made, as it is by Weiner, that the autobiography is Martineau's best literary work. See also F. S. Marvin,

uating her life that she prepared the obituary reprinted here and made it available to the *Daily News*.

Factually full, clear-sighted, and interesting, her own obituary is probably somewhat falsely modest. She accurately assesses herself as a popularizer of others' ideas, but she does not give herself the credit she deserves for being in one after another intellectual and political vanguard. She does not mention her significance in non-office-holding politics. As a woman of her time, she did not in the brief memoir underscore the importance her work took on by the very fact of her being a woman and doing it at all. She does, however, make such an acknowledgment in the *Autobiography*. There she states her belief that for her work it was her good fortune not to have married and remarks that "I long ago came to the conclusion that, without meddling with the case of the wives and mothers, I am probably the happiest single woman in England."[2]

Her recognition that, since she was a woman, her singleness was an important part of her professional success is one indicator of how hard it was for her to achieve what she did. She insisted on support for her status, however. For example, she wrote to her mother when her mother was coming to live with her in London in 1832, "I fully expect that both you and I shall feel as if I did not discharge a daughter's duty, but we shall both remind ourselves that I am now as much a citizen of the world as any professional *son* of yours could be."[3]

The opening selection, preceding the obituary, was also published in Chapman's "Memorials." In it young Martineau set down the guidelines she hoped to follow as a writer. Titled "Private" by Chapman and identified by her as having been written at Norwich in June of 1829, before Martineau had gained much public attention, the piece is full of the Unitarian piety of her early life, yet still consonant with her enduring pattern of being orderly, disciplined, and deliberate.

"Harriet Martineau: Triumph and Tragedy," *Hibbert Journal* 25 (1926): 631–640; Mitzi Myers, "*Harriet Martineau's Autobiography*: The Making of a Female Philosopher," in *Women's Autobiography*, ed. Estelle C. Jelinek (Bloomington and London: Indiana University Press), pp. 53–70; Richard Shannon, "The Consolations of Omniscience," *TLS*, July 1, 1983, 687–688.
[2] More from this passage appears in the fourth selection in Section II.
[3] *Autobiography*, vol. 2, p. 218.

PRIVATE:
A WRITER'S RESOLUTIONS

For some years past my attention has been more and more directed towards literary pursuits; and, if I mistake not, my capacity for their successful prosecution has increased, so that I have now fair encouragement to devote myself to them more diligently than ever. After long and mature deliberation, I have determined that my chief subordinate object in life shall henceforth be the cultivation of my intellectual powers, with a view to the instruction of others by my writings. On this determination I pray for the blessing of God.

I wish to hold myself prepared to relinquish this purpose, should any decided call of duty interfere; but I pray that no indolence or caprice in myself, no discouragement or ill-grounded opposition from others, may prevail on me to relinquish a resolution which I now believe to be rational, and compatible with the highest desire of a Christian.

I am now just twenty-seven years of age. It is my wish to ascertain (should life and health be spared) how much may be accomplished by diligent but temperate exertion in pursuit of this object for ten years.

I believe myself possessed of no uncommon talents, and of not an atom of genius; but as various circumstances have led me to think more accurately and read more extensively than some women, I believe that I may so write on subjects of universal concern as to inform some minds and stir up others. My aim is to become a forcible and elegant writer on religious and moral subjects, so as to be useful to refined as well as unenlightened minds. But, as I see how much remains to be done before this aim can be attained, I wish to be content with a much lower degree of usefulness, should the Father of my

—

Harriet Martineau, *Autobiography*, with Memorials by Maria Weston Chapman, 4th ed. (Boston: Houghton, Osgood and Co., 1879), vol. 2, pp. 166–168. Written in 1829.

spirit see fit to set narrow bounds to my exertions. Of post-humous fame I have not the slightest expectation or desire. To be useful in my day and generation is enough for me. To this I henceforth devote myself, and desire to keep in mind the following rules. (A frequent reference to them is necessary.)

I. To improve my moral constitution by every means; to cultivate my moral sense; to keep ever in view the subordination of intellectual to moral objects; by the practice of piety and benevolence, by entertaining the freedom and cheerfulness of spirit which results from dependence on God, to promote the perfection of the intellectual powers.

II. To seek the assistance of God in my intellectual exertions, and his blessing on their results.

III. To impart full confidence to my family respecting my pursuits, but to be careful not to weary them with too frequent a reference to myself; and to be as nearly as possible silent on the subject to all the world besides.

IV. To study diligently, 1. The Scriptures, good commentators, works of religious philosophy and practice,—*for moral improvement*; 2. Mental philosophy,—*for intellectual improvement*; 3. Natural philosophy and natural history, languages and history,—*for improvement in knowledge*; 4. Criticism, belles-lettres, and poetry,—*for improvement in style*. Each in turn, and something every day.

V. While I have my intellectual improvement ever in view, to dismiss from my thoughts the particular subject on which I have written in the morning for the rest of the day, i.e. to be temperate in my attention to an object.

VI. By *early rising*, and all due economy of time, and especially by a careful government of the thoughts, to employ my life to better purpose than heretofore.

VII. To exalt, enlarge, and refresh my mind by social intercourse, observation of external nature, of the fine arts, and of the varieties of human life.

VIII. To bear in mind that as my determination is deliberately formed and now allowed to be rational, disappointments should not be lightly permitted to relax my exertions. If my object is conscientiously adopted, mortifications of vanity should prove stimulants, rather than discouragements. The same consideration should induce patience under *painful la-*

bour, *delay*, and *disappointment*, and guard me against heat and precipitation.

IX. To consider my own interests as little as possible, and to write with a view to the good of others; therefore to entertain no distaste to the humblest literary task which affords a prospect of usefulness.

X. Should my exertions ultimately prove fruitless, to preserve my cheerfulness, remembering that God only knows how his work may be best performed, and that I have no right to expect the privilege of eminent usefulness, though permitted to seek it. Should success be granted, to take no honour to myself, remembering that I possess no original power or intrinsic merit, and that I can receive and accomplish nothing, except it be given me from Heaven.

June, 1829.

AN AUTOBIOGRAPHIC MEMOIR

"We regret to announce the death of Harriet Martineau. The following memoir, though written in the third person, was from her own pen. The frankness of its self-criticism makes it necessary to guard the reader against confounding her own strict and sometimes disparaging judgment of herself with the impressions made by her upon others."[4]

Harriet Martineau was born in 1802, in the city of Norwich, where the first of the name settled in 1688. David Martineau, the earliest of whom any record remains, was a French

---

Harriet Martineau, *Autobiography*, with Memorials by Maria Weston Chapman, 4th ed. (Boston: Houghton, Osgood and Co., 1879), vol. 2, pp. 562–574. Originally published in *Daily News* (London), June 29, 1876. Written in 1855.

[4] The introduction to the memoir published in the *Daily News*.

Protestant, who came over on the revocation of the Edict of Nantes. He married a French lady, whose family emigrated in the same ship, and pursued his profession as a surgeon in Norwich, where a succession of surgeons of the name existed, till the death of the most eminent of them, Philip Meadows Martineau (the uncle of Harriet), in 1828. He was considered the most eminent provincial surgeon of his day. The eldest brother of Harriet—a man of qualifications so high as to promise to sustain the honour of his name and profession in the old city— died before the age of thirty, and only one member of the family now remains in the city where many generations grew up. Harriet was the third daughter, and the sixth of eight children of Thomas Martineau, who was a manufacturer of the Norwich staples,—bombazine and camlet.[5] His acquaintance with Dr. Parr was kept up and signalized by the gift of a black camlet study-gown every year or so, a piece of the right length being woven expressly for the doctor and dyed with due care.

There was nothing remarkable about the childhood and youth of any of Thomas Martineau's children, unless in the case of Thomas, the eldest son, already referred to. His scholarship was of a high quality, and his mind was altogether of the rare ripeness and richness which comes of the equable cultivation of the intellectual and moral nature. The remarkable feature of the family story, in those days, was the steady self-denial, and clear, inflexible purpose with which the parents gave their children the best education which they could, by all honourable means, command. In those times of war and middle-class adversity, the parents understood their position, and took care that their children should understand it, telling them that there was no chance of wealth for them, and about an equal probability of a competence or of poverty; and that they must, therefore, regard their education as their only secure portion. Harriet came in for her share of this advantage, being well furnished with Latin and French (to which in due time she added Italian and German), and exercised in composition as well as reading in her own language and others. The whole family, trained by parental example, were steady and conscientious workers; but there were no tokens of unusual ability in Harriet during any part of her childhood or

[5] Types of cloth, silk.

youth. Her health was bad, her tone of spirits low, her habit of mind anxious, and her habits of life silent, and as independent as they could be under the old-fashioned family rule of strictness and the strong hand. At her entrance upon womanhood a deafness, unperceived during her childhood and slight in youth, was aggravated by a kind of accident, and became so severe as to compel (for other people's accommodation as well as her own) the use of a trumpet for the rest of her life. This misfortune, no doubt, strengthened her habits of study, and had much to do with the marking out of her career. What other effects it produced upon her she has shown in her "Letter to the Deaf."

Her first appearance in print was before she was out of her teens, in a religious periodical; the same in which the late Judge Talfourd had made his early attempts not very long before.[6] Not only her contributions to the "Monthly Repository," but her first books were of a religious character, her cast of mind being more decidedly of the religious order than any other during the whole of her life, whatever might be the basis and scope of her ultimate opinions. Her latest opinions were, in her own view, the most religious,—the most congenial with the emotional as well as the rational department of human nature. In her youth she naturally wrote what she had been brought up to believe, and her first work, "Devotional Exercises," was thoroughly Unitarian. Of this class, and indeed of all her early writings, the only one worth mention is the little volume "Traditions of Palestine," which first fixed attention upon her, and made her name known in the reviews. There are some even now who prefer that little volume to all her other writings. Before it was out its writer had formed the conception of the very different kind of work which at once and completely opened her career, her "Illustrations of Political Economy." Her stimulus in all she wrote, from first to last, was simply the need of utterance. This need she had gratified early; and those who knew her best were always aware that she was not ambitious, though she enjoyed success, and had pride enough to have suffered keenly under failure. When, in 1829, she and her sisters lost their small fortunes by the failure

---

[6] Sir Thomas Noon Talfourd (1795–1854) was a judge, poet, playwright (*Ion*, 1835), and editor (of Charles Lamb).

of the house in which their money was placed, Harriet continued to write as she had written before, though under the new liability of having no money to spend upon ventures. Without capital, without any literary connections (except the editor of the "Monthly Repository"), without any visible means of accomplishing her object, she resolved to bring out a series of "Illustrations of Political Economy," confident that the work was at that time (1831) very much needed by the working-classes, to say nothing of other persons who had influence in the community, agitated as it then was by the Reform struggle. That Reform struggle and the approach of the cholera on its first visit made the booksellers disinclined to publish any thing. Messrs. Baldwin and Cradock had all but consented to the scheme, and had in fact engaged a stitcher for the monthly volumes, when they took fright and drew back. Harriet Martineau's forthcoming Autobiography will of course tell the story of the struggle she passed through to get her work published in any manner and on any terms. Almost every considerable publisher had refused it; the Diffusion Society had declined it, on the report of their sub-committee against it.[7] It appeared, however, at the beginning of 1832, when its writer was worn out with anxiety and fatigue, and had met with uniform discouragement, except in her own home, where her own confidence that the book would succeed, because it was wanted, commanded the sympathy of her family. In a fortnight after the day of publication her way was open before her for life. The work reached a circulation of about ten thousand in the next few years. The difficulties under which it appeared prevented her being enriched by it; and her own unalterable view of what it could and what it could not effect prevented her expecting too much from it, either in regard to its social operation or its influence on her own fame. The original idea of exhibiting the great natural laws of society by a series of pictures of selected social action was a fortunate one; and her tales initiated a multitude of minds into the conception of what political economy is, and of how it concerns every body living in society. Beyond this, there is no merit of a high order in the

---

[7] The Society for the Diffusion of Useful Knowledge, formed by Henry Brougham (later Lord Brougham) in 1825 to publish new, particularly scientific, information cheaply for the working classes.

work. It did not pretend to offer discoveries, or new applications or elucidations of prior discoveries. It popularized, in a fresh form, some doctrines and many truths long before made public by others. Those were the days of her success in narrative, in fiction. In about ten years from that time she had nearly ceased to write fiction, from simple inability to do it well. On the whole, perhaps, her novel of "Deerbrook" has been the most popular of her works of fiction, though some prefer her history (in the form of a romance) of Toussaint L'Ouverture ("The Hour and the Man"), and others again her story-book for children, written in illness,—"The Playfellow." But none of her novels or tales have, or ever had, in the eyes of good judges or in her own, any character of permanence. The artistic aim and qualifications were absent; she had no power of dramatic construction; nor the poetic inspiration on the one hand, nor critical cultivation on the other, without which no work of the imagination can be worthy to live. Two or three of her Political Economy Tales, are, perhaps, her best achievement in fiction,—her doctrine furnishing the plot which she was unable to create, and the brevity of space duly restricting the indulgence in detail which injured her longer narratives, and at last warned her to leave off writing them. It was fortunate for her that her own condemnation anticipated that of the public. To the end of her life she was subject to solicitations to write more novels and more tales; but she for the most part remained steady in her refusal. Her three volumes of "Forest and Game Law Tales" and a few stories in "Household Words," written at the express and earnest request of Mr. Dickens,[8] and with little satisfaction to herself, are her latest efforts in that direction.*

Her popularity was, however, something extraordinary during the appearance of her "Illustrations of Political Economy." It was presently necessary for her to remove to London, to be within reach of the sources of information rendered indispensable by the success of her scheme and the extension of

*After the above was in the drawer of the "Daily News" office, she wrote some historical fiction for "Once a Week" against her own judgment, and only to gratify Mr. Evans and Mr. Lucas, the proprietor and editor of "Once a Week."

[8] Dickens was the editor of *Household Words* at the time to which she refers.

her influence. She lived in a lodging in Conduit Street for some months, till her mother joined her in London. Their house was in Fludyer Street, Westminster; and there they lived till a serious and long illness compelled Harriet Martineau to leave London, to which she never returned as a resident. On her first taking up her abode there many foolish stories were afloat about the origin of her series, and the aid she received in it from Lord Brougham and others. The facts were that the enterprise was wholly her own, and the execution of it also; and that Lord Brougham in particular knew nothing whatever about her or her work till his secretary sent him the first five numbers half a year after the publication began. His lordship's first thought was to engage her assistance in illustrating the evils of the old poor-law and the intended provisions of the new; and her four little volumes on the poor-laws appeared during the publication of her larger work. The two years which followed her first great success were the busiest of a busy life. All advocates of all schemes applied to her for cooperation. She was plunged at once into such a social whirl that she dined out every day but Sundays. New material for her work was always accumulating on her hands; and besides the production of one number, and occasionally two, of her little volumes per month, she had an unmanageable amount of correspondence always pressing upon her. It was at that time that she formed the habit which she continued for the rest of her life,—of sitting up late, while going on to rise early. She took, on an average, five hours or five and a half of sleep, going to bed at one in the morning, and being at her breakfast at half past seven, to save the precious morning hours for her most serious business. Such was her practice, with few intervals, to the date of her last illness.

Before the publication of her work was completed she had sailed for America. At first her object was simply to travel for the sake of recreation and repose; but, at the suggestion of the late Lord Henley, she turned her face in the direction of the United States, in order to examine some points of social policy and morals, honourable to the Americans and worthy of our emulation, but generally overlooked by European travellers who go to amuse themselves and return to quiz. She hoped to learn some secrets of success in the treatment of criminals, the insane, and other unhappy classes, and in the diffusion of education. She succeeded in her aims in some measure; but the interest of the antislavery question just at that time absorbed every other. She arrived just at the culmination of that reign of terror which she described after her return in the "Westminster Review," in the narrative entitled "The Martyr Age of the United States," which was reprinted as a pamphlet, and by which the nature and significance of the antislavery movement in America (where it involved the entire political and personal liberty of every citizen) were first made known in this country. Harriet Martineau, received with unbounded hospitality and unmeasured flatteries, though known to have written an antislavery story in her series, was not converted to the American view, as had been hoped and expected. Under circumstances in which she had no choice but to speak out she condemned slavery and its political consequences as before; and, for some months preceding her return, she was subjected to insult and injury, and was even for some weeks in danger of her life while travelling where the tar-barrel, the cowhide, and the pistol were the regimen prescribed for and applied to abolitionists, and threatened especially in her case. In her books upon America she said little or nothing of her personal share in the critical troubles of the time, because her purpose was, not to interest the public in her adventures, but to exhibit, without passion or prejudice, the actual condition of society in the United States. Its treatment of herself is rather a topic for her Autobiography, and there, no doubt, it will be found.

After an absence of two years she returned to England in August, 1836, and early in the next spring she published "Society in America." Her own opinion of that work changed much for the worse before her death. It was written while she was in the full flow of sympathy with the theoretical American statesmen of that time, who were all *à priori* political philosophers to a greater or less degree like the framers of the Declaration of Independence. Her intercourse with these may be traced in the structure and method of observation of her book, and her companionship with the adorers of Thomas Carlyle in her style. Some constitutional lawyers of the United States have declared that there is no error in her account of the political structure and relations of the Federal and State governments of that country; and the book contains the only account we have of the condition of slavery, and of the country under it, at the time of the rise of the abolition movement. But, on the whole, the book is not a favourable specimen of Harriet Martineau's writings, either in regard to moral or artistic taste. It is full of affectations and preachments, and it marks the highest point of the metaphysical period of her mind.[9] Little as she valued the second work on America—"Retrospect of Western Travel"—which she wrote at the request of her publishers, to bring into use her lighter observations on scenery and manners, it was more creditable to her mood, and perhaps to her powers, than the more ambitious work. The American abolitionists, then in the early days of their action, reprinted as a pamphlet the parts of these two works which relate to the slave institutions of their country, and sowed it broadcast over the land. The virulence with which the Southern press denounces her to this day, in company with Mrs. [Maria Weston] Chapman and Mrs. [Harriet Beecher] Stowe, seems to show that her representations were not lost on the American public. If they are operating at the end of so many years, there must be truth in them. Though the customary dispensers of hospitality in the United States passed from the extreme of courtesy to that of rudeness to the traveller, she formed valuable friendships in that country which lasted as long as her life. Her connection with the interests of America remained a close one, and its political course was a subject of action to a late period, and of study to the last.

In the interval between her return from America and her leaving London—somewhat less than three years—she wrote "How to Observe Morals and Manners," a volume of a series published by Mr. Knight, of which Sir Henry Delabêche's "How to Observe Geology" was the opening volume; a few of the volumes of the "Guide to Service," issued also by Mr. Knight; and her novel "Deerbrook." The "Guides to Service" were originated by the Poor-law Commissioners, with the object chiefly of training the ideas of children, especially

[9] Here she refers to the second stage of Auguste Comte's epistemology, the first being theological, the second metaphysical, and the final and "best," scientific. By this writing she was a positivist in the Comtean mode. The reference to Carlyle is her way of saying she has rejected the romanticism he represents, it being a metaphysical form of thinking in the scheme she endorses here.

in the workhouse schools, for the occupation of their lives. Harriet Martineau agreed to write the model number, provided she might take the "Maid-of-all-Work" for her subject; which she did, with the amusing result that at various turns of her life afterwards she was met by the popular belief that she had herself been a maid-of-all-work; a mistake which she regarded with some complacency whenever she encountered it. The other volumes of the Series written by her are the "Dressmaker" (in which she had some technical assistance from a professional person), the "Housemaid," and the "Lady's Maid."

On the publication of "Deerbrook," in April, 1839, she went abroad with a party of friends, partly to escort an invalid cousin, and partly for rest and refreshment to herself. She was not aware of the extent of her own illness; and she was brought home on a couch from Venice in June, in a state of health so hopeless that she left London and settled herself at Tynemouth, on the Northumberland coast, within reach of family care and tendance. There she remained, a prisoner to the couch, till the close of 1844. During her illness she wrote her second novel ("The Hour and the Man"), the four volumes of children's tales called "The Playfellow," and "Life in the Sick-Room," originating also, in concert with the present Countess of Elgin and Mr. Knight, the series since so well known as "The Weekly Volume." Of her recovery the public heard at the time much more than she desired and approved. At the instigation of several of her friends, and especially of her medical attendant, she made trial of mesmerism, for the purpose of obtaining some release from the use of opiates. To her own surprise and that of others, the treatment procured her a release from the disease itself, from which several eminent medical men had declared recovery to be impossible. In five months she was perfectly well. Meantime, doctors and strangers in various parts of the kingdom had rushed into print, without her countenance or her knowledge; and the amount of misrepresentation and mischief soon became so great as to compel her to tell the story as it really happened.[10] The commotion

[10] She engages here in a little manipulation of the truth. She published her "Letters on Mesmerism" in the *Athenaeum* in 1844 *first*, claiming among other things that her maid, Jane Arrowsmith, had effectively mesmerized her and was clairvoyant. This caused the biggest commotion, and her medical attendant, her physician and brother-in-law Thomas Greenhow, felt

was just what might have been anticipated from the usual reception of new truths in science and the medical art. That she
recovered when she ought to have died was an unpardonable
offence. According to the doctors who saw her enter society
again from the beginning of 1845, she was in a state of infatua-
tion, and, being as ill as ever in reality, would sink down in six
months. When, instead of so sinking down, she rode on a
camel to Mount Sinai and Petra, and on horseback to Damascus, they said she had never been ill. To the charge that it had
been "all imagination," her reply was that, in that case, it was
the doctor's imagination and not hers that was involved; for
they had told her, and not she them, what and how serious her
illness was. To the friends who blamed her for publishing her
experience before the world was ripe for it, her reply was,
first, that she had no option; and next, that it is hard to see
how the world is to get ripened if experimenters in new departments of natural philosophy conceal their experience. The
immediate consequence of the whole business—the extension
of the practice of mesmerism as a curative agent, and especially
the restoration of several cases like her own—abundantly com-
pensated Harriet Martineau for an amount of insult and ridicule which would have been a somewhat unreasonable penalty
on any sin or folly which she could have committed. As a
penalty on simply getting well when she was expected to die,
the infliction was a curious sign of the times.

Being free to choose her place of abode, on her recovery,
her friends universally supposed she would return to London and its literary advantages and enjoyment. But literature,
though a precious luxury, was not, and never had been, the
daily bread of her life. She felt that she could not be happy, or
in the best way useful, if the declining years of her life were
spent in lodgings in the morning and drawing-rooms in the
evening. A quiet home of her own, and some few dependent
on her for their domestic welfare, she believed to be essential
to every true woman's peace of mind; and she chose her plan
of life accordingly. Meaning to live in the country, she chose

---

compelled to defend his reputation as a doctor. Apparently, he did so without his patient's permission, publishing his *Medical Report of the Case of Miss
H——M——*. See Pichanick, *Martineau*, pp. 129–137, for discussion and
quotations from this exchange.

the most beautiful, and settled at the Lakes. She bought a field near Ambleside, opposite Fox How, and about a mile from Rydal Mount.[11] She built a house, and tried her hand successfully on the smallest of farms,—a farm of two acres. She set on foot some remedial schemes applicable to local mischiefs; and by degrees found herself pledged to a practice of delivering a series of lectures every winter to the mechanics of the little town and their families. She and they were so well acquainted, that there was nothing odd in this in their view, and no strangers were admitted, nor even the gentry of the place, for want of room. Her subjects were Sanitary Principles and Practice, the History of England, the History of North America, and the Scenes of her Eastern Travel. In her Ambleside home she lived for ten years of health and happiness, which, as she was wont to say, was worth all the rest of her life.

At various times since 1832 she had been sounded about accepting a pension on the Civil List; and she had repeatedly replied by objecting to receive one. Her objections remained in full force when Lord Melbourne made an express offer to her of a pension of £150, to be increased as circumstances permitted, as his last act before going out of power in 1841. Lord Melbourne was aware that she had invested her spare earnings in a deferred annuity, and that while hopelessly ill she was very poor. Her objections, however, bore no relation to this class of considerations. Her letter to Lord Melbourne found its way into the newspapers without her knowledge, and it speaks for itself. Not the less for this was she misunderstood. Nothing was further from her thoughts than passing condemnation on the literary pensioners of the time. They must judge for themselves, and their position was different. It was a matter of feeling with her quite as much as of principle; and she would have thankfully received any acknowledgment of past labours which might have been decreed, otherwise than through a method of favouritism. She felt that, once under pecuniary obligation to the sovereign and the minister, she could never again feel perfectly free on political questions, though Lord Melbourne generously deprecated any such conclusion. As it

[11] Fox How was the home of Hartley Coleridge, brother of Samuel Taylor Coleridge, Rydal Mount the home of William and Mary Wordsworth.

happened, she did very well without the money, and she wrote the "History of the Thirty Years' Peace," which she could hardly have done while in receipt of a pension.

This, the bulkiest of her works and the most laborious, was undertaken at the request of Mr. Charles Knight, who had himself written the first few chapters, then deputed the work to another, and presently found it at a stand. Harriet Martineau had no idea whatever whether she could write history; but, on Mr. Knight's pressing his request, she went to work in August, 1848, and completed the work (after an interval of a few weeks) in the autumn of 1849. The introductory volume was written in 1850, also at Mr. Knight's solicitation. Without taking the chronicle form this history could not, from the nature of the case, be cast in the ultimate form of perfected history. All that can be done with contemporary history is to collect and methodize the greatest amount of reliable facts and distinct impressions, to amass sound material for the veritable historian of a future day,—so consolidating, assimilating, and vivifying the structure as to do for the future writer precisely that which the lapse of time and the oblivion which creeps over all transactions must prevent his doing for himself. This auxiliary usefulness is the aim of Harriet Martineau's history; and she was probably not mistaken in hoping for that much result from her labour. It rendered her a personal service which she had not anticipated. There was an impression abroad of her being a sort of demagogue or dangerous Radical, though it is hard to say which of her writings could have originated such an impression. The history dispelled it thoroughly; and if it proved that she belonged to no party, it showed that it was not because she transcended the extremes of all.

The work which she published on her return from her Eastern travels, which she enjoyed as the guest of Mr. and Mrs. Richard V. Yates, of Liverpool, had shown that she was no longer a Unitarian nor a believer in revelation at all. "Eastern Life, Present and Past," exhibits the history and generation of the four great faiths—the Egyptian, the Jewish, the Christian, and the Mohammedan—as they appear when their birthplaces are visited in succession. She had passed from the Nile to Sinai; and thence to Jerusalem, Damascus, and Lebanon. The work in which she gave out her views on her return ranks, on the whole, as the best of her writings; and her reputation assumed a new, a graver, and a broader character after its appearance. It was followed in 1851 by a volume which, though not for the most part written by her, was of her procuring and devising. She took the responsibility of the *Letters on the Laws of Man's Nature and Development*, which were for the greater part written by her friend, Mr. Atkinson, in reply to the short letters of her own which occupy a small proportion of the book. This book brought upon its writers, as was inevitable, the imputation of atheism from the multitude who cannot distinguish between the popular and the philosophical sense of the word,—between the disbelief in the popular theology which has caused a long series of religious men to be called atheists, and the disbelief in a First Cause,—a disbelief which is expressly disclaimed in the book. A full account of Harriet Martineau's faith and philosophy will of course be found in her forthcoming Autobiography, where it is more in place than here. As to the consequences of such an expression of them, they were somewhat different from what might have been expected. The reception of the volume disclosed some curious social facts, revealing to its authors an altogether unexpected proportion between the receivers and repudiators of dogmatic theology in this country. What is called "the entire periodical press" condemned the book, without, however, in any one case meeting its argument or recognizing its main subject; and yet was it excellently received and widely sympathized with. Every body supposed that its authors would be ruined, excluded from society, stopped in their work, and so forth. But the actual result was that this open avowal of heretical opinion made all the relations of life sounder than they had ever been. As Harriet Martineau declared, it dissolved all false relations and confirmed all true ones. At no time of her life was she more occupied, more prosperous, so cheered by sympathy, or so thoroughly happy, as during the interval between the publication of that book and the close of her labours.

Besides some small works, such as "Guide to the Lakes," it remained for her to bring out two of more general importance,—her volume on "Household Education," which is more popular than almost any of her works, and her condensation of Comte's "Positive Philosophy." The story of the intention and achievement of that work is told in its prefaces. Begun in 1852, it occupied the greater part of the year 1853, and appeared in November of that year. It was her last considerable work; and there is no other, perhaps, which so well manifests the real character of her ability and proper direction of her influence,—as far as each went. Her original power was nothing more than was due to earnestness and intellectual clearness within a certain range. With small imaginative and suggestive powers, and therefore nothing approaching to genius, she could see clearly what she did see, and give a clear expression to what she had to say. In short, she could popularize, while she could neither discover nor invent. She could sympathize in other people's views, and was too facile in doing so; and she could obtain and keep a firm grasp of her own, and, moreover, she could make them understood. The function of her life was to do this, and, in as far as it was done diligently and honestly, her life was of use, however far its achievements may have fallen short of expectations less moderate than her own. Her duties and her business were sufficient for the peace and the desires of her mind. She saw the human race, as she believed, advancing under the law of progress; she enjoyed her share of the experience, and had no ambition for a larger endowment, or reluctance or anxiety about leaving the enjoyment of such as she had.

From the early part of 1852 she had contributed largely to the "Daily News," and her "Letters from Ireland" in the summer of that year were written for this paper. As her other works left her hands the connection with the paper became closer, and it was never interrupted except for a few months at the beginning of her last illness, when all her strength was needed for her Autobiography. When she had finished that task she had the work printed, and the engravings prepared for it under her own supervision, partly to avoid delay in its appearance (because any good that it could do would be best done immediately after her death), but chiefly to spare her executors all responsibility about publishing whatever may be found in the Memoir. Her last illness was a time of quiet enjoyment to her, soothed as it was by family and social love, and care, and sympathy, and, except for one heart-grief,—the loss in 1864 of her niece Maria, who was to her as a daughter,—free from anxiety of every kind, and amused by the constant interest of regarding life and its affairs from the verge of the horizon of existence. Her disease was deterioration and en-

largement of the heart, the fatal character of which was discovered in January, 1855. She declined throughout that and
subsequent years, and died—[12]

—And died in the summer sunset of her home amid the
Westmoreland mountains, on the 27th of June, 1876, after
twenty-one more diligent, devoted, suffering, joyful years,—
attended by the family friends she most loved, and in possession of all her mental powers up to the last expiring day; aged
seventy-four years.

If, instead of dying so slowly, she had died as she could
have wished and thought to have done, without delay, what
a treasure of wise counsels, what a radiance of noble deeds,
what a spirit of love and of power, what brave victorious battle
to the latest hour for all things good and true, had been lost to
posterity! What an example of more than resignation, of that
ready, glad acceptance of a lingering and painful death which
made the sight a blessing to every witness, had been lost to the
surviving generation!

During all the last one-and-twenty years death was the
idea most familiar and most welcome. It was spoken of and
provided for with an easy freedom that I never saw approached
in any other home, yet she never expressed a wish respecting a
place of burial.[13] But a few days before her death, when asked
if she would be laid in the burial-place of her family, she assented; and she lies with her kindred, in the old cemetery at
Birmingham.

[12] At this point the obituary written in 1855 by Martineau herself ends.
Note her insertion of the 1864 death of her niece. The material that follows
was written by her friend and literary executor, Maria Weston Chapman.

[13] This is not so. In the library of Manchester College, Oxford, there is
a series of letters from Harriet Martineau, written in 1855, addressed to a
Unitarian minister friend, presumably Philip Carpenter, son of her adoles-
cent mentor, Lant Carpenter, in which she gives detailed directions for her
funeral and burial. She believes that because of her views "which the vulgar w^d call atheistical" some of the people in her parish would object to her
burial there (that is, in the Church of England churchyard a mile up the road
from her house, a church in sight of the Wordsworths' house, Rydal Mount),
so she asks him where the nearest Unitarian burial ground is and if he thinks
she might be buried there. She instructs him in one letter to say in the service for her what he finds most natural. In another, written the next day, she
tells him she forgot the day before to say she wants a simple funeral with no
hatbands or scarves or feasting. It was, of course, more than twenty years
before she died.

II

ON WOMEN'S EQUAL RIGHTS

Let your attack be Evidence softened by Benevolence.

—*Harriet Martineau*
"Criticism on Women"

There can be but one true method in the treatment of each human being of either sex, of any color, and under any outward circumstances—to ascertain what are the powers of that being, to cultivate them to the utmost, and then to see what action they will find for themselves. This has probably never been done for men, unless in some rare individual cases. It has certainly never been done for women.

—*Harriet Martineau*
Letter to an American women's rights convention held at Worcester, Massachusetts

Harriet Martineau c. 1835
Reprinted from Webb, *Harriet Martineau*
Courtesy of R. K. Webb

Harriet Martineau was a lifelong feminist, and she became one early and on her own. "The woman question" was what she and other like-minded nineteenth-century thinkers and activists called what we call feminism.[1] In addition to giving her individual attention to women and women's concerns, Martineau participated in groups in both England and the United States that were fertile environments for deliberate efforts on women's behalf. Probably not too much should be made of the fact that she wrote admiringly of women writers in her first published piece ("Female Writers of Practical Divinity") or that she went to some length to establish the fact that the form she used for her political economy tales was derived from a woman. Still, these attributions acknowledged influences from women that she valued from the first.

Her first intellectual groups, the Norwich and then the London Unitarians and Utilitarians, were probably far more important in her development, since a component of the thought of both Unitarian religion and Utilitarian philosophy was favorable to women having a larger place in intellectual and public pursuits. Although the first of Martineau's several breaches with people she had once favored came with W. J. Fox, the Unitarian editor, because of his setting up a household with Eliza Flowers without marriage, Martineau was surely influenced by Fox's liberality toward talented women and the intellectual role such women as Flowers played in Fox's editorship. Her scruples about sexual liaisons were more stereotypically Victorian than the views and practices of many of her associates. Yet sexuality per se was not a feminist issue in the nineteenth century. To consider it an obstacle to the realization of feminist goals is to interpret nineteenth-century views in light of twentieth-century feminism which has made the link between sexuality and gender role assignment. It is ironic from a contemporary feminist stance, if not from her own, that she regenerated or kept up correspondence or a working relationship with the men in such affairs, but not the women.

The American group with whom Martineau found the greatest affinity during her 1834–1836 travels, the Garrisonian abolitionists, like the British Unitarians and Utilitarians, val-

[1] See note 13, Introduction.

53

ued the activity and importance of women and was markedly more advanced on the question than many other groups. Anti-slavery women's groups in America were to provide leaders and formative ideas in its early years for the movement for women's rights per se, a movement *for* women as well as a movement of and by women on behalf of slaves.

The five pieces that follow are ones in which Martineau addressed feminism in some general way. In the opening selection she questions the advisability of marriage for everyone, a position that required considerable bravery in 1838. She raised the question as a means of making judgments about the character of a society, but whatever its intent, it was a courageous question to ask and one that anticipates such contrasting variations of the theme in the 1970s as Kate Millett's "sexual politics" and Jessie Bernard's study of "his" and "hers" marriages that yield greater benefits to men and lesser benefits to women. Martineau was shrewd and discerning to pick the place of women and the treatment of women in marriage as indices of a society's distinctiveness.

In *How to Observe Morals and Manners* she set up criteria for analyzing a society. Published after her books on the United States, *Society in America* and *Retrospect of Western Travel*, it reflects the method of comparative study of societies used in those books. She set down what she believed to be an appropriate set of principles, laws of right and wrong, if you will, and then gauged the society by how well she thought it met the principles. As the title suggests, these principles had to do with "morals," deep values held and acted upon, and "manners," assumptions and practices of courtesy, kindness, politeness, or the absence thereof, the surface manifestations of moral depth.

This work was indeed an early sociological work on method, as Alice Rossi has claimed. Martineau goes halfway toward what early anthropologists and sociologists several decades later hoped to achieve. That is, her methodological approach involved the attempt to evolve some detached criteria for objectivity. That far, she succeeds in being a primitive scientist. But the other half of her approach provides her limitation. She inserts her *own* values, quite assuredly and dogmatically, as the appropriate criteria. This was, however, four

54

years before Comte's *Positive Philosophy* was published and at least thirteen years before she read it. She was herself to criticize this phase of her thinking as "metaphysical" at a later time. Her feminism and her social science may be in conflict in this article. To raise such questions about women and marriage was important on women's behalf however she did it, but to do it dogmatically is not good enough. Calling monogamy of the English variety "the natural method" for all coupling is application of an unexamined value system. Calling for removal of inferior treatment of women is suggesting a new one.

The second selection, "Criticism on Women," published in 1839, is ostensibly a review essay of three items, but is in fact an essay on the abuse of women and the right of women to be respected and honored or to be criticized according to standards of honesty and fairness to all people. One of the persons she defends so splendidly in this piece is the young Queen Victoria, just come to the throne in 1837. Another (this review is anonymous) is herself, attacked ad hominem for her deafness and her womanhood after daring to write on population.

She had received vicious treatment in the reviews of "Weal and Woe in Garveloch." Writing under the editorship of John Gibson Lockhart in the *Quarterly Review*, John Wilson Croker was the first to damn her. He wrote, "and most of all it is quite impossible not to be shocked, nay, disgusted, with many of the unfeminine and mischievous doctrines on the principles of social welfare. . . . A woman who thinks child-bearing a *crime against society*! An unmarried woman who declaims against marriage!! A *young woman* who deprecates charity and provision for the poor!!!"[2]

The attack was patently unfair, not only for its rejection of the mild story favoring birth control, but also for its sexist rebuke of Martineau personally as a woman who would dare to write on such a subject. In "Criticism on Women," she coins the word "Crokerism" to identify this particular kind of reputation smearing.

The very year (1832) of Croker's article, in fact, she was still allowing for the possibility that she might marry and,

[2]Quoted in Vera Wheatley, *The Life and Work of Harriet Martineau* (London: Secker and Warburg, 1957), pp. 101–102.

hence, bear children herself. Writing to her mother in anticipation of her mother's coming to live with her in London, she laid out, along with her claim to professional independence as a woman, her right to marry: "There is another chance, dear mother, and that is, of my marrying. I have no thoughts of it. I see a thousand reasons against it. But I could not positively answer for always continuing in the same mind. . . . I mean no more than I say, I assure you; but, strong as my convictions are against marrying, I will not positively promise."[3]

The third piece is a marvelous letter written, no doubt, to Maria Weston Chapman and read at an American women's rights convention at Worcester, Massachusetts, in 1851.[4] In the letter, Martineau repeats her themes of the necessity of equal treatment of all humans, of the importance of education to enable women to flourish, of the need for the object of education to be occupation, and of the silliness of the old controversy of influence versus office. However, it is significant here that she couched her persuasive arguments in terms of the need to do a scientific experiment. Although her writing had always been analytical, this letter was written in the year she was first reading Comte's *Positive Philosophy*, and it is clear that she has a new faith that social experiment will yield proof of women's ability. This letter from 1851 is an early example of her work after she had found clarity in science and provides a good exhibit of her utter confidence in the outcome of an experiment not yet conducted. Only to those of us with post-Darwinian, post-Freudian, post-Einsteinian mentalities is such assurance unwarranted. It was entirely earnest and even revolutionary in Martineau.

If the personal is the political is the intellectual, we may have the key to Martineau's vast outpouring of work about

---

[3]Quoted in ibid., p. 94.

[4]I have to thank Joan H. Winterkorn of the Department of Rare Books, Cornell University Libraries, both for providing me with a copy of an undated clipping of the article from the Cornell University Library Anti-Slavery Collection, and for tracing its source of publication to the *Liberator*. Webb in his *Harriet Martineau* (p. 182n) credits its publication to the *National Anti-Slavery Standard*, but Winterkorn speculates that he did so on finding it among other clippings of Martineau's writings from the *National Anti-Slavery Standard* in the Cornell University Libraries.

women. One element in the shaping of her young life was the insanity and apparent suicide of the one man to whom she ever seemed to have had a romantic attachment, her fiancé John Worthington, a college friend of her brother James. I do not think it is the whole story. I do not think it is even a great part of the story. Yet, I take at her word the account she gives in the fourth selection of her singleness being the great benefit to her work, in effect her work being her love. In so doing, I differ with her recent biographers who have speculated about her lesbianism or absence of it, her sexuality, latent or active. R. K. Webb concludes that she was a "latent lesbian." Pichanick disagrees with him, arguing that although Martineau had important "affectionate female friendships," there is no evidence for her being a lesbian.[5] I believe she was probably behaviorally asexual and emotionally sexually naive, and I think she means what she says in her *Autobiography*: that Worthington's death liberated her to be alone and like it.

The fifth selection, on Mary Wollstonecraft, William Godwin, and the woman question, occurs in the context of a description of William Godwin as one of her morning visitors in London in the early days of her fame in 1833.[6] She delighted in Godwin and greatly enjoyed his company, and, seeing no conflict of ideology loyalties, Martineau expressly denied that her interest in him arose because of his connection with Mary Wollstonecraft. Instead, she said, the opposite was true. She had no use for Wollstonecraft, while honoring Godwin. She claimed Wollstonecraft did the cause of woman a disservice, proclaiming Wollstonecraft "a poor victim of passion, with no control over her own peace, and no calmness or content except when the needs of her individual nature were satisfied."

All that, while extolling the pleasure of visiting with the man who loved Wollstonecraft—presumably with a passion

[5] See Webb, *Harriet Martineau*, pp. 50–51; and Pichanick, *Harriet Martineau*, pp. 109–110.

[6] Godwin, a radical philosopher, was briefly the beloved husband of Mary Wollstonecraft, author of *A Vindication of the Rights of Women*, the first English feminist work. The two were a devoted couple but maintained separate households. Wollstonecraft died from complications following the birth of their daughter, Mary Shelley.

of his own—and who had done everything he could to keep her memory alive! The passion she means, of course, is not merely sexual extravagance but the exaggerated romantic flamboyance of a personality like Wollstonecraft's.

Following that judgment of Wollstonecraft, however, her comments on the woman question sound uncharacteristically self-righteous. Her tone is hostile toward some women, but her message is still consistently that of the rational moralist. She writes calmly of her expectation that women will achieve the right to vote.

ON MARRIAGE

The Marriage compact is the most important feature of the domestic state on which the observer can fix his attention. If he be a thinker, he will not be surprised at finding much imperfection in the marriage state wherever he goes. By no arrangements yet attempted have purity of morals, constancy of affection, and domestic peace been secured to any extensive degree in society. Almost every variety of method is still in use, in one part of the world or another. The primitive custom of brothers marrying sisters still subsists in some Eastern regions. Polygamy is very common there, as every one knows. In countries which are too far advanced for this, every restraint of law, all sanction of opinion, has been tried to render that natural method,—the restriction of one husband to one wife,—successful, and therefore universal and permanent. Law and opinion have, however, never availed to anything like complete success. Even in thriving young countries, where no considerations of want, and few of ambition, can interfere with domestic peace,—where the numbers are equal,

—

Harriet Martineau, *How to Observe Morals and Manners* (London: Charles Knight, 1838), pp. 167–182. Probably drafted in 1834.

where love has the promise of a free and even course, and where religious sentiment is directed full upon the sanctity of the marriage state,—it is found to be far from pure. In almost all countries, the corruption of society in this department is so deep and wide-spreading, as to vitiate both moral sentiment and practice in an almost hopeless degree. It neutralizes almost all attempts to ameliorate and elevate the condition of the race.—There must be something fearfully wrong where the general result is so unfortunate as this. As in most other cases of social suffering, the wrong will be found to lie less in the methods ordained and put in practice, than in the prevalent sentiment of society, out of which all methods arise.

It is necessary to make mention (however briefly) of the kinds of false sentiment from which the evil of conjugal unhappiness appears to spring.—The sentiment by which courage is made the chief ground of honour in men, and chastity in women, coupled with the inferiority in which women have ever been sunk, was sure to induce profligacy. As long as men were brave nothing more was required to make them honourable in the eyes of society: while the inferior condition of women has ever exposed those of them who were not protected by birth and wealth to the profligacy of men. . . .

Marriage exists everywhere, to be studied by the moral observer. He must watch the character of courtships wherever he goes;—whether the young lady is negociated for and promised by her guardians, without having seen her intended; like the poor girl who, when she asked her mother to point out her future husband from among a number of gentlemen, was silenced with the rebuke, "What is that to you?"—or whether they are left free to exchange their faith "by flowing stream, through wood, or craggy wild," as in the United States;—or whether there is a medium between these two extremes, as in England. He must observe how fate is defied by lovers in various countries. . . . Scotch lovers agree to come together after so many years spent in providing the "plenishing." Irish lovers conclude the business, in case of difficulty, by appearing before the priest the next morning. There is recourse to a balcony and rope-ladder in one country; a steam-boat and back-settlement in another; trust and patience in a third; and intermediate flirtations, to pass the time, in a fourth. He must note the degree of worldly ambition which attends marriages, and which may therefore be supposed to stimulate them,—how much space the house with two rooms in humble life, and the country-seat and carriages in higher life, occupy in the mind of bride or bridegroom.—He must observe whether conjugal infidelity excites horror and rage, or whether it is so much a matter of course as that no jealousy interferes to mar the arrangements of mutual convenience.—He must mark whether women are made absolutely the property of their husbands, in mind and in estate; or whether the wife is treated more or less professedly as an equal party in the agreement.—He must observe whether there is an excluded class, victims to their own superstition or to a false social obligation, wandering about to disturb by their jealousy or licentiousness those whose lot is happier.—He must observe whether there are domestic arrangements for home enjoyments, or whether all is planned on the supposition of pleasure lying abroad; whether the reliance is on books, gardens, and play with children, or on the opera, parties, the ale-house, or dances on the green.—He must mark whether the ladies are occupied with their household cares in the morning, and the society of their husbands in the evening, or with embroidery and looking out of balconies; with receiving company all day, or gadding abroad; with the library or the nursery; with lovers or with children.—In each country, called civilized, he will meet with almost all these varieties: but in each there is such a prevailing character in the aspect of domestic life, that intelligent observation will enable him to decide, without much danger of mistake, as to whether marriage is merely an arrangement of convenience, in accordance with low morals, or a sacred institution, commanding the reverence and affection of a virtuous people. No high degree of this sanctity can be looked for till that moderation is attained which, during the prevalence of asceticism and its opposite, is reached only by a few. That it yet exists nowhere as the characteristic of any society,—that all the blessings of domestic life are not yet open to all, so as to preclude the danger of any one encroaching on his neighbour,—is but too evident to the travelled observer. He can only mark the degree of approximation to this state of high morals wherever he goes.

The traveller everywhere finds woman treated as the inferior party in a compact in which both parties have an equal interest. Any agreement thus formed is imperfect, and is liable to disturbance; and the danger is great in proportion to the degradation of the supposed weaker party. The degree of the degradation of woman is as good a test as the moralist can adopt for ascertaining the state of domestic morals in any country.

The Indian squaw carries the household burdens, trudging in the dust, while her husband on horseback paces before her, unencumbered but by his own gay trappings. She carries the wallet with food, the matting for the lodge, the merchandize (if they possess any), and her infant. There is no exemption from labour for the squaw of the most vaunted chief. In other countries the wife may be found drawing the plough, hewing wood and carrying water; the men of the family standing idle to witness her toils. Here the observer may feel pretty sure of his case. From a condition of slavery like this, women are found rising to the highest condition in which they are at present seen, in France, England, and the United States,— where they are less than half-educated, precluded from earning a subsistence, except in a very few ill-paid employments, and prohibited from giving or withholding their assent to laws which they are yet bound by penalties to obey. In France, owing to the great destruction of men in the wars of Napoleon, women are engaged, and successfully engaged, in a variety of occupations which have been elsewhere supposed unsuitable to the sex. Yet there remains so large a number who cannot, by the most strenuous labour in feminine employments, command the necessaries of life, while its luxuries may be earned by infamy, that the morals of the society are naturally bad. Great attention has of late been given to this subject in France: the social condition of women is matter of thought and discussion to a degree which promises some considerable amelioration. Already, women can do more in France than anywhere else; they can attempt more without ridicule or arbitrary hinderance: and the women of France are probably destined to lead the way in the advance which the sex must hereafter make. At present, society is undergoing a transition from a feudal state to one of mutual government; and women, gaining in some ways, suffer in others during the process. They have, happily for themselves, lost much of the peculiar kind of observance which was the most remarkable feature of the chivalrous age; and it has been impossible to prevent their sharing in the benefits of the improvement and diffusion of knowledge. All cultivation of their powers has secured to them the use of new power; so that their condition is far superior to what it was in any former age. But new difficulties about securing a maintenance have arisen. Marriage is less general; and the husbands of the greater number of women are not secure of a maintenance from the lords of the soil, any more than women are from being married. The charge of their own maintenance is thrown upon large numbers of women, without the requisite variety of employments having been opened to them, or the needful education imparted. A natural consequence of this is, that women are educated to consider marriage the one object in life, and therefore to be extremely impatient to secure it. The unfavourable influence of these results upon the happiness of domestic life may be seen at a glance.

This may be considered the sum and substance of female education in England; and the case is scarcely better in France, though the independence and practical efficiency of women there are greater than in any other country. The women in the United States are in a lower condition than either, though there is less striving after marriage, from its greater frequency, and little restriction is imposed upon the book-learning which women may obtain. But the old feudal notions about the sex flourish there, while they are going out in the more advanced countries of Europe; and these notions, in reality, regulate the condition of women. American women generally are treated in no degree as equals, but with a kind of superstitious outward observance, which, as they have done nothing to earn it, is false and hurtful. Coexisting with this, there is an extreme difficulty in a woman's obtaining a maintenance, except by the exercise of some rare powers. In a country where women are brought up to be indulged wives, there is no hope, help, or prospect for such as have not money and are not married.

In America, women can earn a maintenance only by teaching, sewing, employment in factories, keeping boarding-houses, and domestic service. Some governesses are tolerably well paid,—comparing their earnings with those of men. Employment in factories, and domestic service, are well paid.

Sewing is so wretched an occupation everywhere, that it is to be hoped that machinery will soon supersede the use of human fingers in a labour so unprofitable. In Boston, Massachusetts, a woman is paid ninepence (sixpence English) for making a shirt.—In England, besides these occupations, others are opening; and, what is of yet greater consequence, the public mind is awakening to the necessity of enlarging the sphere of female industry. Some of the inferior branches of the fine arts have lately offered profitable employment to many women. The commercial adversity to which the country has been exposed from time to time, has been of service to the sex, by throwing hundreds and thousands of them upon their own resources, and thus impelling them to urge claims and show powers which are more respected every day.—In France this is yet more conspicuously the case. There, women are shop-keepers, merchants, professional accountants, editors of newspapers, and employed in many other ways, unexampled elsewhere, but natural and respectable enough on the spot.

Domestic morals are affected in two principal respects by these differences. Where feminine occupations of a profitable nature are few, and therefore overstocked, and therefore yielding a scanty maintenance with difficulty, there is the strongest temptation to prefer luxury with infamy to hardship with unrecognized honour. Hence arises much of the corruption of cities,—less in the United States than in Europe, from the prevalence of marriage,—but awful in extent everywhere. Where vice is made to appear the interest of large classes of women, the observer may be quite sure that domestic morals will be found impure. If he can meet with any society where the objects of life are as various and as freely open to women as to men, there he may be sure of finding the greatest amount of domestic purity and peace; for, if women were not helpless, men would find it far less easy to be vicious.

The other way in which domestic morals are affected by the scope which is allowed to the powers of women, is through the views of marriage which are induced. Marriage is debased by being considered the one worldly object in life,—that on which maintenance, consequence, and power depend. Where the husband marries for connexion, fortune, or an heir to his estate, and the wife for an establishment, for consequence, or influence, there is no foundation for high domestic morals and lasting peace; and in a country where marriage is made the single aim of all women, there is no security against the influence of some of these motives even in the simplest and purest cases of attachment. The sordidness is infused from the earliest years; the taint is in the mind before the attachment begins, before the objects meet; and the evil effects upon the marriage state are incalculable.

All this—the sentiment of society with regard to Woman and to Marriage, the social condition of Woman, and the consequent tendency and aim of her education,—the traveller must carefully observe. Each civilized society claims for itself the superiority in its treatment of woman. In one, she is indulged with religious shows, and with masquerades, or Punch, as an occasional variety. In another, she is left in honourable and undisputed possession of the housekeeping department. In a third, she is allowed to meddle, behind the scenes, with the business which is confided to her husband's management. In a fourth, she is satisfied in being the cherished domestic companion, unaware of the injury of being doomed to the narrowness of mind which is the portion of those who are always confined to the domestic circle. In a fifth, she is flattered at being guarded and indulged as a being requiring incessant fostering, and too feeble to take care of herself. In a sixth society, there may be found expanding means of independent occupation, of responsible employment for women; and here, other circumstances being equal, is the best promise of domestic fidelity and enjoyment.

It is a matter of course that women who are furnished with but one object,—marriage,—must be as unfit for anything when their aim is accomplished as if they had never had any object at all. They are no more equal to the task of education than to that of governing the state; and, if any unexpected turn of adversity befals them, they have no resource but a convent, or some other charitable provision. Where, on the other hand, women are brought up capable of maintaining an independent existence, other objects remain where the grand one is accomplished. Their independence of mind places them beyond the reach of the spoiler; and their cultivated faculty of reason renders them worthy guardians of the rational beings whose weal or woe is lodged in their hands. There is yet, as may be seen by a mere glance over society, only a very imperfect provision made anywhere for doing justice to the next generation by qualifying their mothers; but the observer of morals may profit by marking the degrees in which this imperfection approaches to barbarism. Where he finds that girls are committed to convents for education, and have no alternative in life but marriage, in which their will has no share, and a return to their convent, he may safely conclude that there a plurality of lovers is a matter of course, and domestic enjoyments of the highest kind undesired and unknown. He may conclude that as are the parents, so will be the children; and that, for one more generation at least, there will be little or no improvement. But where he finds a variety of occupations open to women; where he perceives them not only pursuing the lighter mechanic arts, dispensing charity and organizing schools for the poor, but occupied in education, and in the study of science and the practice of the fine arts, he may conclude that here resides the highest domestic enjoyment which has yet been attained, and the strongest hope of a further advance. . . .

From observation on these classes of facts,—the Occupation of the people, the respective Characters of the occupied classes, the Health of the population, the state of Marriage and of Women, and the character of Childhood,—the moralist may learn more of the private life of a community than from the conversation of any number of the individuals who compose it.

CRITICISM ON WOMEN

Art. VII.—1. *A Letter to the Queen on the State of the Monarchy.* By a Friend of the People.

2. *A Letter to the Lord Chancellor on the Infants' Custody Bill.* By Pierce Stevenson, Esq.

3. A few Plain Words to the Author of 'A Letter to the Queen.'

These publications, though their subjects are very different, have one common feature, for the sake of which we have put them together, at the head of this article. They all either contain or comment on the topic we have chosen for a few remarks—Abuse of Women;—the question never more urgently pressed on our attention than at the present moment— How ought women to be treated in controversy?

The whole morality of controversy is so very new to literature and literary journals, that (like the man who was astonished when told that he had spoken prose all his life, without knowing it), it will be a surprise to some to be told there is such a thing as a morality of literary controversy. But literature is, however lamentably, amenable to moral rules as well as to artistical ones, and even critics are responsible to moral obligations, like ordinary mortals; . . .

In consequence of the change of the relations between authors and reviewers—*slashing* articles have become more valuable to reviews. They are really very stirring reading: even when stupidly done they are not dull. If it be the interest of most men to be civil and decorous even to their enemies (on the principle of the Spaniard, who called the devil, my lord), because they may one day fall into their hands, the reviewer is an exception. The more spicy and personal he can make his article the better, provided he has enough of tact and taste to

—

London and Westminster Review 32 (1838–1839):454–475.

carry the malice of his readers along with him. Hence, it is this circumstance, we presume, which accounts for the existence of a very curious thing in literature, called Crokerism. There are several clever and amusing writers of the present day who owe much notoriety, and sale, to the regularity with which they season their journals with attacks on men, and especially on women. The morality of controversy among these men, is a fear of the law of libel, and the rules of duelling, and nothing more. They hold, that in politics and literature everything is fair against an opponent that is safe; at least this is the only morality they practise, and, therefore, their only real morality. In slang parlance, their attacks are called by the strange word we have used—they are called Crokerisms: a word of mysterious origin and import. Philologists and lexicographers are divided regarding its origin; for ourselves, we are opposed to the opinion that it is derived from a venomous reptile. No reptile could write reviews; at least our acquaintance with natural history does not furnish us with the slightest knowledge of any such, since the fish which yields a fluid like ink, does not, from want of early instruction in caligraphy, put its ink into a form adapted to the printers. We can only inform our readers what the usage is regarding the word. If a man is addicted to abuse—if he is an animal who lives by it,—and if he exhibits a "wonderful accession of courage," to quote the words of a great wit, "when he attacks a woman," he is called a Crokerite. When a general of great and well-merited fame—the greatest marshal a great people have amongst them, arrives, bearing the congratulations of a nation to the foot of the English throne on the occasion of the coronation of a young Queen,—if, instead of a generous admiration of distinguished genius, and a proud and noble superiority, to national prejudices, and the base ashes of old feuds, a writer selects this very moment for the fabrication of a tissue of unworthy insinuations addressed to the meanest capacities and hearts,—and if, when from the magnificent aisles of Westminster Abbey, the assembled aristocracy of the empire, and from the thronged streets and allies of the metropolis, the toil-worn democracy of England—both unite to give an utterance in shouts from the great heart of manhood, in admiration of an old, brave, and fame-covered foe,—if at this hour of national generosity and enthusiasm, a writer is found who mutters feebly from the dirt, weak innuendoes and insinuated lies, the name which describes him to all men is a "Crokerite." When a woman who has had her name blighted by slander, and her honour implicated by imbecility—has obtained a verdict of acquittal from a jury of her countrymen, and her husband himself has declared her innocence—if a set of men are found who, under the shelter of the anonymous, and laws which give no redress for the foulest wrong which words can inflict on a human being—the sullying of the fair fame of a woman—still brutally denounce her as guilty, they, whatever may be the vehicle they use—are a set of Crokerites. If a writer, who carefully and skilfully avoids duellable matter when attacking men, unscrupulously publishes things which can receive no other reply from women, who cannot fight—the man or thing is a Crokerite. When the successful sycophant of a debauched king sneers at a gifted man, made poor by sufferings for his honest convictions for being poor, the sneer is a Crokerism. If a man, who by no merit of his, has ears to hear, sneers at a woman for being deaf; a man who is not lame ridicules another man for being halt; a man who has the use of his eyesight throws jokes at a man who is blind—adding the scoffer's sting to the afflicting dispensations of Providence; and if this ribald scoffer has not even the excuse of the children who cried "bald-head" at the prophet in the scriptures, being neither young nor thoughtless, the irreverend mocker, with a heart of blackness and a soul of slime—is a Crokerite. If a woman, virtuous and gifted, whose genius sheds a lustre on the nation which gave her birth, and showers benefits on the people who are proud when they call her countrywoman—complies with the dying wish of her father, and before her eyes are dry from the tears she dropped over his sacred grave, completes and publishes his Life,—if this woman is abused for being too partial to that pious and holy memory, accused of too much love to that dead and departed one, and because she has been too partial and too loving to her father, charged with caring no more for the death of her mother than for the death of a kitten, the man who sends his slanders all over the world against the mourner beside that grave,—is a Crokerite. Were a stranger to seek throughout the empire for the men who have spared no woman who has dared to differ from them in politics—not even those across the purity of whose fame the breath of no slander but theirs was ever breathed—an Austen, an Edgeworth,[7] or a Martineau,— for the men whom all manly men who speak the English tongue would clothe in recreant calf-skin, or substitute for it the red stripes of the horsewhip,—he would find them in the Crokerites.

We shall now, by a selection of instances, show that there is not a single syllable of exaggeration in the general statement we have made of the conduct of the Crokerites towards distinguished women. Women are not protected by law from the worst slander to which they can be subjected, unless they can prove special damages. They cannot have the miserable protection of the duel, because every affection of their natures rises up to make them use their influence to prevent their brothers and husbands from taking up their quarrels. They are the most piquant and the safest objects of abuse a reviewer can select. . . .

The Queen is the first woman of whose treatment by anonymous writers we have to speak. When, at the early age of eighteen, this young and blooming girl was called by the laws to the throne of the British empire—that throne became, we do believe, a greater object of interest to all Europe than it had been for many generations; and at home there were, no doubt, various feelings entertained by different parties, but indifference was felt nowhere. A human interest was imparted to a gorgeous pageant—royalty was made attractive by womanhood—the chief magistrate enlisted all sympathies as a youthful girl. It is true that to the office-hunting Tories her accession was detestable. Amidst the universal sympathy and affection which prevailed in society at that hour, it is true that from men of this class might be heard muttered curses on the laws which placed the Queen in her powerful position; and it is equally true, whatever may have been the father to his thought, that Sir Robert Peel[8] compared her to Marie Antoinette, a glittering star which set in blood. But these were the only excep-

[7] Jane Austen (1775–1817) and Maria Edgeworth (1767–1849). Edgeworth was also a novelist, highly thought of in Martineau's time.

[8] Leader of the opposition when Queen Victoria came to the throne.

tions. In the assembled crowd which saw her with tearful eyes appear at the window of the palace of St. James's[9] on the lovely summer morning of her proclamation,—among the eager crowds who hedged her state carriage as, drawn along the Strand towards Guildhall on the 9th of November 1837, by cream-coloured horses, it floated—a fairy vision—there was one common feeling of sympathy, and hope of kindness and good-will: and from St. James's these circling feelings extended and widened through the length and breadth of the empire. A gifted lady traveller, Mrs. Jameson,[10] has told us how they sprung up in her heart in the far west on the Lake Huron, when in the east the lake and sky were intermingling radiance, and then, just there, where they seemed flowing and glowing together like a bath of fire, the huge black hull of a vessel loamed, lessened, and became distinct as a heavy-built schooner, with one man on her bows slowly pulling a large oar by walking backwards and forwards, who, when asked what news, answered, "William the Fourth is dead, and Queen Victoria reigns in his stead."

"As many hopes hang on that youthful head
As there hang blossoms on the boughs in May."

These feelings have not yet passed away. True it is, the Queen has done little to increase those feelings towards her: but *she* has done nothing to alter them.

Though we have enjoyed, we do not think, the satire quite just of the caricature of her which represents Britannia patronizing the drama;—the Queen patting the lions which are trampling upon Shakspeare. The Queen, though at first, when the lion novelty was at its height, she went more frequently to Drury Lane than to Covent Garden theatre, has since, by the frequency of her visits, shown a disposition to appreciate the noble exertions of Mr. Macready[11] in a great national cause—the restoration of Shakspeare to the stage and

[9]Royal residence from 1697 to 1837, hence the starting point for the coronation procession.

[10]Anna Brownell Jameson (1794–1860), writer on art, literature, religion, and charity, best known for her works on art history.

[11]William Charles Macready (1793–1873), prominent Shakespearean actor, at this time (1837–1839) manager of Covent Garden theater.

the people. It was a fit and proper feeling which dictated the fear that these services were not appreciated by the occupant of the throne; it was a just and rightly informed taste which was apprehensive that the Queen was wanting in a due and becoming loyalty and homage to Shakspeare—a man greater in real greatness than all her line—and to the admirable and exquisite delineations of his great creations which Covent Gardens presents, the Lear, Othello, Hamlet, and Prospero of a Macready, the first tragedian of his time—and the Hermione, Miranda, Cordelia, and Desdemona of Miss Helen Faucit, a young actress of unrivalled grace, and power, and tenderness, omitting all mention for the present of the excellent performers who support them, Horton, Elton, and Bartley, and the rest,—but however praiseworthy the feelings may have been which dictated the fears and suspicions in question, the Queen deserved them not; since we doubt if there be a single member of the upper classes who has, more frequently than she has done, encouraged and applauded by her presence the efforts now made to support and perpetuate the legitimate drama.

When it is considered that the Queen, whether fit or otherwise for the position she occupies, was put into it by no seeking of hers,—that laws to the making of which she was not a party, and a Providence in the decrees of which she had no voice, dragged her from the studies of girlhood to the cares of empire, the man who reproaches her or insults her, or mentions so as to pain her, the inevitable consequences of the laws and of Providence, is guilty of an immorality and a cruelty akin to his who scoffs the baldness of the old or the blindness of the blind. . . .

. . . [A] writer, who is said to be a man whose sycophancy to a brave and stout-hearted old man, William the Fourth, was as conspicuous and odious as his rude and base insolence to a defenceless girl—the most defenceless and exposed in matters of this sort in the empire,—is unworthy of manhood;—this virtuous, experienced, aged, dignified, and much read patriot, compares the Queen to Louis XIV, an infant called to grasp the sceptre when his fingers were too tiny to grasp its narrow end, and to Henry VI, a slavering idiot, called upon to satisfy the "longing desire of his faithful Commons" by making a sign that he heard their prayers.

It is true, doubtless, that great qualifications for government cannot be possessed by a girl of twenty; we could name orators of sixty who have not an atom of them; but it is false that a young woman of twenty is a child, and every one who has seen her intelligent face knows that the comparisons by which utter incapacity is insinuated against the Queen are alike unfeeling and false. We believe this writer equally far from the truth when he says, the feelings of loyalty and affection with which the accession of the Queen to the throne was greeted were unmeaning, and that they have already changed into feelings of unpopularity. The human sympathy for one so young, and so perilously placed, which fused itself through the habitual loyalty of a monarchical people—even the Chartists[12] are not Republicans—sprung from feelings too deeply planted in the natures of all generous and kind-hearted people to be erased until its object shall have done, instead of nothing, many things, to cause its erasure. . . .

[There follow examples of critical slander of Mrs. Norton, Lady Morgan, Mrs. Jameson, and Miss Edgeworth.]

MISS MARTINEAU.—We have found it to be impossible to give any examples from the Crokerite reviews of the worst and coarsest attacks which they have made on this lady. Our pages have never contained a line or an allusion calculated to bring a blush on the cheek of any woman; and we will not sully them now with the pollutions of the Crokerites. Miss Martineau happened to differ with the Crokerite review regarding the new Poor-law Bill: she approved in 1833 of a measure which their slower appreciation approved a few years later. But, owing to this she was made the object of attacks in which every joke a coarse but stupid writer could invent in the subject of population was applied to her.

Of the abuse of another sort we can furnish specimens. Miss Martineau is, as everybody knows, so deaf that she is obliged to use an ear-trumpet, which, however, she does so well, that very few persons indeed surpass her in the ability with which she collects information, whether from seeing or listening. This infirmity is thus brutally alluded to by the Cro-

---

[12] A reform group of the 1830s and 1840s concerned with electoral and social reform. Martineau's point here is that even these reformers, feared as extremists by many, were not opposed to the monarchy.

kerite review—the sneer at the blind is directed against Mr. Holman, the traveller.

—"We cannot answer these questions; but Miss Martineau's inference is plain and undeniable—none of these persons could be expected in their present state to write an instructive book of travels, whereas, if any of them, after losing eyes and ears, should by any means become acquainted with this excellent work, and thereby learn *how to observe*, &c."

—"Very few indeed; and considering that there are but two *blind* travellers extant, and only *one* that we know of, stone *deaf*, we cannot but wonder where Miss Martineau has collected all this valuable information."

The editors of the periodicals in which these things appear, complain most piteously against being held responsible for the slanders they are said to insert by the contributors who proclaim everywhere, that they despise and detest the insertions which are forced upon them by editorial omnipotence. No man owns these things: the owning of them would be incompatible with a reception into the society of honourable men. The editors, it is true, are liable to be asked, why they insert passages which expose them to imputations on their personal honour and respectability; and the contributors to the enquiry, why they send their articles to men who issue them to the world with detestable and despicable additions. But the cowardice of the anonymous, covers both editors and contributors. The baseness of equivocation conceals them. The women who are slandered are known: they stand clearly and distinctly in the public gaze—the men who slander them are hidden: their names are denied; their deeds are repudiated even by themselves. Their friends would not stand up for them were their names or their initials attached to their articles. We remember having seen a caricature, in which a gentleman is represented asking a villanous-looking cabman to drive him to the Old Bailey,[13] who replies, that he had never heard of the place. Mention Crokerism to a Crokerite, and he assures you he never heard of such a thing.

The disgust which the account we have given of abuse of women, must have excited, in every manly breast, is likely to be less than it ought to be, owing to the lax morality prevalent

[13] Famous London criminal court.

73

on the subject of satire. When benevolent writers have said that pity and compassion, rather than anger and reprobation, were the fit feelings with which men ought habitually to regard even the crimes of their fellows, they have been told that the Creator would not have implanted the emotions of anger and reprobation in our natures, had he not intended them to be exercised on appropriate and deserving objects. . . .

We had almost forgotten the Crokerites. As an improvement on their mode of warfare, clever and witty men, have said it is not the interest of our class to fight with the weapons of abuse and slander, at which the worst men are the best fighters, and therefore they have recommended the use only of the weapons of cleverness and wit. This is a great improvement, but somewhat selfish of the wits: the true morality of controversy seems however to be, to avoid all personalities with an avoidance proportioned to the defencelessness of their object, and when the duty of attack comes to discharge it even against a Crokerite,—hesitatingly as one awed by the realized presence of both Truth and Charity: let your attack be Evidence softened by Benevolence.

LETTER TO AMERICAN WOMEN'S RIGHTS CONVENTION

The following Letter from Miss Martineau was read to the Convention:—

Cromer, [England], Aug. 3, 1851.

MY DEAR MADAM: I beg to thank you heartily for your kindness in sending me the Report of the Proceedings of your 'Woman's Rights Convention.' I had gathered what I could from the newspapers concerning it, but I was gratified at being able to read, in a collected form, addresses so full of ear-

Liberator 21 (November 1, 1851).

nestness and sound truth as I found most of the speeches to be. I hope you are aware of the interest excited in this country by that Convention; the strongest proof of which is the appearance of an article on the subject in *The Westminster Review*, (for July,) as thorough-going as any of your own addresses, and from the pen (at least, as it is understood here,) of one of our very first men, Mr. John S. Mill. I am not without hope that this article will materially strengthen your hands, and I am sure it cannot but cheer your hearts.

As for me, my thoughts and best wishes will be with you when you meet in October. I cannot accept your hearty invitation to attend your Convention, as my home duties will not allow of my leaving my own country. But you may be assured of my warm and unrestricted sympathy. Ever since I became capable of thinking for myself, I have clearly seen—and I have said it till my listeners and readers are probably tired of hearing it—that there can be but one true method in the treatment of each human being of either sex, of any color, and under any outward circumstances—to ascertain what are the powers of that being, to cultivate them to the utmost, and *then* to see what action they will find for themselves. This has probably never been done for men, unless in some rare individual cases. It has certainly never been done for women: and, till it is done, all debating about what woman's intellect is—all speculation, or laying down the law, as to what is woman's sphere, is a mere beating of the air. *A priori* conceptions have long been found worthless in physical science, and nothing was really effected till the experimental method was clearly made out and strictly applied in practice, and the same principle holds most certainly through the whole range of Moral Science. Whether we regard the physical fact of what women are able to do, or the moral fact of what woman ought to do, it is equally necessary to abstain from making any decision prior to experiment. We see plainly enough the waste of time and thought among the men who once talked of Nature abhorring a vacuum, or disputed at great length as to whether angels could go from end to end without passing through the middle; and the day will come when it will appear to be no less absurd to have argued, as men and women are arguing now, about what woman ought to do, before it was ascertained what woman can do. Let us once see a hundred women educated up to the highest point that education at present reaches—let them be supplied with such knowledge as their faculties are found to crave, and let them be free to use, apply and increase their knowledge as their faculties shall instigate, and it will presently appear what is the sphere of each of the hundred. One may be discovering comets, like Miss Herschel; one may be laying upon the mathematical structure of the universe, like Mrs. Somerville;[14] another may be analyzing the chemical relations of Nature in the laboratory; another may be penetrating the mysteries of physiology; others may be applying Science in the healing of diseases; others may be investigating the laws of social relations, learning the great natural laws under which society, like every thing else, proceeds; others, again, may be actively carrying out the social arrangements which have been formed under these laws; and others may be chiefly occupied in family business, in the duties of the wife and mother, and the ruler of a household. If, among the hundred women, a great diversity of powers should appear, (which I have no doubt would be the case), there will always be plenty of scope and material for the greatest amount and variety of power that can be brought out. If not—if it should appear that women fall below men in all but the domestic function—then it will be well that the experiment has been tried; and the trial had better go on forever, that woman's sphere may forever determine itself, to the satisfaction of everybody.

It is clear that Education, to be what I demand on behalf of woman, must be intended to issue in active life. A man's medical education would be worth little, if it was not a preparation for practice. The astronomer and the chemist would put little force into their studies, if it was certain that they must leave off in four or five years, and do nothing for the rest of their lives; and no man could possibly feel much interest in political and social morals, if he knew that he must all his life long, pay taxes, but neither speak nor move about public affairs. Women, like men, must be educated with a view to

[14]Caroline Lucretia Herschel (1750–1848), astronomer, discovered eight comets, prepared an index of all the known stars, was made an honorary member of the Royal Astronomical Society. Mary Somerville (1789–1872), writer on science, became famous with her translation of Laplace's *Mécanique céleste*. Also wrote *The Connection of the Physical Sciences* (1834), *Physical Geography* (1848), and *Molecular and Microscopic Science* (1866).

action, or their studies cannot be called Education, and no judgment can be formed of the scope of their faculties. The pursuit must be the life's business, or it will be mere pastime or an irksome task. This was always my point of difference with one who carefully cherished a reverence for woman—the late Dr. Channing.[15] How much we spoke and wrote of the old controversy—INFLUENCE *vs.* OFFICE! He would have had any woman study any thing that her faculties led her to, whether physical science, or law, government and political economy; but he would have had her stop at the study. From the moment she entered the hospital as physician, and not nurse; from the moment she took her place in a court of justice in the jury-box, and not the witness-box; from the moment she brought her mind and her voice into the legislature, instead of discussing the principles of laws at home; from the moment she enounced and administered justice, instead of looking upon it from afar, as a thing with which she had no concern— she would, he feared, lose her influence as an observing intelligence, standing by in a state of purity, 'unspotted from the world.' My conviction always was, that an intelligence never carried out into action could not be worth much; and that, if all the action of human life was of a character so tainted as to be unfit for woman, it could be no better for men, and we ought all to sit down together to let barbarism overtake us once more. My own conviction is, that the natural action of the whole human being occasions not only the most strength, but the highest elevation: not only the warmest sympathy, but the deepest purity. The highest and purest beings among women seem now to be those who, far from being idle, find among their restricted opportunities some means of strenuous action; and I cannot doubt that, if an active social career were open to all women, with due means of preparation for it, those who are high and holy now would be high and holy then, and would be joined by an innumerable company of just spirits from among those whose energies are now pining and fretting in enforced idleness or unworthy frivolity, or brought down into pursuits and aims which are any thing but pure and peaceable. In regard to this old controversy—of Influence *vs.* Of-

[15] William Ellery Channing (1780–1842), American Protestant clergyman and intellectual, a founder of American Unitarianism.

fice—it appears to me that, if Influence is good and Office is bad for human morals and character, Man's present position is one of such hardship as it is almost profane to contemplate; and if, on the contrary, Office is good and a life of Influence is bad, Woman has an instant right to claim that her position be amended.

With every wish that your meeting may be a happy one, and your great cause a flourishing one, I am, dear Madam, yours, faithfully,

HARRIET MARTINEAU

SINGLE LIFE

And now my own special trial was at hand. It is not necessary to go into detail about it. The news which got abroad that we had grown comparatively poor,—and the evident certainty that we were never likely to be rich, so wrought up the mind of one friend as to break down the mischief which I have referred to as caused by ill-offices. My friend had believed me rich, was generous about making me a poor man's wife, and had been discouraged in more ways than one. He now came to me, and we were soon virtually engaged. I was at first very anxious and unhappy. My veneration for his *morale* was such that I felt that I dared not undertake the charge of his happiness: and yet I dared not refuse, because I saw it would be his death blow. I was ill,—I was deaf,—I was in an entangled state of mind between conflicting duties and some lower considerations; and many a time did I wish, in my fear that I should fail, that I had never seen him. I am far from wishing

—

Harriet Martineau, *Autobiography*, with Memorials by Maria Weston Chapman, 4th ed. (Boston: Houghton, Osgood and Co., 1879), vol. 1, pp. 130–133. Written in 1855.

that now;—now that the beauty of his goodness remains to
me, clear of all painful regrets. But there was a fearful period
to pass through. Just when I was growing happy, surmount-
ing my fears and doubts, and enjoying his attachment, the
consequences of his long struggle and suspense overtook him.
He became suddenly insane; and after months of illness of
body and mind, he died. The calamity was aggravated to me
by the unaccountable insults I received from his family, whom
I had never seen. Years afterwards, when his sister and I met,
the mystery was explained. His family had been given to understand, by cautious insinuations, that I was actually engaged
to another, while receiving my friend's addresses! There has
never been any doubt in my mind that, considering what I
was in those days, it was happiest for us both that our union
was prevented by any means. I am, in truth, very thankful for
not having married at all. I have never since been tempted, nor
have suffered any thing at all in relation to that matter which is
held to be all-important to woman,—love and marriage. Nothing, I mean, beyond occasional annoyance, presently disposed
of. Every literary woman, no doubt, has plenty of importu-
nity of that sort to deal with; but freedom of mind and coolness of manner dispose of it very easily: and since the time I
have been speaking of, my mind has been wholly free from all
idea of love-affairs. My subsequent literary life in London was
clear from all difficulty and embarrassment,—no doubt because I was evidently too busy, and too full of interest of other
kinds to feel any awkwardness,—to say nothing of my being
then thirty years of age; an age at which, if ever, a woman is
certainly qualified to take care of herself. I can easily conceive
how I might have been tempted,—how some deep springs in
my nature might have been touched, then as earlier; but, as a
matter of fact, they never were; and I consider the immunity a
great blessing, under the liabilities of a moral condition such
as mine was in the olden time. If I had had a husband dependent on me for his happiness, the responsibility would have
made me wretched. I had not faith enough in myself to endure
avoidable responsibility. If my husband had *not* depended on
me for his happiness, I should have been jealous. So also with
children. The care would have so overpowered the joy,—the
love would have so exceeded the ordinary chances of life,—
the fear on my part would have so impaired the freedom

on theirs, that I rejoice not to have been involved in a relation for which I was, or believed myself unfit. The veneration in which I hold domestic life has always shown me that life was not for those whose self-respect had been early broken down, or had never grown. Happily, the majority are free from this disability. Those who suffer under it had better be as I,—as my observation of married, as well as single life assures me. When I see what conjugal love is, in the extremely rare cases in which it is seen in its perfection, I feel that there is a power of attachment in me that has never been touched. When I am among little children, it frightens me to think what my idolatry of my own children would have been. But, through it all, I have ever been thankful to be alone. My strong will, combined with anxiety of conscience, makes me fit only to live alone; and my taste and liking are for living alone. The older I have grown, the more serious and irremediable have seemed to me the evils and disadvantages of married life, as it exists among us at this time: and I am provided with what it is the bane of single life in ordinary cases to want—substantial, laborious and serious occupation. My business in life has been to think and learn, and to speak out with absolute freedom what I have thought and learned. The freedom is itself a positive and never-failing enjoyment to me, after the bondage of my early life. My work and I have been fitted to each other, as is proved by the success of my work and my own happiness in it. The simplicity and independence of this vocation first suited my infirm and ill-developed nature, and then sufficed for my needs, together with family ties and domestic duties, such as I have been blessed with, and as every woman's heart requires. Thus, I am not only entirely satisfied with my lot, but think it the very best for me,—under my constitution and circumstances: and I long ago came to the conclusion that, without meddling with the case of the wives and mothers, I am probably the happiest single woman in England. Who could have believed, in that awful year 1826, that such would be my conclusion a quarter of a century afterwards!

THE WOMAN QUESTION

The mention of Coleridge reminds me, I hardly know why, of Godwin, who was an occasional morning visitor of mine. I looked upon him as a curious monument of a bygone state of society; and there was still a good deal that was interesting about him. His fine head was striking, and his countenance remarkable. . . . and I fear there was no other portrait, after the one corresponding to the well-known portrait of Mary Wollstonecraft. It was not for her sake that I desired to know Godwin; for, with all the aid from the admiration with which her memory was regarded in my childhood, and from my own disposition to honour all promoters of the welfare and improvement of Woman, I never could reconcile my mind to Mary Wollstonecraft's writings, or to whatever I heard of her. It seemed to me, from the earliest time when I could think on the subject of Woman's Rights and condition, that the first requisite to advancement is the self-reliance which results from self-discipline. Women who would improve the condition and chances of their sex must, I am certain, be not only affectionate and devoted, but rational and dispassionate, with the devotedness of benevolence, and not merely of personal love. But Mary Wollstonecraft was, with all her powers, a poor victim of passion, with no control over her own peace, and no calmness or content except when the needs of her individual nature were satisfied. I felt, forty years ago, in regard to her, just what I feel now in regard to some of the most conspicuous denouncers of the wrongs of women at this day;—that their advocacy of Woman's cause becomes mere detriment, precisely in proportion to their personal reasons for unhappiness, unless they have fortitude enough (which loud complainants usually have not) to get their own troubles under

—

Harriet Martineau, *Autobiography*, with Memorials by Maria Weston Chapman, 4th ed. (Boston: Houghton, Osgood and Co., 1879), vol. 1, pp. 399–403. Written in 1855.

their feet, and leave them wholly out of the account in stating
the state of their sex. Nobody can be further than I am from
being satisfied with the condition of my own sex, under the
law and custom of my own country; but I decline all fellowship and co-operation with women of genius or otherwise
favourable position, who injure the cause by their personal
tendencies. When I see an eloquent writer insinuating to every
body who comes across her that she is the victim of her husband's carelessness and cruelty, while he never spoke in his
own defence: when I see her violating all good taste by her
obtrusiveness in society, and oppressing every body about her
by her epicurean selfishness every day, while raising in print
an eloquent cry on behalf of the oppressed; I feel, to the bottom of my heart, that she is the worst enemy of the cause she
professes to plead. The best friends of that cause are women
who are morally as well as intellectually competent to the
most serious business of life, and who must be clearly seen to
speak from conviction of the truth, and not from personal unhappiness. The best friends of the cause are the happy wives
and the busy, cheerful, satisfied single women, who have no
injuries of their own to avenge, and no painful vacuity or mor-
tification to relieve. The best advocates are yet to come,—in
the persons of women who are obtaining access to real social business,—the female physicians and other professors in
America, the women of business and the female artists of
France; and the hospital administrators, the nurses, the educators and substantially successful authors of our own country.
Often as I am appealed to speak, or otherwise assist in the promotion of the cause of Woman, my answer is always the
same:—that women, like men, can obtain whatever they show
themselves fit for. Let them be educated,—let their powers be
cultivated to the extent for which the means are already provided, and all that is wanted or ought to be desired will follow
of course. Whatever a woman proves herself able to do, society will be thankful to see her do,—just as if she were a man.
If she is scientific, science will welcome her, as it has welcomed
every woman so qualified. I believe no scientific woman com-
plains of wrongs. If capable of political thought and action,
women will obtain even that. I judge by my own case. The
time has not come which certainly will come, when women
who are practically concerned in political life will have a voice

in making the laws which they have to obey; but every woman who can think and speak wisely, and bring up her children soundly, in regard to the rights and duties of society, is advancing the time when the interests of women will be represented, as well as those of men. I have no vote at elections, though I am a tax-paying housekeeper and responsible citizen; and I regard the disability as an absurdity, seeing that I have for a long course of years influenced public affairs to an extent not professed or attempted by many men. But I do not see that I could do much good by personal complaints, which always have some suspicion or reality of passion in them. I think the better way is for us all to learn and to try to the utmost what we can do, and thus to win for ourselves the consideration which alone can secure us rational treatment. The Wollstonecraft order set to work at the other end, and, as I think, do infinite mischief; and, for my part, I do not wish to have any thing to do with them. Every allowance must be made for Mary Wollstonecraft herself, from the constitution and singular environment which determined her course: but I have never regarded her as a safe example, nor as a successful champion of Woman and her Rights.

III

ON WOMEN'S EDUCATION

When I was young, it was not thought proper for young ladies to study very conspicuously; and especially with pen in hand. Young ladies (at least in provincial towns) were expected to sit down in the parlour to sew,—during which reading aloud was permitted,—or to practice their music; but so as to be fit to receive callers, without any signs of bluestockingism which could be reported abroad. Jane Austen herself, the Queen of novelists, the immortal creator of Anne Elliott, Mr. Knightley, and a score or two more of unrivalled intimate friends of the whole public, was compelled by the feelings of her family to cover up her manuscripts with a large piece of muslin work, kept on the table for the purpose, whenever any genteel people came in. So it was with other young ladies, for some time after Jane Austen was in her grave; and thus my first studies in philosophy were carried on with great care and reserve.

—*Harriet Martineau*
AUTOBIOGRAPHY

Teacher and Pupils

Teacher. "I wonder what your mother would say if she knew how backward you are in geography?"

Girl. "Oh, my mother says she never learnt jogfry and she's married, and Aunt Sally says *she* never learnt jogfry and *she's* married; and you did and you ain't."

Reproduced by permission of *Punch*

A central doctrine of Martineau's feminist thought from the very start of her writing career was the importance of education for women. Excerpts from her second *Monthly Repository* article, "On Female Education," written in 1822, open this section. In that piece, written when she was barely twenty years old, Martineau made the claim, amazing for her youth and period, that women's intellectual inferiority to men is based on women's lack of mental training, others' expectations of women, and women's circumstances rather than women's ability. She cleverly sidestepped the issue of whether women *can* be men's equals, saying instead she was looking "to show the expediency of giving proper scope and employment to the powers which they [women] do possess."

Similarly, she avoided the nature versus nurture argument of whether educational potential is dependent on "the structure of the body" or "bodily frame." Although in this youthful argument, published in the organ of Unitarian Christianity to which she was then faithful, she allowed that women should be educated to enhance their relationships to men and make them better mothers and held that the greatest value of education is to give women a better understanding of Christianity, she nevertheless had a very clear-sighted perception of the dreariness and degradation, the retrogression that lack of education means in women's lives.

In later life, Martineau was to abandon and even to repudiate the religion that this early essay relied upon, but she was always to believe in the great importance of education for women.

Forty years later she was of a different mind on the *purpose* but not on the benefit of women's education. Writing in *Once a Week* in 1861, she deplored the justification of "good intellectual training as fitting women to be 'mothers of heroes,' 'companions to men,' and so on. . . . Till it is proposed, in educating girls, to make them, in themselves and for their own sakes, as good specimens of the human being as the conditions of the case allow, very little will be effected by any expenditure of pains, time, and money."

Included here are pieces on basic education for women, including a section from her 1848 book, *Household Education*, which was a kind of popular manual for the moral and practical instruction of a household, and a long article from *Cornhill*

Magazine (1864) entitled "Middle-Class Education in England: Girls." In both of these she held that education should be for the sake of improving the person. She insisted that girls should study the same subjects as boys, that both should have time in school for both study and play, mental exercise and physical exercise, but that girls should study the domestic arts as well.

Never did she question that women should become skillful at housekeeping; rather she claimed that education would make them better at it. This is drawn from her own life, for she prided herself on her needlework, her household management, and the sensible way in which she entertained. She argues in several contexts that not all Englishwomen are cared for by a man and that women need to be educated for an occupation so that they can earn their own way. These ideas came out of Martineau's own middle-class experience of having been left with a small legacy poorly invested. It did not occur to her to argue for universal education. She did, however, favor higher education for qualified women early on and enthusiastically supported the establishment in London of Queen's College in Hartley Street and the Ladies' College in Bedford Square (now Bedford College). An article on higher education, "What Women are Educated For," forms the third selection in this section.

ON FEMALE EDUCATION

Norwich, November, 1822

In discussing the subject of Female Education, it is not so much my object to inquire whether the natural powers of women be equal to those of men, as to shew the expediency of giving proper scope and employment to the powers which they do possess. It may be as well, notwithstanding, to in-

Monthly Repository 17 (October 1822):77–81.

quire whether the difference be as great as is generally supposed between the mental structure of men and of women.

Doubtless the formation of the mind must depend in a great degree on the structure of the body. From this cause the strength of mind observable in men is supposed to arise; and the delicacy of the female mind is thought to be in agreement with the bodily frame. But it is impossible to ascertain how much may depend on early education; nor can we solve our doubts on this head by turning our view to savage countries, where, if the bodily strength be nearly equal in the two sexes, their minds are alike sunk in ignorance and darkness. In our own country, we find that as long as the studies of children of both sexes continue the same, the progress they make is equal. After the rudiments of knowledge have been obtained, in the cultivated ranks of society, (of which alone I mean to speak,) the boy goes on continually increasing his stock of information, it being his only employment to store and exercise his mind for future years; while the girl is probably confined to low pursuits, her aspirings after knowledge are subdued, she is taught to believe that solid information is unbecoming her sex, almost her whole time is expended on light accomplishments, and thus before she is sensible of her powers, they are checked in their growth; chained down to mean objects, to rise no more; and when the natural consequences of this mode of treatment arise, all mankind agree that the abilities of women are far inferior to those of men. But in the few instances where a contrary mode of treatment has been pursued, where fair play has been given to the faculties, even without much assistance, what has almost invariably been the result? Has it not been evident that the female mind, though in many respects differently constituted from that of man, may be well brought into comparison with his? If she wants his enterprising spirit, the deficiency is made up by perseverance in what she does undertake; for his ambition, she has a thirst for knowledge; and for his ready perception, she has unwearied application.

It is proof sufficient to my mind, that there is no natural deficiency of power, that, unless proper objects are supplied to women to employ their faculties, their energies are exerted improperly. Some aim they must have, and if no good one is presented to them, they must seek for a bad one.

We may find evidence in abundance of this truth in the condition of women before the introduction of Christianity.

Before the revelation of this blessed religion, (doubly blessed to the female sex,) what was their situation? They were either sunk almost to the level of the brutes in mental darkness, buried in their own homes, the slaves instead of the companions of their husbands, only to be preserved from vice by being excluded from the world, or, not being able to endure these restraints, employing their restless powers and turbulent passions in the pursuit of vicious pleasures and sensual gratifications. And we cannot wonder that this was the case, when they were gifted with faculties which they were not permitted to exercise, and were compelled to vegetate from year to year, with no object in life and no hope in death. Observe what an immediate change was wrought by the introduction of Christianity. Mark the zeal, directed by knowledge, of the female converts, of so many of whom St. Paul makes honourable mention as his friends, on account of their exertions in the great cause. An object was held out for them to obtain, and their powers were bent to the attainment of it, instead of being engaged in vice and folly. The female character has been observed to improve since that time, in proportion as the treasures of useful knowledge have been placed within the reach of the sex.

I wish to imply by what I have said, not that great stores of information are as necessary to women as to men, but that as much care should be taken of the formation of their minds. Their attainments cannot in general be so great, because they have their own appropriate duties and peculiar employments, the neglect of which nothing can excuse; but I contend that these duties will be better performed if the powers be rationally employed. If the whole mind be exercised and strengthened, it will bring more vigour to the performance of its duties in any particular province.

The first great objection which is made to enlightening the female mind is, that if engaged in the pursuit of knowledge, women neglect their appropriate duties and peculiar employments.

2nd. That the greatest advances that the female mind can make in knowledge, must still fall far short of the attainments of the other sex.

3rd. That the vanity so universally ascribed to the sex is apt to be inflated by any degree of proficiency in knowledge, and that women therefore become forgetful of the subordinate station assigned them by law, natural and divine.

To the first objection I answer, that such a pursuit of knowledge as shall lead women to neglect their peculiar duties, is not that cultivation of mind for the utility of which I am contending. But these duties may be well performed without engaging the whole time and attention. If "great thoughts constitute great minds," what can be expected from a woman whose whole intellect is employed on the trifling cares and comparatively mean occupations, to which the advocates for female ignorance would condemn her? These cares and these occupations were allotted to women to enable them to smooth our way through life; they were designed as a means to this end, and should never be pursued as the end itself. The knowledge of these necessary acts is so easily acquired, and they are so easily performed, that an active mind will feel a dismal vacuity, a craving after something nobler and better to employ the thoughts in the intervals of idleness which must occur when these calls of duty are answered, and if nothing nobler and better is presented to it, it will waste its energies in the pursuit of folly, if not of vice, and thus continually perpetuate the faults of the sex. . . .

It must be allowed by all, that one of woman's first duties is to qualify herself for being a companion to her husband, or to those with whom her lot in life is cast. She was formed to be a domestic companion, and such an one as shall give to home its charms, as shall furnish such entertainment that her husband need not be driven abroad for amusement. This is one of the first duties required from a woman, and no time can be misemployed which is applied to the purpose of making her such a companion, and I contend that a friend like this cannot be found among women of uncultivated minds. If their thoughts are continually occupied by the vanities of the world, if that time which is not required for the fulfilment of household duties, is spent in folly, or even in harmless trifles in which the husband has no interest, how are the powers of pleasing to be perpetuated, how is she to find interesting subjects for social converse? . . .

If we consider woman as the guardian and instructress of

infancy, her claims to cultivation of mind become doubly urgent. It is evident that if the soul of the teacher is narrow and contracted, that of the pupil cannot be enlarged. . . .

With respect to the second objection, viz., That the greatest advances which the female mind can make in knowledge must fall far short of the attainments of the other sex,—I allow that the acquirements of women can seldom equal those of men, and it is not desirable that they should. I do not wish to excite a spirit of rivalry between the sexes; I do not desire that many females should seek for fame as authors. I only wish that their powers should be so employed that they should not be obliged to seek amusements beneath them, and injurious to them. I wish them to be companions to men, instead of playthings or servants, one of which an ignorant woman must commonly be. If they are called to be wives, a sensible mind is an essential qualification for the domestic character; if they remain single, liberal pursuits are absolutely necessary to preserve them from the faults so generally attributed to that state, and so justly and inevitably, while the mind is buried in darkness.

If it be asked what kind and degree of knowledge is necessary to preserve women from the evils mentioned as following in the train of ignorance, I answer that much must depend on natural talent, fortune and station; but no Englishwoman, above the lower ranks of life, ought to be ignorant of the Evidences and Principles of her religious belief, of Sacred History, of the outline at least of General History, of the Elements of the Philosophy of Nature, and of the Human Mind; and to these should be added the knowledge of such living languages, and the acquirement of such accomplishments, as situation and circumstances may direct.

With respect to the third objection, viz., that the vanity so universally ascribed to the sex is apt to be inflated by any degree of proficiency in knowledge, and that women, therefore, become forgetful of the subordinate station assigned them by law, natural and divine: the most important part of education, the implanting of religious principles must be in part neglected, if the share of knowledge which women may appropriate, should be suffered to inflate their vanity, or excite feelings of pride. Christian humility should be one of the first requisites in female education, and till it is attained every acquirement of every kind will become a cause of self-exaltation, and those accomplishments which are the most rare, will of course be looked upon with the most self-complacency. But if the taste for knowledge were more generally infused, and if proficiency in the attainments I have mentioned were more common, there would be much less pedantry than there is at present; for when acquirements of this kind are no longer remarkable, they cease to afford a subject for pride. . . .

Let woman then be taught that her powers of mind were given her to be improved. Let her be taught that she is to be a rational companion to those of the other sex among whom her lot in life is cast, that her proper sphere is *home*—that there she is to provide, not only for the bodily comfort of the man, but that she is to enter also into community of mind with him; . . . As she finds nobler objects presented to her grasp, and that her rank in the scale of being is elevated, she will engraft the vigorous qualities of the mind of man on her own blooming virtues, and insinuate into his mind those softer graces and milder beauties, which will smooth the ruggedness of his character. . . .

DISCIPULUS

HOUSEHOLD EDUCATION

I mention girls, as well as boys, confident that every person able to see the right, and courageous enough to utter it, will sanction what I say. I must declare that on no subject is more nonsense talked, (as it seems to me) than on that of female education, when restriction is advocated. In works otherwise really good, we find it taken for granted that girls are not to learn the dead languages and mathematics, because they are not to exer-

—

Harriet Martineau, *Household Education* (London: E. Moxon, 1848), pp. 240–245.

cise professions where these attainments are wanted; and a little further on we find it said that the chief reason for boys and young men studying these things is to improve the quality of their minds. I suppose none of us will doubt that everything possible should be done to improve the quality of the mind of every human being.—If it is said that the female brain is incapable of studies of an abstract nature,—that is not true: for there are many instances of women who have been good mathematicians, and good classical scholars. The plea is indeed nonsense on the face of it; for the brain which will learn French will learn Greek; the brain which enjoys arithmetic is capable of mathematics.—If it is said that women are light-minded and superficial, the obvious answer is that their minds should be the more carefully sobered by grave studies, and the acquisition of exact knowledge.—If it is said that their vocation in life does not require these kinds of knowledge,—that is giving up the main plea for the pursuit of them by boys;—that it improves the quality of their minds.—If it is said that such studies unfit women for their proper occupations,—that again is untrue. Men do not attend the less to their professional business, their counting-house or their shop, for having their minds enlarged and enriched, and their faculties strengthened by sound and various knowledge; nor do women on that account neglect the work-basket, the market, the dairy and the kitchen. If it be true that women are made for these domestic occupations, then of course they will be fond of them. They will be so fond of what comes most naturally to them that no book-study (if really not congenial to their minds) will draw them off from their homely duties. For my part, I have no hesitation whatever in saying that the most ignorant women I have known have been the worst housekeepers; and that the most learned women I have known have been among the best,—wherever they have been early taught and trained to household business, as every woman ought to be. A woman of superior mind knows better than an ignorant one what to require of her servants, how to deal with tradespeople, and how to economise time: she is more clear-sighted about the best ways of doing things; has a richer mind with which to animate all about her, and to solace her own spirit in the midst of her labours. If nobody doubts the difference in pleasantness of having to do with a silly and narrow-minded woman and with one who is intelligent and enlightened, it must be clear that the more intelligence and enlightenment there is, the better. One of the best housekeepers I know,—a simple-minded, affectionate-hearted woman, whose table is always fit for a prince to sit down to, whose house is always neat and elegant, and whose small income yields the greatest amount of comfort, is one of the most learned women ever heard of. When she was a little girl, she was sitting sewing in the window-seat while her brother was receiving his first lesson in mathematics from his tutor. She listened, and was delighted with what she heard; and when both left the room, she seized upon the Euclid that lay on the table, ran up to her room, went over the lesson, and laid the volume where it was before. Every day after this, she sat stitching away and listening, in like manner, and going over the lesson afterwards, till one day she let out the secret. Her brother could not answer a question which was put to him two or three times; and, without thinking of anything else, she popped out the answer. The tutor was surprised, and after she had told the simple truth, she was permitted to make what she could of Euclid. Some time after, she spoke confidentially to a friend of the family,—a scientific professor,—asking him, with much hesitation and many blushes, whether he thought it was wrong for a woman to learn Latin. "Certainly not," he said; "provided she does not neglect any duty for it.—But why do you want to learn Latin?" She wanted to study Newton's Principia: and the professor thought this a very good reason. Before she was grown into a woman, she had mastered the Principia of Newton. And now, the great globe on which we live is to her a book in which she reads the choice secrets of nature; and to her the last known wonders of the sky are disclosed: and if there is a home more graced with accomplishments, and more filled with comforts, I do not know such an one. Will anybody say that this woman would have been in any way better without her learning?—while we may confidently say that she would have been much less happy.

As for women not wanting learning, or superior intellectual training, that is more than any one should undertake to say in our day. In former times, it was understood that every woman, (except domestic servants) was maintained by her father, brother or husband; but it is not so now. The footing of women is changed, and it will change more. Formerly, every woman was destined to be married; and it was almost a matter of course that she would be: so that the only occupation thought of for a woman was keeping her husband's house, and being a wife and mother. It is not so now. From a variety of causes, there is less and less marriage among the middle classes of our country; and much of the marriage that there is does not take place till middle life. A multitude of women have to maintain themselves who would never have dreamed of such a thing a hundred years ago. This is not the place for a discussion whether this is a good thing for women or a bad one; or for a lamentation that the occupations by which women might maintain themselves are so few; and of those few, so many engrossed by men. This is not the place for a speculation as to whether women are to grow into a condition of self-maintenance, and their dependence for support upon father, brother and husband to become only occasional. With these considerations, interesting as they are, we have no business at this moment. What we have to think of is the necessity,—in all justice, in all honour, in all humanity, in all prudence,—that every girl's faculties should be made the most of, as carefully as boys'. While so many women are no longer sheltered, and protected, and supported, in safety from the world (as people used to say) every woman ought to be fitted to take care of herself. Every woman ought to have that justice done to her faculties that she may possess herself in all the strength and clearness of an exercised and enlightened mind, and may have at command, for her subsistence, as much intellectual power and as many resources as education can furnish her with. Let us hear nothing of her being shut out, because she is a woman, from any study that she is capable of pursuing: and if one kind of cultivation is more carefully attended to than another, let it be the discipline and exercise of the reasoning faculties. From the simplest rules of arithmetic let her go on, as her brother does, as far into the depths of science, and up to the heights of philosophy as her powers and opportunities permit; and it will certainly be found that the more she becomes a reasoning creature, the more reasonable, disciplined and docile she will be: the more she knows of the value of knowledge and of all other things, the more diligent she will be;—the more sensible of duty,—the more interested in occupations,—the more womanly. This is only coming round to the points we started from; that every human being is to be made as perfect as possible: and that this must be done through the most complete development of all the faculties.

WHAT WOMEN ARE EDUCATED FOR

Among the observances of the London summer are now the annual meetings of the authorities of the Ladies' Colleges, which are a new feature in English society. The kinds of attention paid to these meetings, and of comment made upon them are very various. I am at present concerned with only one of the many points of view from which these institutions are regarded.

At the recent annual meeting of Queen's College (for Ladies), Harley Street, the chair was filled by the Right Honourable W. Cowper. The Dean of the College, and some of the Professors, several clergymen, and many friends of the pupils were present, as well as the main body of the pupils. Having had opportunity to see, through a long life, what men have, at this age of the world, been thinking for two generations about the education of women, I always read with interest the reports of such annual meetings as that at the Harley Street College, and amuse myself with marking the progress of opinion disclosed by the speakers. On the late occasion (July 4th), the chairman's speech was perhaps better understood in its bearings by some hearers and readers than by himself. My experience of men's minds on this particular subject satisfies me that Mr. Cowper believed himself to be exceedingly liberal in his views, so that he was doing something virtuous,—something that would win gratitude from one sex, if it did not inspire re-

Once a Week, August 10, 1861, pp. 175–179.

spect for his courage in the other, in asserting the claims of women to a good education. I have usually traced in the gentlemen present at such meetings a happy complacency, an air of amiable magnanimity, which it was unnecessary to find fault with,—it was so natural and so harmless;—a keen sense of the pleasures of generous patronage, in seeing that women have a fair opportunity of a better cultivation than had been given before; but it is not often that the complacency is so evident, and so self-confident, as in Mr. Cowper's speech of the 4th instant. He has evidently no misgiving about the height of his own liberality when he assumes that the grand use of a good education to a woman is that it improves her usefulness to somebody else. This is the turn that praise of female enlightenment has always taken among men till very lately, when one here and there ventures to assume that the first object of a good education is to improve the individual as an individual. Mr. Cowper has not got beyond the notion of the majority of the friends of female education, who think they have said everything when they have recommended good intellectual training as fitting women to be "mothers of heroes," "companions to men," and so on. No great deal will be done for female improvement while this sort of sentiment is supposed to be the loftiest and most liberal.

Girls will never make a single effort, in any length of school years, for such an object as being companions to men, and mothers of heroes. If they work, and finally justify the pains taken for them in establishing such colleges as these, it will be for the same reasons that boys work well, and come out worthy of their schooling;—because they like their studies, and enjoy the sense of mental and moral development which is so strong in school and college years; and because their training is well adapted to educe, develop, and strengthen their powers, and render them as wise and good as their natures, years, and circumstances permit.

Till it is proposed, in educating girls, to make them, in themselves and for their own sakes, as good specimens of the human being as the conditions of the case allow, very little will be effected by any expenditure of pains, time, and money. . . .

The common plea is that the boys are so expensive that there is not much to spare for the girls' education. This is no particular concern of the college managers; but there are parents who seem to think that they are doing something virtuous in coming to bargain and haggle for the greatest amount of instruction for the smallest possible sum. They would not think of haggling with the master of the public school their boys go to. They pay down their hundred or two a-year for each boy; but, when it comes to the girls, they contrive, and assume, and beg, till they get in one or two younger girls on cheap terms, or send the governess to sit by as guardian, and pick up a lesson without pay. The mothers are apt to take credit for such management, on the ground of the trouble they have with the fathers to get any money out of them for college-lessons, when a governess (if they could find a paragon of one for a reasonable salary) might "educate" any number of girls for the same terms as one. It does not particularly concern the college managers what the fathers say at home about family plans: but they hear a good deal about it, through the expositions the mothers think fit to make of their own virtue and ability in contriving to get their daughters' education done as cheaply as possible.

But this may not be a true account of the fathers' notions, I may be reminded. I rather think it is, in the majority of cases. It is not only in newspapers, in angry letters called forth by some new phase of female education or employment, that fathers inquire what possible use there can be in learning this or that. While a narrow-minded commercial man says, in a newspaper effusion, that girls should be fitted for managing the house and doing the needlework, and that all study beyond this is mischievous; a common-place professional man says, at his own table or his club, that it ought not to cost much to teach his girls as much as it is good for them to know: that the whole college course at Harley Street or Bedford Square is more than he thinks it right to afford while his boys are at school. Not that it is a costly education: it is very much otherwise, considering its quality: but he cannot see the use of making the girls so learned. In fact, he has told his wife how much he will spend on the girls, and she may get for them as much as she can for the money.

And what are the girls thinking meantime? An old hermit cannot undertake to report their views, which are probably very seldom uttered. But it is clear, from the college reports, and by what is known in the world of the results thus far, that the young ladies are disposed to be industrious, are highly intelligent, and cheerful and happy amidst their intellectual pursuits. We may fairly suppose therefore that they either see a use in what they learn, or learn for other reasons than the thought of utility: that in school and classrooms they are, in short, like their brothers. The boys are not encouraged to study for such a reason as becoming intelligent companions to somebody hereafter, or being the fathers of great men. The boys know that they are to be made as wise as they can be made under their conditions; that the knowledge they gain is a good in itself; and that their fathers do not, in paying their bills, pause in doubt whether they are justified in spending so much money for such an object as the enlightenment of their children. If at their desks, I should say that they have higher and truer notions of the operation, value, and fitness of knowledge in their own case than many of their parents. Possibly some of them could teach the chairman of their annual meeting that there are better reasons for their being well educated than the prospect he holds out of their "influence" hereafter— the use they are to be of furthering the objects of men.

I am not unmindful, however, of the great advance made— the remarkable conquest of prejudice—within a few years. It required some courage, till within a few years, to speak of any sort of college in connection with female studies: and nothing short of heroism and every kind of magnanimity was requisite to make any man offer himself for a professorship in such colleges. It is very different now, though too many of my acquaintances still perpetually fall into the old notion that women have no occasion for intellectual cultivation. I have never wondered at, nor much regretted, the dislike to the very name of "college," considering what we have seen done, and heard said, in foreign institutions bearing that title. There are great joint-stock company's schools in America, advertised and glorified under the name of colleges, from which English parents and brothers would flee away, and take refuge in the wild woods, rather than "assist" at an annual meeting. The public exhibition of intellect and sensibility, the recitations, the compositions, the essays on metaphysical or moral subjects, the prize-giving, the newspaper reports of the pupils,—all this, and the dreadful hollowness and abominable taste of the whole display, might well cause English fathers to start back from the first mention of female colleges at home. So might the continental celebrations which we still witness occasionally, where the most virtuous school girl is crowned in the presence of a throng of visitors; and where virtue in detail— honour, sensibility, fidelity, &c., &c.—is rewarded by prizes and praises. But it is now understood that our colleges for ladies have nothing in common with institutions in which these terrible exhibitions can take place. Our young maidens altogether decline publicity, and could not condescend to try for prizes or accept praises. They are plainly zealous for the honour of their college; but no one of them has anything to gain for herself beyond the privileges of learning and art. There is a wider difference between such colleges as we see annually glorified in American journals and those of Bedford Square and Harley Street than between these last and the closest and narrowest education given in an aristocratic school-room, by an unrelieved governess, to two or three secluded and spiritless girls who never heard a masterly exposition of anything in their lives. But due credit should be given to such fathers of the present generation as have surmounted their horror at the name of colleges for young ladies.

The whole significance of the matter—the whole importance of the assumption involved in Mr. Cowper's speech about qualifying women by education to "stir up man" and improve the nation—can hardly be seen without reverting to some of the stages that women have passed through within two or three generations, and then turning to some recent discussions which have caused a strong sensation in London society, and a good deal beyond it.

There was a great notion of making women learned several times during the last century. We know almost as much of the reign of the female pedants as of the history of any political party in the time of George III. I do not wish to dwell on the subject, for there was nothing in the writings of the Blues[1] of the last century which need detain us now, or which would

---

[1] Refers to bluestockings, British society women of the eighteenth century who attempted to arrange intellectual "conversations" with literary figures as social events. A term commonly used derisively for intellectual women with affectations, although some of the original bluestockings were quite capable.

have obtained praise in any society where women were duly respected,—which is the same thing as being truly appreciated. We need not trouble ourselves now with the Sewards, the Carters, the Veseys, Hamiltons, Mores, Montagues, and others who, without anything like the genuine knowledge now attainable by women, poured out sentiment and fancies which they mistook for intellectual products. We need not pause on these, nor criticise their works; but I must mention them, in order to recall the Blue-stocking stage of female education, and also because they are a foil to the really well-educated women of the period. I knew the Miss Berrys, and the Miss Baillies, and the empress of her sex in her own time and after,—Mrs. Barbauld.[2] The Miss Berrys were a favourable specimen of the Blue order: not only clever and well-read, but enlightened;—rather blue, certainly, but sensible, kindly, sufficiently practical for their position—in short, certainly the better for their intellectual cultivation, and in no way the worse for it. The Baillies were not Blue. Joanna's genius was too strong and natural to be overlaid by any amount of reading she was disposed to undertake. All the sources of wisdom were open to her;—Nature, books, and life: and she drew from them all in happy proportion; so that she became the wise and happy woman that every wise father would desire his daughter to be in herself, whatever she might also do for, and be to other people. If Joanna Baillie had written nothing, she would have been the beloved and revered being that she is in all memories. The only difference is that her lot as an author affords further evidence of the robust character of her mind, in the equal serenity with which she regarded the rise, and culmination, and decline of her own fame. No seat of irritability seems to have been ever touched, more or less, by such a celebrity as very few women have ever attained, or by that extinction of her fame, which must have appeared to her unjust, if the fame had not been itself a delusion. Less celebrated, but

[2] Mary (1763–1852) and Agnes (1764–1852) Berry. Mary edited a posthumous edition of Horace Walpole's collected works and wrote plays, memoirs, and social history. The two were close friends of Walpole. Joanna Baillie (1762–1851), Scottish poet and dramatist. She and her sister lived on Hampstead Heath many years and received such visitors as Sir Walter Scott. Mrs. Letitia Aikin Barbauld (1743–1825), a neighbor and friend of the Misses Baillie, was a poet and essayist.

hardly less highly endowed, and more thoroughly educated than Joanna Baillie, or perhaps any other woman of her time, was Mrs. Barbauld, whose few but exquisite writings still kindle enthusiasm in duly qualified readers who happen to pick up anything of hers in their path of study.

Her father educated her with her brother; and we see in her noble style, full of power, clearness, and grace, one of the results of her sound classical training. We see others in her compactness of thought, and closeness of expression; while the warm glow of sentiment, pure as the sunlight, excludes all appearance of pedantry, or unsuitableness to the hour in which she wrote. Fox pronounced her "Essay on the Inconsistency of Human Expectations," "the finest essay in the English language,"—no one being more aware than he must have been of the classical origin of the train of thought, so admirably conveyed in vivid English. The strength and discipline of her moral nature were only too well proved by the experience of her married life. She underwent, with noble outward serenity, a long and excruciating trial from her husband's insanity, which ended in suicide. The "Dirge," which remains among her poems, discloses to those who knew her something of what lay under the dignity and calm which she preserved for his sake. The strain and shock induced an indolence, or reluctance to act, and make any appearance, which has deprived us of much which she would no doubt have written, if she had not lost the spirit and gaiety of her early life; but we have enough to understand how it was that her reason and fancy swayed all minds that approached her own, and her words burned themselves in on the memories of all who fell in with them. . . .

Her father certainly did not train her to be somebody's companion, or somebody's mother. He treated her and her brother alike, with the view of freely opening to both the way to wisdom. Her education was a pure blessing to her. It was to her what she briefly and brilliantly describes intellectual pursuits to be in her celebrated essay. Her firm grasp of philosophy, her student-like habit of mind, and the scholarly discipline she underwent did not impair, in the slightest degree, her womanly grace, her delicate reserve, or the glow of her friendships. It is true, she was not much of a needlewoman. There is a tradition that the skeleton of a mouse was found in her workbag; but this kind of disinclination is seen in women who know no language but their own, and whose ideas do not range beyond their own street. As her husband's aider in the work of his great school at Palgrave, and as a motherly hostess to the little boys, she was tenderly remembered by some men of distinction who had stood at her knee. A nobler and sweeter presence than Mrs. Barbauld's I have never witnessed; and I have heard from some of her own generation that her sprightliness was once as bewitching as her composure was afterwards pathetic.

In the next generation after the Blues of the last century, there seems to have been a sort of reaction in regard to the education of at least the middle-class girls. As far as I have heard from many quarters, the mothers of the early part of this century were less informed, less able in even the common affairs of life, than those who immediately preceded and followed them. There were, of course, reasons for this: but I cannot go into them now. It is enough to recall to the memory of old people what they heard in their childhood of the boarding-schools, sewing-schools, and day-schools in which their mothers had received their education, as it was called. . . . There was, however, a marked improvement: and the hardness of the times, introducing competition into the governess department, directed more attention upon education. From that day to this the whole conception of the objects and methods of education has been expanding and improving; and perhaps not even the city Arabs now gathered into ragged schools have more reason to be thankful for the change than the girlhood of England and Scotland. As Mr. Cowper justly observed at Harley Street, it is the well-grounded and systematic instruction, the habit of co-ordinated study, which is so valuable to the minds of women. Our Ladies' Colleges are rapidly familiarising society with this view of female study; schools are formed for the purpose of preparing pupils for the college, and the quality of governesses is rising in full proportion to the new means of training now put within their reach. Through them, as well as by natural incitements of example and sympathy, the improvement will spread from the middle classes upwards. If aristocratic parents will not as yet send their daughters to colleges, where future governesses and professional and mercantile men's daughters study together, they will soon demand a higher order of instruction from the exclusive schoolmistresses, governesses, and masters whom they employ. Hitherto their children have undoubtedly had the advantage in learning well what they do learn,—modern languages, English reading and writing, and the practice of the arts. Now, they must extend their scheme. . . .

I have seen something of that order of young ladies; and what I have observed obliges me to believe that they are at least as well provided with independent objects and interests as middle-class girls. One family rises up before my mind,—sensible parents and their five daughters (saying nothing here of the sons). The parents provided instruction for each girl, according to her turn and ability: and when each grew up to womanhood, she had free scope for her own pursuit. One was provided with a painting-room, and another with a music-room, and all appliances and means: a third had a conservatory and garden; and all lived in a society of the highest cultivation. They had as much as they wished of the balls and fêtes we hear so much about; and there was nothing to distinguish them from other young ladies who are now subjected to such insolent speculation from below: but I am confident that it could never have entered the head of the veriest coxcomb of their acquaintance that any of the family were speculating in marriage. Four of them married well, in the best sense, though not all grandly. The fifth died, after many years of illness. There is every reason to believe that English girls have the simplicity, intelligence, and kindliness of their order in one rank of life as in another; and certainly not least in that class which is surrounded, from its birth upwards, by an atmosphere of refinement derived from intelligence.

What, then, are they educated for? This is the great question, in their case as in that of middle-class girls.

For the most part, their education is probably a matter of sympathy and imitation. In this or that way they may best learn what every girl is expected to learn. Beyond this, there is usually but a dim notion of the object, and as little notion as elsewhere of the great single or paramount aim of education,—to raise the quality of the individual to the highest attainable point. I believe that the parents fall short of this conception, like most other parents of daughters: but I am confident that they are yet further from the other extreme,—

of universally and audaciously breeding up their daughters for the matrimonial market. One evidence that is before our eyes tells a great deal. The unmarried women of the upper classes seem to be at least as well occupied with natural and useful pursuits as those of any other rank; and more so perhaps, in proportion to their greater command of means for accomplishing their purposes and gratifying their tastes. Some may do a little mischief in attempting to do good: some may get into a foolish metaphysical school in their study of German: some may lose themselves among the religious sects of the day in the course of their polemical or antiquarian studies: but I doubt whether one could anywhere find more satisfactory specimens of single women, amiable and cheerful, because satisfied and occupied,—with friends enough for their hearts, and business enough for head and hands.

What is the truth, I wonder, about the "fast young ladies" we read so much about? I am out of the world; but I cannot find that anybody who is in it has actually seen the young ladies who talk of "awful swells" and "deuced bores," who smoke, and venture upon free discourse, and try to be like men. In Horace Walpole's time, as in Addison's, there were "fast young ladies," as we see in many a letter of Walpole's, and many a paper of the "Spectator." Probably there were some in every age, varying their doings and sayings, according to the fopperies of the time. Have we more than the average proportion? I do not know. One obvious remark on the case of the girls so freely discussed has scarcely, I think, been sufficiently made; that the two commonest allegations against them are incompatible. We hear of their atrocious extravagance in dress and peculiarity of personal habits; and, in the next breath, of their lives being one unremitting effort to obtain a husband. Now, in my long life, I have witnessed nothing like the opposition set up by men, within the last seven years, to certain modes of female dress and manners: yet the modes remain. The ladies are steady. I wish their firmness was shown in a better cause; for I admire the fashions of the day as little as any man: but it is plain that the ladies, young and old, daughters and mothers, do not try to please men in their dress and behaviour. They choose to please themselves: and, whatever we may think of their taste, we cannot but admit their spirit of independence.

On the whole, I cannot see any evidence that women of any rank are, generally speaking, educated with a view to getting married: nor yet for the purpose of being companions to men, or the mothers of heroes; nor yet for the purpose of inspiring men to great deeds, and improving society; nor yet, except in a few scattered instances, to make the most of their own individual nature. There will be less confusion of thought, and dimness of aim, when the better instructed generation grows up. Meantime, in the midst of the groping among sympathies and sentiments, and imitations, and ambitions, and imperfect views of all sorts, let us only have some few who uphold the claim of every human being to be made the most of, in all the provinces of its nature, and the female sex is redeemed. Women will quietly enter into their "rights," without objection on any hand, when those rights consist in their being more reasonable, more able, more useful, and more agreeable than ever before, without losing anything in exchange for the gain.

FROM THE MOUNTAIN

MIDDLE-CLASS EDUCATION IN ENGLAND: GIRLS

If the education of middle-class Boys is a vague and cloudy subject to treat in writing, what is that of Girls? At first sight, the subject seems to be too chaotic to be examined on any principle or in any method at all; and perhaps the best purpose to be answered by any examination at all is that of exposing the confusion itself. In the Boys' case there is something like firm ground to stand on in the universal agreement that boys should be somehow educated, and in the old custom of mak-

Cornhill Magazine 10 (November 1864):549–569.

ing Latin and Greek the chief studies; but in the case of the Girls, there is no tradition, no common conviction, no established method, no imperative custom,—nothing beyond a supposition that girls must somehow learn to read and write, and to practise whatever accomplishment may be the fashion at the time. As a matter of fact, some of us have an impression that things are not so bad as they were at the beginning of the century; and there are evidences that this is true: but still, the way in which girls generally spend their time from seven years old to twenty is so desperately unfavourable to mind and character or (to speak more moderately) so inferior to what it might be, and to the way in which their grandmothers passed their precious youth, nearly as far back as we can trace them, that we may well feel a sort of despair in approaching the subject with any practical aim.

The custom of giving girls a classical education three centuries ago, ought to have settled for ever the pretended doubt whether the female intellect is adequate to the profitable study of the classics; and, as the practice was by no means confined to the aristocracy, the results should have left no room to question the benefit of such studies. But the religious struggle of the seventeenth century disturbed the natural course of women's training, as it disturbed everything else; and a manifest decline of female intelligence and manners followed the abatement of Puritanism, and the enlargement of social liberty or licence. Our grandmothers did, however, learn something well. Their parents had not fallen into the modern temptation of being ashamed of their station in life, and anxious that their children should attain a higher. The daughters were prepared to be what their mothers had been before them; and the children therefore learned early and thoroughly what their mothers could teach them. They had better health than modern children,—little as was then popularly known of sanitary truths and methods. They were more in the open air, had rougher sports, were not over-worked in their brains, and had a larger variety of occupations. In times when every woman below the highest ranks knew how to cook, to prepare medicines, to wash laces and iron cambrics, and plait shirt-frills, and manage the garden, and take care of the domestic pets, there was exercise and variety enough to counteract the mischiefs of long hours at the needle, under the conditions of a high seat and a straight back, or no back at all, to the bench. What the literary pursuit of those days was, and what the spelling, and what the general cultivation of mind among young women of the middle class, their letters, and even their receipt-books show; but it was the advantage of their time that the middle classes knew what they would be at in the training of their daughters; and they mainly accomplished their purpose. Generally speaking, the girls knew no language but their own, and that only by ear and instinct; they had no conception of the meaning of any of the *ologies*, and they were rarely accomplished, except in the arts of the needle; but there was a sterling quality in what they did which ought to be taken into the account. As far as appears, nearly all the handwritings were good,—that is, legible and neat. In the domestic arts it was a disgrace to be incompetent: and the mastery of these brought with it,—as it always does and always will bring with it,—an opening and a call to that grand function of domestic administration which is at once education and the fruition of education. It was the reality of this rule in the household which gave so much character to our grandmothers, enriched them with good sense, ripened them by experience of human life and character, and helped them to some of the best results of learning. They wrote letters as good, in essential respects, as if they had been taught composition; and their conversation with their husbands, brothers, and pastors, was perhaps as good in its way as if it had had a savour of book-learning. Add to this the sound health (small-pox and fevers apart), and the natural and unconcealed relish of life, and we may ask whether the chief end of education,—the *educing* the powers of the individual—might not be nearly as well attained by that generation as by any since. It is true, it was dreadful that they misunderstood the treatment of husband or children in small-pox; it was a pity that they feared and despised everything that was foreign; it was disastrous that they supposed they held a despotism by divine right over their children and servants up to any age; it might be amusing that they thought they could have been close to an eclipse by sailing in the clouds, or that they supposed Euclid to be a Latin poet, or that they did not know where to find our colonies of Virginia and Massachusetts Bay on the map; but there were countervailing advantages belonging to those days and that training. The health and soundness of their neighbourhoods were sustained very much by the knowledge and skill of women who really understood the qualities and uses of vegetable medicines, and who could practise simple surgery. The doctors of those days held many of them in high respect, and committed to them the care and cure of wounds, sores, burns, dislocations, and a wide range of ordinary diseases. If they did not respect the wills of their children, they did not overtask their brains. If they held a strict rule over their servants, they took them first for pupils and then for friends; they first trained them in domestic business, and then made common cause with them in it. If they knew nothing of foreign nations and notions, they were good judges of foreign commodities; and if they were not clear as to where tea and spices and silks and shawls came from, they could appreciate them when under their hands. They no doubt inflicted some pain and fell short of much good by the narrowness of view and scantiness of intellectual culture; but they were what they were intended by their parents to be; and they were tolerably complete as far as they went and professed to go. And certainly they were less in the rear of the boys of their generation than girls are now.

Their acquirements, such as they were, were obtained at home for the most part; and further, at the writing-school, the sewing-school, or the general day-school. Then followed the period of middle-class girls' boarding-schools. There was a great expansion and multiplication of these during the war which followed the French Revolution. It was a period of high prosperity for certain middle-class interests, while so costly to the country on the whole. I need not describe it, for it was not so long ago but that we have all heard our elders speak of it if we have not ourselves witnessed the effects of it. There can be no doubt that we are suffering now from the sort of education which then became common among the farming and shopkeeping classes. As the parents made war and monopoly profits, an evil emulation entered into too many of them to rise in gentility; and one of the first methods they took was to make sportsmen of their sons, and fine ladies of their daughters. Hence the low condition of agriculture before the repeal of the corn laws;[3] hence the deteriorated household character of women of the shopkeeping, and even the farming class for a generation past; hence the mushroom "Ladies' Seminaries" which became a byword long ago,—a representative term for false pretension, vulgarity, and cant. The complaints of dismayed parents that their girls at eighteen could do no one thing well, and pretended only to read a little French with difficulty, play badly on the piano, and ornament screens, are still fresh in our ears. How low this sort of parental vanity and filial failure descended in the gradation of the middle class could scarcely be believed by any who do not know that class well throughout. It is enough to say here that "the butcher, the baker, the candlestick-maker," were as anxious about their girls playing a tune on the piano, and having a water-colour daub to show, as the richest tenant-farmer in the days of the sliding scale.

There has certainly been some improvement since that time,—half a century ago; and the most striking part of the improvement has been within the last half, and especially the last quarter of those fifty years. This is an encouragement to look into the present state of things,—chaotic as it appears from the highest point of view. What, then, is the state of Girls' education now?

The improvement might not be distinctly proposed half a century ago; but it can hardly be doubted that the stir was beginning. One evidence of this is that some girls of the middle class were allowed to learn Latin and Greek; and that some others who were not permitted desired it. . . . There were few women qualified to teach the dead languages; but out of that generation of pupils those ladies were to arise who have established Preparatory Schools for boys of such merit as to be considered some of the best schools in the country. Masters in our most eminent public schools have openly rejoiced over boys who have come to them from this or that Preparatory School, because the mistresses grounded the boys so well in Latin and Greek grammar.

[3] Laws designed to discourage the importation of grain, repealed in 1846. At various times the duties varied with the domestic price of grain, hence the "sliding scale" at the end of the paragraph.

At the beginning of this change, towns where there was a grammar school were usually the first scene of the experiment. Among several reasons for this, one was that the undermasters were available for teaching in families on reasonable terms. Where Latin is once fairly established as a girl's study there is sure to be presently a particularly good master ready to teach it. . . .

As there is no standard for the education of girls, and no basis of principle or consent on which to establish it, there are frequent changes of fashion or fancy in practice. On this very point there have been fluctuations down to the present hour: and no one would undertake to say what proportion of the girlhood of the country has the advantage of any classical training at all. Some of us think that the practice is more common among the aristocracy than the middle class. . . .

The social condition which just now renders the inquiry into the education of girls particularly interesting, is that the present is a period of transition for that class. Within half a century the girlhood of the upper middle class has gone through an experience of permanent historical importance. At the beginning of that time, it was assumed in ordinary practice, as in law and politics, that every woman is maintained by her father or her husband, or other male relative. . . .

At the time at which we are living, it is an indisputable fact that above two millions of the women of England are self-supporting workers: it is an admitted truth that while the customs of English society remain what they are, there must be tens of thousands of middle-class women dependent on their own industry: and it can hardly be doubtful, even to the most reluctant eyes, that the workers ought to be properly trained to the business of their lives.

The interest of the present time, then, is in its being the date of an opening of a new line of life for a considerable proportion of middle-class women; and the date therefore of a radical change in the principle and conduct of the intellectual culture of the educators of the next generation. It is settled that marriage is much less general than formerly; that while it remains so a multitude of women must work for the support of themselves, and sometimes their connexions; that the excessive badness of the girls' schools and domestic schoolrooms of the last generation must be retrieved; and that the retrieval has been really begun in a partial way.

So much is agreed: the next question is,—What means of education are actually in use at this moment for middle-class girls?

The daughters of wealthy commoners go through much the same training as the classes above them. Those who are educated by governesses and masters at home, exclusively, may be well-mannered, and have some general culture. . . .

The "genteel" schools, which are merely an imitation of . . . [very exclusive schools]—the fantastical households in which the pupils are elegantly dressed,—probably in uniform, with a marked style of bonnet, and veils all hanging down on the same side; in which every movement is measured, and the pupils all speak alike, and walk alike, and write the same hand, and utter the same pretty sentiments. . . .

The greatest, or most conspicuous change which has taken place is in the next and far larger class of boarding-schools,—the schools filled from the manufacturers' houses, and the surgeons', and lawyers', and country-gentlemen's, and large tenant-farmers'. It is scarcely credible now what some of those schools were like during and after the critical financial period which cast so many poor ladies adrift to get their bread as they might. Those were the days when girls took their exercise, walking two and two, in melancholy procession; and not seldom with books in their hands, learning their lessons as they walked. Those were the days when half-a-dozen of them were crammed into a bedroom not airy enough for two; and when they washed their feet all round on Saturday nights with a limited supply of water and towels. Those were the days when saucy girls invented names of European capitals, and found the most extraordinary places on the map, with full approbation from a short-sighted teacher. Those were the days when the Sunday morning lesson might be learning four lines of *Paradise Lost* by heart, leaving off whether there was a stop or not. . . . Even the best of such schools, however, had its idiosyncrasy, which, during such a period of debased education, was the same thing as a drawback or defect. All the girls in such a school,—or all but the reckless and unworthy— had one style of thinking, and of expression of their thought;

or, rather, what they expressed was not thought, but sentiment. In one such school, the girls all wrote demonstrative
letters; in another, the style was poetical; in another moral, or
sprightly. The handwriting of one set of elderly ladies now
living tells where they were educated, as does the epistolary
style of another set; and the open-air gait and salutations of
another, and the drawing-room manners of yet another. While
this result was produced, each establishment was thus conspicuously marked as having failed of the true aim of education—however honourable, in such times, might be the comparative character and achievement of the school. . . .

The girls of the lower middle class have, all the while,
had little choice and little chance. Their educational lot has
been truly dreary. Wherever it can be managed, the children
of small farmers, country shopkeepers, and poor professional
men naturally go to a day-school, as the cheapest plan. The
day-school may be good, bad, or indifferent, according to
the accident of a better or worse master or mistress; but it
seems to be too true that the low-priced boarding-schools for
girls of that rank do the pupils more harm than good. . . .

Take a country neighbourhood, where the old-fashioned
farming ways assume that the girls are to be handy in domestic business. "The girls are not what they used to be," the
complaint is in such places. "The poultry don't answer as they
did, nor does the dairy. The girls must have schooling; but
there is no seeing what good it does; for they forget their
school learning before they have been home two years; and
they have all real business still to learn." A lady who happens
to be fond of teaching, and who is eminently skilled in it, sees
what a field there is in such a place; and she opens such a
school as was never heard of before, far or near. There are
other teachers besides herself—chosen for their special qualifications and their training. Among them, these ladies can
teach, in the best modern methods, whatever can be useful to
girls of this class, either in training their faculties—as Latin
and geometry; or in expanding their range of reading and general intelligence—as the French language, History, and English literature; or in fitting them for the business of life as
helpers of their parents—as writing a good hand, arithmetic,
and bookkeeping, and such study of Natural Philosophy and
Natural History as will at once make them more sensible

women generally, and operate favourably on their special objects, improving their dairy produce, and their poultry, and their honey, and putting them in the way of important economy in every branch of management.

There is a liberal apparatus provided; the hours are fixed considerately, to suit farmhouse ways; the girls bring their own sewing to do in the hours appropriated to genuine instruction in needlework, and cheered by pleasant readings. The terms are very low, complete and liberal as is the establishment; and those of the pupils who choose may dine there (due notice of numbers being given) for scarcely more than the cost-price of the provisions. Yet such a school as this goes a-begging. For one father and mother who appreciate it, there are half a dozen who find fault, and yet more who stand shilly-shallying till their opportunity is lost. Though aware that everybody else's daughters have for two generations past come back from school fit for neither one thing nor another, they don't know what to think of anything so new as this school. If the lady would charge half her terms for just the French, and the writing, and ciphering, with, perhaps, a little geography, and leave out all the rest, they might be glad to send their girls to her. And so the lady, having waited as long as she,— far from being poor—can afford, carries her benefits elsewhere. It is an occasional question among neighbours, whether they had not better have kept her; but she is gone, and it is no use talking now.

Take a town case. In a large, old-fashioned, but growing town, there seems to be no such thing as a school appropriate to the wants of the small shopkeeping and superior artisan class. Moreover, there is no saying when there ever was such a school; for it is the universal complaint that the domestic comfort, abilities and manners of that class are of a very low order from the defective training of the women. Their houses are not well kept; the rooms are untidy and not even clean; the ways are unpunctual; the meals are badly cooked; the clothes are badly got up; and if there is a servant, there is endless turmoil with her. The mistress says the maid does not do her work; the maid finds the mistress unreasonable and harsh; and the master and the children feel that both the charges are true. There has been so much crying out, all over the country, for something which shall be to this order of society what our regulated and assisted schools are to the labouring class, that many good citizens and sensible women bestir themselves to see what they can do among their neighbours. Of these, one lady has an experiment of her own. She fits up and opens a convenient house, in an easily accessible situation, settles in it a mistress of high qualifications, and a housekeeper who has risen through the ranks of domestic service to be fit for the present business. Under her, the girls are to learn household work in the best style,—cleaning, cooking, laying the table, and so on; while the proper school-learning is of a better quality than can be found anywhere else within reach. When the plans are got fairly to work, there will be a regular dinner provided for the smallest payment, for girls from a distance; meantime, the lesson of laying the cloth, &c. goes on, for the sake of those who bring their dinners. This lesson is rather baulked, however, and the superiors are much vexed, by the sort of dinners disclosed,—viz. stale pastry bought with money given at home for the girls to spend as they like. This phenomenon hastens the plan for the good hot dinner at the school,—the roast leg of mutton or sirloin, with vegetables, the Irish stew, and other good things, to be cooked by the girls, in turn, in view of the table to be kept in the future home of each. But the girls have no mind for the roast beef and Yorkshire pudding, or the stew, or anything else that sensible people like: they go on buying stale pastry on their way to school, and pay more for it than for the confortable dinner at their command. In a little while difficulty arises about the industrial part of the schooling. Strange to say, the mothers do not like that their daughters should learn to wash china properly, to clean furniture, rub up silver, and spread a table; and even the fathers object to any time being given to the art of cookery. On the whole, the very superior school-learning is graciously accepted, if not appreciated; but the industrial element is fatal. The pawnbroker's daughter is absent on the days when it is her turn to sweep a room or make the bread; the cabinet-maker's girls are always missing on ironing days; the linen-draper's girls cannot come any more, unless they are excused from all but book, and map, and pen work; and thus the scheme is brought to an end, the school is closed, and the husbands and children of these unhappy pupils will have to go through the wretched old experience of domestic discomfort and wrangling, because the wife and mother does not know how to keep house.

After this review of the late and present condition of middle-class female education in England, what should we desire? what may we hope? and what should we aim at? . . .

The case of the Girls differs from that of the Boys, in the absence of all need to consider the question of appeal to the State. Probably there is nobody in England who for a moment dreams of asking the State to undertake, or to touch more or less, the education of the daughters of the most active, intelligent, practical, and domestic class of English citizens. Only a word is necessary on this head; but that word is of some importance, and at present, if ever, needing attention.

The Royal Commissioners on Education reported, three years since, in favour of applying to the improvement of education the incomes of charities which have become by lapse of time useless or pernicious. The annual amount thus proposed to be transferred exceeds 100,000£. In considering how such a sum would be best applied, attention was fixed on the proportion of girls to boys profiting, really or ostensibly, by old educational endowment. In common endowed schools, the girls are little more than half as many as the boys; and in grammar-schools they are only a tenth of the scholars. After the appearance of the Commissioners' Report, it was strongly urged by some sensible people that the great new educational want which had arisen since those old bequests were made, should be first attended to in the disposal of this fund, viz. the need among middle-class women of an education for teaching. Model schools—training schools—of this character are an urgent want of the time and of the country; and something of the sort was claimed for the sex, on the unquestionable ground that the charities to be superseded were for the equal benefit of men and women, and that it would be a manifest unfairness to apply the income for the benefit of boys alone. At that very time, an income from land bequeathed in an old century to needy persons of both sexes was used, under the sanction of the Court of Chancery, for the erection of a school for boys exclusively. If this example were to be followed all over the country while there is no provision for instructing and training middle-class women as teachers, and while many counties of England contain no endowed schools at all for girls, it would be as pitiful a cowardice on the one hand as it would be an insolent aggression on the other to permit such a thing to be done. It is one thing to beg from the State help which would involve subservience to State administration in a matter of which Government is not a particularly good judge; and it is another thing to claim from Government a just share of existing funds, to be applied under conditions agreed upon. Repugnant to English notions and feelings as would be a system of public-school education for girls, under the management of the Government, or any ecclesiastical party, or a joint-stock company, there can be no doubt of the eagerness with which the establishment of a few model and training schools of a high order would be hailed by women whose lot is to work, and who need a good education for the purpose. It will be a cruel injustice if they are denied their fair share of funds intended for the aid of equal numbers of men and women.

Even in the three years which have passed since the Commissioners reported, advances have been made in female education which have produced a great change of feeling. The timid can now hear the mention of things which sounded very terrible even so short a time ago; and the chances of a really good education becoming attainable are so far improved.

Let it be understood at once that in claiming for middle-class girls a substantial and liberal development and training of the mind, and, for those who desire it, a special preparation for the educational or other profession in life, nobody contemplates the use of any method which is not in accordance with national custom and English feelings. . . .

Both French and Americans, but particularly the latter, teach us that there is nothing insuperable in the greatest seeming difficulty about girls,—the difficulty which makes the main difference between their case and that of boys,—the claim of the household arts as an essential part of education. Boys have two things to divide their days between: study and play. Girls have three: study, the domestic arts, and play. At boarding-school the domestic training is dropped out of the life altogether; and a home life, without any school at all, almost nullifies study. Here is the dilemma. But French and American women excel our middle-class women in both departments. How do they manage it?

How it may be in the French household, I do not know; but in the American it is a matter of course for little girls to be much more useful than damsels of double their age are in England. I never could make out why English little girls are not gratified in their liking for housekeeping from the beginning. Every healthy and happy child enjoys the dignity and amusement of household business, unless it be the early stage of needlework. There seems to be no reason why she should not know perfectly well how things should be done, and be familiar with the doing of them, before the boarding-school time arrives. If this is not made secure, boarding-school is so far an evil. A girl who at seventeen has everything to learn about the shopping, and the management of the table, and nursing the sick, and the economy of the house, is at a disadvantage which she will hardly get over. We see much of this among our middle-class brides, who feel it a heavy care on their minds that they have no confidence and no knowledge about housekeeping. It is well if they do not grow afraid of their husbands; they are certainly afraid of their husbands' family, and of their own servants; and all for want of simple knowledge and skill which they ought to have attained before they went to school. The deficiency of domestic service in America, and the habits of society, preclude this mischief; and it may be taken for granted that ladies who obtain their diploma as physicians, and who read Greek plays, and who thoroughly understand the Differential Calculus are as dexterous in making beds, and turning out a good batch of bread and pies, and administering medicines and blisters, as ever their grandmothers were.

With us the best chance seems to be for those who are within reach of a first-class day-school, or of one of the colleges which are springing up among us. A combination of the domestic and academical life is a very high privilege indeed. Where this cannot be had, the domestic training should, in the first place, be given to such an extent as that it can never be lost, and may be easily resumed on the verge of womanhood. But there is a happy possibility opening before us, through the recent discoveries of the benefits of half-time in school work.

Inspectors declare that in schools where boys have given six hours per day to book-work, while the girls have spent three in book-work, and three in sewing and other domestic arts, the girls are by no means behind the boys in attainments. Before this discovery, girls had benefited by the new lights (very old lights, disastrously eclipsed for a time) on the necessity of play and of a sensible care of the bodily frame. Instead of the pale-faced, languid, crooked, fretful type of school-girl, we now have before our eyes the well-grown and well-exercised young maiden who is excellent at ball play and the skipping-rope in its advanced stages, and archery; and if at gymnastics and foot races and swimming, so much the better. This is a vast improvement; but there may be room for another; for the appropriation of a part of the day to domestic business. Where girls board together in a house, under the superintendence of a lady, for the object of attending a school or college, this kind of training might surely go on together with the book study; and if in large boarding-schools the thing cannot be done— this is, as I have said, so far an objection to that mode of education. As the praise and adoption of the half-time method spread, means may be found of administering a complete feminine training, so as to save governesses and other professional women from an ignorance and inaptitude as disadvantageous to their purse as to their dignity and peace of mind. It is to no purpose saying that intellectual women should leave the housekeeping to servants, and that the sewing-machine puts the needle out of court altogether. The truth is, that servants cannot do their work well under any mistress but one who understands their business at least as well as they do. It is also true that a change has come over the servant-maid class, throughout the country—a change which we need not discuss here, but which renders the capacity for domestic administration more than ever necessary to middle-class women. And it is true, again, that the sewing-machine is useless in hands which are not thoroughly skilled in sewing without the machine. Under all circumstances, therefore, let middle-class parents regard household qualifications as sacred, not to be encroached upon or slighted for the sake of any other attainments whatever.

This being understood and admitted, it does not appear that there is any limit to what women may desire and attempt to learn. The case of the dead languages was settled as soon as the objectors were brought to state their objections.

Q. "What should women do with their Latin and Greek when they enter on practical life?"

A. "That is exactly the objection made to the amount of time spent on the classics by boys in public schools. When they become members of Parliament, or physicians, or manufacturers, or shopkeepers, we are told, they never open a Greek or Latin book again."

Q. "But the literature, beyond the school range, is not the only, nor the main, consideration. It is the exercise and discipline of the faculties in the study of the languages which is the inestimable benefit."

A. "Very well, so be it: and this is the very best argument in favour of a sound classical training for girls. If women are usually slovenly in thought, inaccurate in intellectual perception, and weak in reasoning, they should be more and not less exercised in processes which will remedy their defects."

This is so clear that the claim of the female mind to instruction in the classics and mathematics will not be again denied by sensible people of either sex. And they have equally firm ground to stand upon in regard to every other kind of knowledge which is open to anybody.

That this is widely admitted appears by the rapidity with which the resources for female education are extending.

The *Scottish Institution* at Edinburgh has gone through thirty sessions. It was probably the first attempt to combine the advantages of the boarding and day school with the privileges of a collegiate system. There is no doubt that a large number of middle-class women have obtained a high order of education there; but the general impression seems to be that there are mistakes in the scheme—such as prize-giving, and a public distribution of honours—which operate mischievously. Studious or clever girls engross most of the benefits; pursuits are determined, and studies urged in an arbitrary way by these prizes and honours; and girls of slow-moving minds— often the best quality of mind—have no chance under the pressure of the system, while idle ones have no appropriate stimulus, and reckless ones no check. All this may naturally be true in an institution so new and strange as this great school was in its early days; and there must always be grave drawbacks in a scheme which involves public prize-giving to girls. But it was a great day for the sex when such ranges of study were thrown open to women as are under the charge of the professors of the *Scottish Institution*. They offer Latin and three modern languages; and, besides the ordinary school studies, mathematics, natural philosophy, and natural history, and scientific instruction in music. Lectures on scientific and literary subjects give a still further collegiate character to the place and its work.

The two colleges in London, *Queen's College* in Harley Street, with its Preparatory School, and the *Ladies' College* in Bedford Square, were striking signs of the times in their institution, and are becoming more and more so in their success. They were sure to bring out all the weaknesses and vices of the popular mind in regard to female education, and to raise up a host of enemies, and treacherous or mischievous friends; and their gradual triumph over such opposition and embarrassment is a sufficient assurance that the cause is safe. If a full disclosure could be made of the experience of the conductors in regard to the applications and criticisms of parents and guardians, one wonders what proportion of the middle class would be astonished, and how many more would be astonished at their astonishment. One wonders whether these colleges have brought into notice all the fathers who grumble over paying five-pound notes for their daughters' education, while cheerfully spending hundreds a year for their boys, at Eton or Harrow. One wonders where the perplexity is when the father first tells his girls that he can give them no fortune whatever, because their brothers cost him so much, and then declares in their hearing that he can't see what women want, beyond what they might easily pick up at home. One wonders whether he ever considers what is to become of them if he dies untimely, leaving them without a maintenance, and without education wherewith to gain one. One wonders how much dread of the father operates on the mother when she slily and yet audaciously manoeuvres to get two girls into a course for the fees of one; or contrives to introduce the governess "just to sit by during the lessons," so that she may learn without pay, and save sending the younger girls at all. Things like these on the one hand, and, on the other, the honest eagerness of the young pupils themselves, and of grown women who enter as pupils, afford guidance and stimulus to all who witness them. So does the generous zeal of the professors. Those who desire a high order of instruction for girls, whether women and girls, or parents and friends, or patriots and philosophers, should persist in the demand; and the right answer will come. Not all the ignorance, the jealousy, the meanness, the prudery, or the profligate selfishness which is to be found from end to end of the middle class, can now reverse the destiny of the English girl, or retard that ennobling of the sex which is a natural consequence of its becoming wiser and more independent, while more accomplished, gracious, and companionable. The briars and brambles are cleared away from the women's avenue to the temple of knowledge. Now they have only to knock, and it will be opened to them.

The examinations which female students may now command are a sufficient warrant for saying this. The mere knowledge that there is a spirit of superintendence abroad, that there is any system of testing in existence, any means of verification by which female students may ascertain their own standing, is an effectual assurance to them of justice at the hands of their instructors; and accordingly we find a striking improvement from year to year in the spelling, arithmetic, and other ordinary studies of school-girls who come under the examinations of the Society of Arts. There is now an ascending scale of examinations, of one kind or another, till we arrive at that professional testing from which Miss Garrett[4] has come out qualified and certified as a medical practitioner. Of all the kinds of examination now at the service of female students, none are more valuable than those belonging to the Harley Street and Bedford Square Colleges, by which certificates of proficiency in learning are obtainable by women proposing to be educators, or professional workers in one way or another. The entrance thus opened to such a career, and thus zealously sought, the first step in the great reform is securely taken. The State, however well-disposed, could do nothing for the middle-class

---

[4]Elizabeth Garrett Anderson (1836–1917), pioneer British physician, advocate of opening the professions to women, first woman to serve as a mayor in England.

that could compare in value with what has been done by a very small portion of that class for itself. The State could not so well judge of its wants,—could not so wisely provide the agency of instruction needed,—could not so touch and fire the great heart of the nation as this spontaneous effort will soon be seen to have touched and fired it. Let the members of that great middle class help one another from year to year to ascertain distinctly what education they desire for their daughters, and they can have it to their wish. Last year an experiment of immense significance was tried in the extension of the Cambridge examination, framed for boys, to the case of girls. At the short notice of a fortnight, eighty-one entered their names; and they went through with it admirably. In the quietest way, and in the privacy of silent school-rooms, these girls did their work, in the presence of friendly ladies who sat with them to certify to the propriety and fair play of the whole procedure. To use the words of the committee, "In every point of view, the experiment was completely successful." As students, teachers, friends, and patriotic observers all desire that this "might be the first step towards the establishment of a regular and permanent system," it is reasonable to expect to see principle and method introduced into the chaos from which something like order is beginning to arise, and even the next generation much better qualified than the present and the last to justify and confirm the traditional lofty and benign reputation of the womanhood of England.

IV

ON AMERICAN
WOMEN

Garrison was quite right, I think, to sit in the gallery [with the rejected women delegates] at [the 1840 London International Antislavery] Convention. . . . It has done much for the woman question, I am persuaded. You will live to see a great enlargement of our scope, I trust; but, what with the vices of some women and the fears of others, it is hard work for us to assert our liberty. I will, however, till I die, and so will you; and so make it easier for some few to follow us than it was for poor Mary Wollstonecraft to begin.

—*Harriet Martineau to Maria Weston Chapman*

Maria Weston Chapman
From the daguerreotype in the collection of the Boston Public
Library
Reprinted by courtesy of the Trustees of the Boston Public Library

N eeding a holiday after the strains of producing her political economy manuscripts and being the centerpiece of
nightly dinners and parties as a result of her literary fame,
Harriet Martineau sailed for the United States in August 1834.
She insisted that she did not intend to write about her journey,
though that is hard to believe from a writer of her fame and
ambition at a time when European travel accounts of America
were much in demand. With her companion, Louisa Jeffrey,
she disembarked in New York in September and was caught
up in a social whirl in the United States as well. Immersing
herself in American culture, seeking every experience available to her in the new nation, reading everything American
she could acquire, talking to hundreds of people from every
occupation and social status, and using her prominent hosts to
full advantage, she saturated herself in the life of the Americans.[1] In the two years of her visit she traveled more than
10,000 miles in New England, the South, and the West. Her
hosts included Andrew Jackson, James Madison, John C. Cal-
houn, Catherine Sedgwick, George Bancroft, Ralph Waldo
Emerson, William Ellery Channing, and William Lloyd Garrison. She met Martin Van Buren, Nicholas Biddle, John
H. B. Latrobe, Thomas Hart Benton, Daniel Webster, Henry
Clay, and John C. Marshall, a roll call of the political, intellectual, artistic, and literary leaders of the period. In what
was the West of the time, Cincinnati, in June of 1835, she
met "Dr. Beecher and his daughters," probably including
Catharine and Harriet. (Catharine Beecher was two years her
senior; Harriet, not yet married to Calvin Stowe, was nine
years younger than Martineau.) In Boston she met Margaret
Fuller and Elizabeth Peabody. These four women, all roughly
her age, were destined to play important, though different,
roles as intellectuals and feminists in America, but the woman
Martineau chose as her enduring friend and lifelong correspondent was another Bostonian, Maria Weston Chapman.

Although Martineau had already published her views opposing slavery, she was welcome in the slave-holding South

---

[1] *Autobiography*, "Period IV," vol. 1, pp. 139–438; *Retrospect of Western
Travel*, 2 vols. (New York: Saunders & Otley, 1838); *Society in America*; and
William R. Seat, Jr., "Harriet Martineau in America," *Notes and Queries* 204
(June 1959): 207–208.

and feted throughout the country even at this time of high-pitched agitation about the abolition question. However, upon attending an abolitionist meeting of the Boston Female Anti-Slavery Society in 1835 and speaking up at the urging of her host, Mr. Loring, and to the delight of Chapman, she became unwelcome in many places, most Americans save the abolitionists turning on her. As Sir Leslie Stephen says in his piece about her in the *Dictionary of National Biography*, "She naturally came home a determined abolitionist."

Society in America has lasted as Martineau's major work. Published in 1837, it is a serious and thorough critical analysis of the society she visited, set down according to the method she later published in *How to Observe Morals and Manners*. She followed its publication with the lighter *Retrospect of Western Travel*, a book full of enjoyable portraits of people and detailed descriptions of landscapes and customs. However, in *Society in America* she investigated the new state in terms we would now call sociological. She determined to examine American society in the light of what the Americans maintained to be their foundation principle, democracy. From that perspective, she looked at various aspects of society: politics, government, newspapers, economy, religion, civilization, honor, women, children, sufferers. She assumed it was important to inquire into the manners practiced in and the morals undergirding each of these areas in reference to the principle of democracy.

In its treatment of women, she found the United States flagrantly lacking. Setting down her principles, she wrote,

> If a test of civilisation be sought, none can be so sure as the condition of that half of society over which the other half has power,—from the exercise of the right of the strongest. Tried by this test, the American civilisation appears to be of a lower order than might have been expected from some other symptoms of its social state. The Americans have, in the treatment of women, fallen below, not only their own democratic principles, but the practice of some parts of the Old World.
>
> The unconsciousness of both parties as to the injuries suffered by women at the hands of those

who hold the power is a sufficient proof of the low degree of civilisation in this important particular at which they rest. While woman's intellect is confined, her morals crushed, her health ruined, her weaknesses encouraged, and her strength punished, she is told that her lot is cast in the paradise of women: and there is no country in the world where there is so much boasting of the 'chivalrous' treatment she enjoys.[2]

Suggesting that women are not educated either in matters of health or in intellectual disciplines, Martineau contended that the only objects for women were marriage and religion. Yet, marriage for such a limited woman is far from a partnership, and uninformed religion is vapid. Such a social condition for women originates in a failure of politics, and Martineau held, discussing the "morals of politics," that Americans support the "political non-existence of women." She began her argument with the statement that the Declaration of Independence announces "that governments derive their just powers from the consent of the governed," yet women are not asked for their consent.

She goes on to make the comparison of woman's status with that of the slave, ridiculing Thomas Jefferson's reservation that women must not be politically active because they "could not mix promiscuously in the public meetings of men" and James Mill's claim that women's interests are represented by their fathers and husbands. Like the slave, Martineau asserted, woman is not free until she speaks and acts on her own behalf.

Martineau's book is often compared with the better-known *Democracy in America*, written during the same period by the Frenchman Alexis de Tocqueville. Up until the 1830s the explanation of a society was usually made in historical terms, what leaders (who were usually male) had done in what sequences to what effects in political and military engagements. Tocqueville and Martineau attacked the problem of explaining what a country is like differently. They sought to analyze it

---

[2] *Society in America*, Lipset, ed., p. 291.

into its component contemporary social parts. Being conservative, Tocqueville wrote a conservative book. Being radical, Martineau wrote a radical one. Martineau paid close attention to women in hers. "Political Non-Existence of Women," the first selection in this section, is a leading document in American—and British—women's political theory.

There is often a discrepancy between the tough Martineau of political theory and criticism and the tender Martineau of relationships. It is that all-too-human inconsistency of ideas and feelings that enabled her to make a scathing judgment of the political ill-treatment of womankind in America and at the same time to admire personally many leading men in American government. There is, I believe, just a touch of hyperbole in her assessment of Chief Justice John Marshall's kindness to women. She wrote of her visit with him:

> With Judge Story sometimes came the man to whom he looked up with feelings little short of adoration— the aged Chief-justice Marshall. There was almost too much mutual respect in our first meeting; we knew something of his individual merits and services; and he maintained through life, and carried to his grave, a reverence for women as rare in its kind as in its degree. It had all the theoretical fervour and magnificence . . . with the advantage of being grounded upon an extensive knowledge of the sex. He was the father and the grandfather of women; and out of this experience he brought, not only the love and pity which their offices and position command, and the awe of purity which they excite in the minds of the pure, but a steady conviction of their intellectual equality with men; and, with this, a deep sense of their social injuries. Throughout life he so invariably sustained their cause, that no indulgent libertine dared to flatter and humour; no skeptic, secure in the possession of power, dared to scoff at the claims of woman in the presence of Marshall, who, made clearsighted by his purity, knew the sex far better than either.[3]

[3] *Retrospect of Western Travel*, vol. 1, pp. 149–150.

After her return to England in 1836, Martineau kept in close touch with her American friends, particularly the abolitionists and especially Maria Weston Chapman, who visited her in England and with whom she corresponded over the years. Chapman was a very beautiful, stylish, wealthy woman, who devoted herself to the antislavery cause. She and her sisters gave an annual bazaar for the cause in Boston. She published a journal, the *Liberty Bell*, wrote frequently for several antislavery publications, and at one point turned down a major office in the American Anti-Slavery Society. When the two women met, there seemed to have been an immediate recognition of their affinity. Martineau's description of Chapman years later, telling of their meeting, is one of effusive affection: "I still see the exquisite beauty which took me by surprise that day;—the slender, graceful form,—the golden hair which might have covered her to her feet;—the brilliant complexion, noble profile, and deep blue eyes;—the aspect, meant by nature to be soft and winning only, but that day, (as ever since) so vivified by courage, and so strengthened by upright conviction, as to appear the very embodiment of heroism."[4]

Martineau wrote voluminously about the abolitionist cause. In 1855 she stated in a letter to William Lloyd Garrison that "twenty years ago, I considered the Abolition question in your country the most important concern of the century; and my sense of its significance has deepened with every passing year."[5]

She wrote about her American friends and their work in British journals of the day. In an article on the abolitionists published in the *London and Westminster Review* in 1838, an article that was quickly brought out as a separate volume under the title *The Martyr Age of the United States* and widely read, she again took occasion to write about the politics of American women, this time the practical politics of women organizing themselves in the antislavery cause.[6] She reported on the "first General Convention of women that was ever assembled," held in New York for three days during the second week of May

[4] *Autobiography*, vol. 1, p. 349.
[5] Ms. letter to W. Lloyd Garrison, written from Ambleside, February 16, 1855. Harriet Martineau Mss. Collection. Manchester College, Oxford.
[6] Selections from this article appear in this section.

with 174 delegates "from all parts of the Union" and presided over by Lucretia Mott, "an eminent Quaker preacher of Philadelphia—a woman of an intellect as sound and comprehensive as her heart is noble."

Though the resolutions of the women's convention pertained only to the issue of slavery, Martineau claimed that it was because the convention discredited the women's work that the issue of the rights of woman became publicly connected with the issue of the rights of slaves.

This connection extended not just to the abolitionists' awareness of women's political deprivation and the organization of separate women's societies in the antislavery cause, but erupted in controversy over whether women should hold office. The *National Anti-Slavery Standard* reports that this issue was a prominent reason the American and Foreign Anti-Slavery Society broke away from the American Anti-Slavery Society: "The occasion embraced by a considerable minority, of retiring from our ranks at the late Annual Meeting and forming a separate National Anti-Slavery Society, was the appointment of a woman [Abby Kelley], a member of the Society, and a delegate to that meeting, on the Business Committee."[7]

Martineau was identified with the original group of abolitionists in Boston, whose best-known leader was William Lloyd Garrison, often considered the greatest of all the radical abolitionists. Women had always been leaders in the Boston group, and the Garrisonians were generally more favorable to woman than the New York abolitionists. Maria Weston Chapman is sometimes ranked with Garrison and Wendell Phillips as one of the group's three main forces, Lydia Maria Child was a career editor and writer in the abolition cause, and women took the lead in the American Anti-Slavery Association. At the core of the American Anti-Slavery Society was often an alliance between Boston and Philadelphia, Unitarian and Quaker. The post-schism American and Foreign Anti-Slavery Society was financed by Lewis and Arthur Tappan and led by Theodore Weld and Henry Stanton. Weld and Stanton will be recognized as the husbands of Angelina Grimké and Elizabeth Cady Stanton, women who contributed more as

[7] July 23, 1840, p. 25.

feminists to women's rights than did either Child or Chapman. Their husbands' organization, however, came into being at least partially around a dispute over women, including Child and Chapman, holding positions of leadership.

The Boston-Philadelphia group had elected women delegates to the 1840 International Convention on Anti-Slavery in London, which provoked a furor when the American women led by Lucretia Mott were refused seats as delegates. The reports of the convention ring with indignation as the American male delegates showed that they supported the elected women. The *National Anti-Slavery Standard* anticipated that "a World's Convention will be assembled, whose dimensions will include a representation from the American Anti-Slavery Society. Such women as Lucretia Mott, Maria Weston Chapman, Ann Phillips and Lydia Maria Child, will be admitted as members and the land of Hannah Moore, Elizabeth Fry and Harriet Martineau, will yet acknowledge women to be possessed of souls and minds."[8]

In a later issue of the *Standard*, Garrison wrote in a letter that follows one from the rejected women delegates: "These are the times that try the souls of WOMEN, as well as men. The Moloch of slavery has, from the first, sought to frighten them from an equal participation in the anti-slavery cause, by howling about the indelicacy of their publicly pleading for their imbruted sex."[9] After sitting in the balcony with the refused women delegates through the convention, Garrison went to visit Martineau, who was then ill at Tynemouth. Her letter to Chapman about his visit is included here.

Two other pieces complete the section. When an English publisher brought out pieces from *The Lowell Offering*, the creative writing of Lowell, Massachusetts, factory "girls," Martineau wrote the introductory letter for it. Her letter is characteristically effusive about self-reliant workers and about the nobility of minds elevated with high-minded thoughts. No union organizer she, no machine breaker. Cooperative association, industrious effort, and high-mindedness show the truly worthy person. She believed in workers' associations, but for

[8] Ibid., p. 27.
[9] October 22, 1840, p. 78.

worker-owner cooperation, not for adversarial roles, in the true political economist, rationalist manner. She overstated the case for factory cooperation when she saw a single example of how she thought it ought to work.

The final piece is an 1855 editorial from the *Daily News* about women's temperance efforts. Not written as part of an organized campaign, and praising an Englishwoman along with an American, this article is an example of that nineteenth-century female thinking that linked drink with male moral impurity and asserted indirectly that women were more up-right than men in trying to right the wrong of men's abuse of alcohol.

POLITICAL NON-EXISTENCE
OF WOMEN

One of the fundamental principles announced in the Declaration of Independence is, that governments derive their just powers from the consent of the governed. How can the political condition of women be reconciled with this?

Governments in the United States have power to tax women who hold property; to divorce them from their husbands; to fine, imprison, and execute them for certain offences. Whence do these governments derive their powers? They are not "just," as they are not derived from the consent of the women thus governed.

Governments in the United States have power to enslave certain women; and also to punish other women for inhuman treatment of such slaves. Neither of these powers are "just;" not being derived from the consent of the governed.

Governments decree to women in some States half their husbands' property; in others one-third. In some, a woman, on

---

Harriet Martineau, *Society in America* (New York: Saunders & Otley, 1837), vol. 1, pp. 148–154.

her marriage, is made to yield all her property to her husband; in others, to retain a portion, or the whole, in her own hands. Whence do governments derive the unjust power of thus disposing of property without the consent of the governed?

The democratic principle condemns all this as wrong; and requires the equal political representation of all rational beings. Children, idiots, and criminals, during the season of sequestration, are the only fair exceptions.

The case is so plain that I might close it here; but it is interesting to inquire how so obvious a decision has been so evaded as to leave to women no political rights whatever. The question has been asked, from time to time, in more countries than one, how obedience to the laws can be required of women, when no woman has, either actually or virtually, given any assent to any law. No plausible answer has, as far as I can discover, been offered; for the good reason, that no plausible answer can be devised. The most principled democratic writers on government have on this subject sunk into fallacies, as disgraceful as any advocate of despotism has adduced. In fact, they have thus sunk from being, for the moment, advocates of despotism. Jefferson in America, and James Mill at home,[10] subside, for the occasion, to the level of the author of the Emperor of Russia's Catechism for the young Poles.

Jefferson says,* "Were our State a pure democracy, in which all the inhabitants should meet together to transact all their business, there would yet be excluded from their deliberations,

"1. Infants, until arrived at years of discretion;

"2. Women, who, to prevent depravation of morals, and ambiguity of issue, could not mix promiscuously in the public meetings of men;

"3. Slaves, from whom the unfortunate state of things with us takes away the rights of will and of property."

If the slave disqualification, here assigned, were shifted

---

*Correspondence, vol. iv. p. 295.

[10] Thomas Jefferson was regarded as one of the leading theorists of democracy. James Mill was an important English Utilitarian philosopher of Martineau's time. It is interesting to note in this connection that the authors of the English Reform Bill of 1832 thought it necessary to name "male persons" as those to whom the franchise was being extended.

up under the head of Women, their case would be nearer the truth than as it now stands. Woman's lack of will and of property, is more like the true cause of her exclusion from the representation, than that which is actually set down against her. As if there could be no means of conducting public affairs but by promiscuous meetings! As if there would be more danger in promiscuous meetings for political business than in such meetings for worship, for oratory, for music, for dramatic entertainments,—for any of the thousand transactions of civilized life! The plea is not worth another word.

Mill says, with regard to representation, in his Essay on Government, "One thing is pretty clear; that all those individuals, whose interests are involved in those of other individuals, may be struck off without inconvenience. . . . In this light, women may be regarded, the interest of almost all of whom is involved, either in that of their fathers or in that of their husbands."

The true democratic principle is, that no person's interests can be, or can be ascertained to be, identical with those of any other person. This allows the exclusion of none but incapables.

The word "almost," in Mr. Mill's second sentence, rescues women from the exclusion he proposes. As long as there are women who have neither husbands nor fathers, his proposition remains an absurdity.

The interests of women who have fathers and husbands can never be identical with theirs, while there is a necessity for laws to protect women against their husbands and fathers. This statement is not worth another word.

Some who desire that there should be an equality of property between men and women, oppose representation, on the ground that political duties would be incompatible with the other duties which women have to discharge. The reply to this is, that women are the best judges here. God has given time and power for the discharge of all duties; and, if he had not, it would be for women to decide which they would take, and which they would leave. But their guardians follow the ancient fashion of deciding what is best for their wards. The Emperor of Russia discovers when a coat of arms and title do not agree with a subject prince. The King of France early perceives that the air of Paris does not agree with a free-thinking foreigner. The English Tories feel the hardship that it would be to impose the franchise on every artizan, busy as he is in getting his bread. The Georgian planter perceives the hardship that freedom would be to his slaves. And the best friends of half the human race peremptorily decide for them as to their rights, their duties, their feelings, their powers. In all these cases, the persons thus cared for feel that the abstract decision rests with themselves; that, though they may be compelled to submit, they need not acquiesce.

It is pleaded that half of the human race does acquiesce in the decision of the other half, as to their rights and duties. And some instances, not only of submission, but of acquiescence, there are. Forty years ago, the women of New Jersey went to the poll, and voted, at state elections. The general term, "inhabitants," stood unqualified;—as it will again, when the true democratic principle comes to be fully understood. A motion was made to correct the inadvertence; and it was done, as a matter of course; without any appeal, as far as I could learn, from the persons about to be injured. Such acquiescence proves nothing but the degradation of the injured party. It inspires the same emotions of pity as the supplication of the freed slave who kneels to his master to restore him to slavery, that he may have his animal wants supplied, without being troubled with human rights and duties. Acquiescence like this is an argument which cuts the wrong way for those who use it.

But this acquiescence is only partial; and, to give any semblance of strength to the plea, the acquiescence must be complete. I, for one, do not acquiesce. I declare that whatever obedience I yield to the laws of the society in which I live is a matter between, not the community and myself, but my judgment and my will. Any punishment inflicted on me for the breach of the laws, I should regard as so much gratuitous injury; for to those laws I have never, actually or virtually, assented. I know that there are women in England who agree with me in this—I know that there are women in America who agree with me in this. The plea of acquiescence is invalidated by us.

It is pleaded that, by enjoying the protection of some laws, women give their assent to all. This needs but a brief answer. Any protection thus conferred is, under woman's circumstances, a boon bestowed at the pleasure of those in whose power she is. A boon of any sort is no compensation for the privation of something else; nor can the enjoyment of it bind to the performance of anything to which it bears no relation.

Because I, by favour, may procure the imprisonment of the thief who robs my house, am I, unrepresented, therefore bound not to smuggle French ribbons? The obligation not to smuggle has a widely different derivation.

I cannot enter upon the commonest order of pleas of all;—those which relate to the virtual influence of woman; her swaying the judgment and will of man through the heart; and so forth. One might as well try to dissect the morning mist. I knew a gentleman in America who told me how much rather he had be a woman than the man he is;—a professional man, a father, a citizen. He would give up all this for a woman's influence. I thought he was mated too soon. He should have married a lady, also of my acquaintance, who would not at all object to being a slave, if ever the blacks should have the upper hand; "it is so right that the one race should be subservient to the other!" Or rather,—I thought it a pity that the one could not be a woman, and the other a slave; so that an injured individual of each class might be exalted into their places, to fulfil and enjoy the duties and privileges which they despise, and, in despising, disgrace.

The truth is, that while there is much said about "the sphere of woman," two widely different notions are entertained of what is meant by the phrase. The narrow, and, to the ruling party, the more convenient notion is that sphere appointed by men, and bounded by their ideas of propriety;—a notion from which any and every woman may fairly dissent. The broad and true conception is of the sphere appointed by God, and bounded by the powers which he has bestowed. This commands the assent of man and woman; and only the question of powers remains to be proved.

That woman has power to represent her own interests, no one can deny till she has been tried. The modes need not be discussed here: they must vary with circumstances. The fearful and absurd images which are perpetually called up to perplex the question,—images of women on woolsacks in England, and under canopies in America, have nothing to do with the matter. The principle being once established, the methods will follow, easily, naturally, and under a remarkable transmutation of the ludicrous into the sublime. The kings of Europe would have laughed mightily, two centuries ago, at the idea of a commoner, without robes, crown, or sceptre, stepping into the throne of a strong nation. Yet who dared to laugh when Washington's super-royal voice greeted the New World from the presidential chair, and the old world stood still to catch the echo?

The principle of the equal rights of both halves of the human race is all we have to do with here. It is the true democratic principle which can never be seriously controverted, and only for a short time evaded. Governments can derive their just powers only from the consent of the governed.

WOMEN IN THE ANTI-SLAVERY MOVEMENT

Art. I.—1. *Right and Wrong in Boston in 1835.* Boston, U.S.: Isaac Knapp.

2. *Right and Wrong in Boston in 1836.* Boston, U.S.: Isaac Knapp.

3. *Right and Wrong in Boston in 1837.* Boston, U.S.: Isaac Knapp.[11]

There is a remarkable set of people now living and vigorously acting in the world, with a consonance of will and understanding which has perhaps never before been witnessed among so large a number of individuals of such diversified powers, habits, opinion, tastes, and circumstances. The body comprehends men and women of every shade of colour, of every degree of eduction, of every variety of religious opinion, of every gradation of rank, bound together by no vow, no pledge, no stipulation but of each preserving his individual liberty; and

---

"The Martyr Age of the United States," *London and Westminster Review* 32 (1838–1839): 1–59.

[11] The works being reviewed are by Maria Weston Chapman.

yet they act as if they were of one heart and of one soul. Such union could be secured by no principle of worldly interest; nor, for a term of years, by the most stringent fanaticism. A well-grounded faith, directed towards a noble object, is the only principle which can account for such a spectacle as the world is now waking up to contemplate in the abolitionists of the United States.

Before we fix our attention on the history of the body, it may be remarked that it is a totally different thing to be an abolitionist on a soil actually trodden by slaves, and in a far-off country, where opinion is already on the side of emancipation, or ready to be converted; where only a fraction of society, instead of the whole, has to be convicted of guilt; and where no interests are put in jeopardy but pecuniary ones, and those limited and remote. Great honour is due to the first movers in the anti-slavery cause in every land: but those of European countries may take rank with the philanthropists of America who may espouse the cause of the aborigines: while the primary abolitionists of the United States have encountered, with steady purpose, such opposition as might here await assailants of the whole set of aristocratic institutions at once, from the throne to pauper apprenticeship. Slavery is as thoroughly interwoven with American institutions—ramifies as extensively through American society, as the aristocratic spirit pervades Great Britain. The fate of Reformers whose lives are devoted to making war upon either the one or the other must be remarkable. . . .

Ten years ago there was external quiet on the subject of slavery in the United States. Jefferson and other great men had prophesied national peril from it: a few legislators had talked of doing something to ameliorate the "condition of society" in their respective States; the institution had been abolished in some of the northern States, where the number of negroes was small, and the work of emancipation easy and obviously desirable: an insurrection broke out occasionally, in one place or another; and certain sections of society were in a state of perplexity or alarm at the talents, or the demeanour, or the increase of numbers of the free blacks. But no such thing had been heard of as a comprehensive and strenuously active objection to the whole system, wherever established. The surface of society was heaving; but no one surge had broken into voice, prophetic of that chorus of many waters in which the doom of the institution may now be heard. Yet clear-sighted persons saw that some great change must take place ere long; for a scheme was under trial for removing the obnoxious part of the negro population to Africa. Those of the dusky race who were too clever, and those who were too stupid, to be safe, or useful at home, were to be exported; and slave-owners who had scruples about holding man as property might, by sending their slaves away over the sea, relieve their consciences without annoying their neighbours. Such was the state of affairs previous to 1829.

The Colonization Society originated abolitionism. It acted in two ways. It exasperated the free blacks by the prospect of exile, and it engaged the attention of those who hated slavery, though the excitement it afforded to their hopes was illusory. Its action in both ways became manifest in the year 1829. In spring of this year the stir began at Cincinnati, where a strenuous effort was made to induce the white inhabitants to drive away the free coloured people, by putting in force against them the atrocious state laws, which placed them in a condition of civil disability, and providing at the same time the means of transportation to Africa. . . .

William Lloyd Garrison is one of God's nobility—the head of the moral aristocracy whose prerogatives we are contemplating. . . .

Garrison's lectures were now upon abolition, not colonization. He was listened to with much interest in New York; but at Boston he could obtain no place to lecture in; and it was not till it was clear that he intended to collect an audience on the Common, in the midst of the city, that a door was opened to him. . . .

The time was ripe for Garrison's exertions. A pamphlet appeared in the autumn of 1829, at Boston, from the pen of a man of colour, named Walker, which alarmed society not a little. It was an appeal to his coloured brethren, to drown their injuries in the blood of their oppressors. Its language is perfectly appalling. It ran through several editions, though no bookseller would publish it. Not long after, the author was found murdered near his own door; but whether he had been assassinated for his book, or had been fatally wounded in a fray, is not known. If the slave-owners could but have seen it,

Garrison was this man's antagonist, not his coadjutor. Garrison is as strenuous a "peace-man" as any broad-brimmed Friend in Philadelphia; and this fact, in conjunction with his unlimited influence over the Negro population, is the chief reason why no blood has been shed,—why no insurrectionary movement has taken place in the United States, from the time when his voice began to be heard over the broad land till now. . . .

On the 2nd of March, 1833, there appeared in the 'Liberator' the following advertisement—

"PRUDENCE CRANDALL,

"Principal of the Canterbury (Connecticut) Female Boarding School, returns her most sincere thanks to those who have patronized her School, and would give information that, on the first Monday of April next, her School will be opened for the reception of young Ladies and little Misses of colour. The branches taught are as follows:—Reading, Writing, Arithmetic, English Grammar, &c."

The advertisement closed with a long list of references to gentlemen of the highest character.

The reason of this announcement was, that Miss Crandall, a young lady of established reputation in her profession, had been urgently requested to undertake the tuition of a child of light colour, had admitted her among the white pupils, had subsequently admitted a second, thereby offending the parents of her former pupils; and, on being threatened on the one hand with the loss of all her scholars, and urged on the other to take more of a dark complexion, had nobly resolved to continue to take young ladies of colour, letting the whites depart, if they so pleased. We relate the consequences, because this is, as far as we know, the first instance in the struggle of a protracted persecution of a peaceable individual by the whole of the society of the district.

A town-meeting was called on the appearance of the advertisement, and the school was denounced in violent terms. Miss Crandall silently prosecuted her plan. The legislature was petitioned, through the exertions of a leading citizen of Canterbury, Mr. Judson, and a law was obtained in the course of the month of May, making it a penal offence to establish any school for the instruction of coloured persons, not inhabitants of the State, or to instruct, board, or harbour persons entering the State for educational purposes. This law was clearly unconstitutional, as it violated that clause in the constitution which gives to the citizens of each State all the privileges and immunities of the citizens of the several States.* Perceiving this, Miss Crandall took no notice, but went on with her school. She was accordingly arrested, and carried before a justice of the peace; and the next spectacle that the inhabitants of Canterbury saw was Miss Crandall going to jail. She was bailed out the next day, and her trial issued in nothing, as the jury could not agree. She was again prosecuted, and again; and at length convicted. She appealed to a higher Court, and struggled on through a long persecution till compelled to yield, from the lives of her pupils being in danger. Her neighbours pulled down her fences, and filled up her well. All the traders in the place refused to deal with her, and she was obliged to purchase provisions and clothing from a great distance. She and her pupils were refused admission to the churches; her windows were repeatedly broken during the night; and, at length, the attacks upon her house became so alarming, and the menaces to her pupils on their way to school so violent, that their parents were compelled to hide the children in their own houses, and Miss Crandall retired from the place. Her conduct was to the last degree meek and quiet; nothing need be said about its courage.

By this time the abolition cause was supported by twenty-six periodicals, circulating from Maine to Virginia and Indiana. Some excellent individuals had done the brave deed of publishing books in aid of the same cause. Among these was Mrs. Child, a lady of whom society was exceedingly proud before she published her 'Appeal,' and to whom society has been extremely contemptuous since. Her works were bought with avidity before, but fell into sudden oblivion as soon as she had done a greater deed than writing any or all of them. Her noble-minded husband lost his legal practice, sound and respected as were his talents, from affording his counsel to citi-

*Laws which are infringements of the constitution are not binding upon the Court of Judicature in the last resort, the Supreme Court of the United States.

zens of colour; and he was maliciously arrested on the quays of New York, for a fictitious or extremely trifling old debt, when he was just putting his foot on board a vessel for England. The incident affected him deeply; and his brave wife was, for once, seen to sit down to weep: but she shook off her trouble, packed up a bundle of clothes for him, and went to cheer him in his prison, whence, it is needless to say, he was presently released, crowned in the eyes of his friends with fresh honours. A circumstance which we happen to know respecting this gentleman and lady illustrates well the states of feeling on the great question in the different classes of minds at the time. Mr. Child was professionally consulted by a gentleman of colour. The client and his lady visited Mr. Child at his residence at Boston, one afternoon, and staid beyond the family tea-hour. Mrs. Child at length ordered up tea; but before it could be poured out the visitors took their leave, not choosing to subject Mr. and Mrs. Child to the imputation of sitting at table with people of colour. Boston soon rang with the report that Mr. and Mrs. Child had given an entertainment to coloured people. Some aristocratic ladies, seated in one of the handsomest drawing-rooms in Boston, were one day canvassing this and other abolition affairs, while Dr. Channing appeared absorbed in a newspaper by the fireside. The ladies repeated tale after tale, each about as true as the one they began with, and greeted with loud laughter every attempt of one of the party to correct their mistakes about the ladies who were then under persecution, and in peril for the cause. At length Dr. Channing turned his head, and produced a dead silence by observing, in the sternest tone of his thrilling voice, "The time will come when the laughers will find *their* proper place." This happened, however, not in 1833, but when the persecution of the women had risen to its height. . . .

Our historical review has not brought us up to the date of the first of the works whose titles we have prefixed to this article, and which are, substantially, Annual Reports of the proceedings of the Massachusetts Female Anti-Slavery Society. We have arrived at the most remarkable period of the great struggle, when an equal share of its responsibility and suffering came to press upon women. We have seen how men first engaged in it, and how young men afterwards, as a separate element, were brought in. Many women had joined from the first, and their numbers had continually increased: but their exertions had hitherto consisted in raising funds, and in testifying sympathy for the coloured race and their advocates. Their course of political action, which has never since been checked, began in the autumn of 1835.

The Female Anti-Slavery Society in Boston is composed of women of every rank, and every religious sect, as well as of all complexions. The president is a Presbyterian; the chief secretary is an Unitarian; and among the other officers and members may be found Quakers, Episcopalians, Methodists, and Swedenborgians. All sectarian jealousy is lost in the great cause; and these women have, from the first day of their association, preserved, not only harmony, but strong mutual affection, while differing on matters of opinion as freely and almost as widely as if they had kept within the bosom of their respective sects. Upon such a set of women was the responsibility thrown of vindicating the liberty of meeting and of free discussion in Boston; and nobly they sustained it.

Before we proceed, it is necessary to say a few words upon the most remarkable of these women,—the understood author of the books whose titles stand at the head of our article. Maria Weston was educated in England, and might have remained here in the enjoyment of wealth, luxury, and fashion: but with these she could not obtain sufficient freedom of thought and action to satisfy her noble nature; and, no natural ties detaining her, she returned to New England, to earn her bread there by teaching, and breathe as freely as she desired. She has paid a heavy tax of persecution for her freedom; but she has it. She is a woman of rare intellectual accomplishment, full of reading, and with strong and well-exercised powers of thought. She is beautiful as the day, tall in her person, and noble in her carriage, with a voice as sweet as a silver bell, and speech as clear and sparkling as a running brook. Her accomplishments have expanded in a happy home. She has been for some years the wife of Mr. Henry Chapman, a merchant of Boston, an excellent man, whose spirit of self-denial is equal to his wife's, and is shown no less nobly in the same cause. A woman of genius like her's cannot but take the lead wherever she acts at all; and she is the life and soul of the enterprise in Boston. The foes of the cause have nicknamed her "Captain Chapman;" and the name passes from mouth to mouth as she walks up Washington street,—not less admired, perhaps, all the while than if she were only the most beautiful woman in the city. This lady, with all her sisters, took her ground early, and has always had sober reason to plead for every one of her many extensions of effort. She is understood to have drawn up the petition which follows,—a fair specimen of the multitudes of petitions from women which have been piled up under the table of Congress, till the venerable John Quincy Adams has been roused to the remarkable conflict which we shall presently have to relate:—

"PETITION
"*To the Honourable Senate and House of Representatives in Congress assembled*,
"The undersigned, women of Massachusetts, deeply convinced by the sinfulness of slavery, and keenly aggrieved by its existence in a part of our country over which Congress possesses exclusive jurisdiction in all cases whatsoever, do most earnestly petition your honourable body immediately to abolish slavery in the District of Columbia, and to declare every human being free who sets foot upon its soil.

"We also respectfully announce our intention to present the same petition yearly before your honourable body, that it may at least be a 'memorial of us' that in the holy cause of Human Freedom 'we have done what we could.'"

In answer to objections against such petitioning, the author of 'Right and Wrong in Boston' says—

"If we are not enough grieved at the existence of slavery to ask that it may be abolished in the ten miles square over which Congress possesses exclusive jurisdiction, we may rest assured that we are slave-holders in heart, and indeed under the endurance of the penalty which selfishness inflicts,—the slow but certain death of the soul. We sometimes, but not often, hear it said—'It is such an odd, *unladylike* thing to do!' We concede that the human soul, in the full exercise of its most god-like power of self-denial and exertion for the good of others, is, emphatically, a very unladylike thing. We have never heard this objection but from that sort of woman who is dead while she lives, or to be pitied as the victim of domestic tyranny. The woman who makes it is generally one who has struggled from childhood up to womanhood through a process of spiritual suffocation. Her infancy was passed in serving as a convenience for the display of elegant baby-linen. Her youth, in training for a more public display of braiding the hair, and wearing of gold, and putting on of apparel; while the ornament of a meek and quiet spirit,—the hidden man of the heart, is not deemed worthy the attainment. Her summers fly away in changes of air and water; her winters in changes of flimsy garments, in inhaling lamp-smoke, and drinking champagne at midnight with the most dissipated men in the community. This is the woman who tells us it is *unladylike* to ask that children may no longer be sold away from their parents, or wives from their husbands, in the District of Columbia, and adds, 'They ought to be mobbed who ask it.' . . . O how painful is the contemplation of the ruins of a nature a little lower than the angels!"—*Right and Wrong in Boston in 1836*, p. 27.

"We feel," she elsewhere declares, "that we may confidently affirm that no woman of Massachusetts will cease to exercise for the slaves the right of petition (her only means of manifesting her civil existence) for which Mr. Adams has so nobly contended. Massachusetts women will not forget in their petitions to Heaven the name of him who upheld their prayer for the enslaved of the earth, in the midst of sneers and wrath, bidding oppressors remember that *they*, too, were woman-born, and declaring that he considered the wives, and mothers, and daughters of his electors, as his constituents". . . . —*Right and Wrong in Boston in 1837*, p. 84.

To consult on their labours of this and other kinds, the ladies of the Boston Anti-Slavery Society intended to meet at their own office, 46 Washington street, on the 21st of October. Handbills had been circulated and posted up in different parts of the city the day before, offering a reward to any persons who would commit certain acts of violence,—such as "bringing Thompson to the tar-kettle before dark." The ladies were informed that they would be killed; and when they applied at the Mayor's office for protection to their lawful meeting, the City Marshal replied—"You give us a great deal of trouble."

This trouble, however, their consciences compelled them to give. They could not decline the duty of asserting their liberty of meeting and free discussion. But Mrs. Chapman felt that every member should have notice of what might await her; and she herself carried the warning from house to house, with all discretion and quietness. Among those whom she visited was an artizan's wife, who was sweeping out one of her two rooms as Mrs. Chapman entered. On hearing that there was every probability of violence, and that the warning was given in order that she might stay away if she thought proper, she leaned upon her broom and considered for awhile. Her answer was—"I have often wished and asked that I might be able to do something for the slaves; and it seems to me that this is the very time and the very way. You will see me at the meeting, and I will keep a prayerful mind, as I am about my work, till then."

Twenty-five reached the place of meeting, by presenting themselves three-quarters of an hour before the time. Five more struggled up the stairs, and a hundred were turned back by the mob. It was well known how these ladies were mobbed by some hundreds of gentlemen in fine broad-cloth"—(Boston broad-cloth has become celebrated since that day). It is well known how these gentlemen hurraed, broke down the partition, and threw orange-peel at the ladies while they were at prayer: but Mrs. Chapman's part in the lessons of the hour has not been made public.

She is the Foreign Corresponding Secretary of the society; and she was in the midst of reading her Report, in a noise too great to allow of her being heard, when the mayor of Boston, Mr. Lyman, entered the room in great trepidation—

"Ladies," said he, "I request you to dissolve this meeting."

"Mr. Mayor," said Mrs. Chapman, "we desire you to disperse this mob."

"Ladies," the mayor continued, "you must dissolve this meeting; I cannot preserve the peace."

"Mr. Mayor," replied Mrs. Chapman, "we are disturbed in our lawful business by this unlawful mob, and it is your business to relieve us of it."

"I know it, Mrs. Chapman, I know it; but I cannot: I cannot protect you; and I entreat you to go."

"If that be the case," answered she, "as we have accomplished our object, and vindicated our right of meeting, we will, if the meeting pleases, adjourn." She looked round upon her companions, and proposed that, to accommodate the authorities, they should adjourn their meeting. This was agreed to, and the women passed down the stairs, and through the mob, and, as the business of the day was finished, each to her own home. Certain of the fine broad-cloth men observed afterwards that Mrs. Chapman, in the high excitement of the hour, looked more like an angel than a woman who is visible every day. She was not aware that her friend Garrison was in the hands of the mob, and she therefore went home, as she had advised her companions to do, and sat down to her needle. Presently several gentlemen entered without asking admission. She recognized among them some members of Dr. Channing's church, whom she was accustomed to meet at worship Sunday by Sunday. They demanded Mr. Thompson, saying that they had reason to believe he was in that house. They wanted Mr. Thompson.

"I know it," said she; "and I know what you want with Mr. Thompson; you want his blood."

They declared they would not shed his blood; but she held off till they had pledged themselves that under no circumstances should Mr. Thompson receive bodily harm.

"This pledge is what I wanted," said she; "and now I will tell you that Mr. Thompson is not here, and I am sure I don't know where he is."

She then told the gentlemen that she had something to say to them, and they must hear her. On a day like this, when the laws were broken, and the peace of society violated by those who ought best to know their value, it was no time for ceremony; she should speak with the plainness which the times demanded. And she proceeded with a remonstrance so powerful that, after some argument, her adversaries fairly succumbed: one wept, and another asked as a favour that she would shake hands with him. But at this crisis her husband came in. The sight of him revived the bad passions of these gentry. They said they had to inform him that they had obtained the names of his commercial correspondents in the South, and were about to deprive him of his trade, by informing his southern connexions that the merchants of Boston disowned him for a fellow-citizen, and had proscribed him from their society. Mr. Chapman quietly replied that by their thus coming to see him he was enabled to save them the trouble of writing to the South; and he proceeded to explain that, finding his southern commerce implicated with slave labour, he had surrendered more and more of it, and had this very week declined to execute orders to the amount of three thousand dollars. There was nothing left for these magnanimous gentlemen but to sneak away.

The women who were at the meeting of this memorable day were worthy of the occasion, not from being strong enough to follow the lead of such a woman as Maria Chapman, but from having a strength independent of her. The reason of Garrison being there was, that he went to escort his young wife, who was near her confinement. She was one of the last to depart, and it could not be concealed from her that her husband was in the hands of the mob. She stepped out of the window upon a shed, in the fearful excitement of the moment. He was in the extremest danger. His hat was lost, and brickbats were rained upon his head, while he was hustled along in the direction of the tar-kettle, which was heating in the next street. The only words which escaped from the white lips of the young wife were—"I think my husband will not deny his principles: I am sure my husband will never deny his principles." Garrison was rescued by a stout truck-man, and safely lodged in jail (the only place in which he could be secure), without having in the least flinched from the consequences of his principles. The differences in the minds of these women, and the view which they all agree to take of the persecution to which they are subjected, may be best shown in the eloquent words of the author of 'Right and Wrong:'—

"Our common cause appears in a different vesture as presented by differing minds. One is striving to unbind a slave's manacles—another to secure to all human souls their inalienable rights; one to secure the temporal well-being, and another the spiritual benefit, of the enslaved of our land. . . ."

. . . "Angelina E. Grimké." Who is she? She and her sister Sarah are Quaker ladies of South Carolina. Our author says of their visit to Boston, to act and speak in this cause—"It might have been anticipated that they would have met with a friendly reception from those calling themselves the better sort, for they were highly connected. Unfortunately, they were but women, though the misfortune of that fact was greatly abated by their being sisters of the Hon. Thos. S. Grimke." This gentleman was, in point of scholarship, the greatest ornament of the United States, and his character was honoured by the whole community. After his death his sisters strove by all the means which could be devised by powerful intellects and kind hearts to ameliorate the condition of the slaves they had inherited. In defiance of the laws, they taught them, and introduced upon their estates as many as possible of the usages of free society. But it would not do. There is no infusing into slavery the benefits of freedom. When these ladies had become satisfied of this fact, they surrendered their worldly interests instead of their consciences. They freed their slaves, and put them in the way of providing for themselves in a free region, and then retired to Philadelphia, to live on the small remains of their former opulence. It does not appear that they had any intention of coming forward publicly, as they have since done; but the circumstances of their possessing the knowledge, which other abolitionists want, of the minute details and less obvious workings of the slavery system, was the occasion of their being applied to, more and more frequently and extensively, for information, till they publicly placed their knowledge at the service of all who needed it, and at length began to lecture wherever there was an audience who requested to hear them. Their Quaker habits of speaking in public rendered this easy to them; and the exertion of their great talents in this direction has been of most essential service to the cause. . . .

In answer to an overwhelming pressure of invitations, these ladies have lectured in upwards of sixty towns of the United States to overflowing audiences. Boston itself has listened to them with reverence. Some of the consequences of their exertions will be noticed as we proceed: meantime we must give our author's report of this novelty in the method of proceeding:—

"The idea of a woman's teaching was a startling novelty, even to abolitionists; but their principled and habitual reverence for the freedom of individual action induced them to a course unusual among men—to examine before they condemned. Only a short examination was needed to convince them that the main constituents in the relation of teacher and taught are ignorance on one side and knowledge on the other. They had been too long accustomed to hear the Bible quoted in defence of slavery, to be astonished that its authority should be claimed for the subjugation of woman the moment she should act for the enslaved. The example and teaching of the Grimkes wrought conviction as to the rights and consequent duties of women in the minds of multitudes." . . .—*Right and Wrong in Boston in 1837*, p. 61.

Angelina E. Grimké was married, last spring, to Theodore D. Weld, a man worthy of her, and one of the bravest of the abolition confessors. There were some remarkable circumstances attending the wedding. It took place at Philadelphia, and, the laws of Pennsylvania constituting any marriage legal which (the parties being of age) is contracted in the presence of twelve persons, was attended neither by clergyman nor magistrate. Mr. Weld, in promising to be just and affectionate to his wife, and to protect and cherish her, expressly abjured all use of the power which an unjust law put into his hands over her property, her person, and her will. Angelina having promised to devote herself to her husband's happiness, they proceeded to hallow their agreement by prayer from the lips of two of the party. Among those assembled, besides the near connections of the bride and bridegroom, there was Garrison, who took charge of the certifying part of the business, and two persons of colour, friends of the Grimkés, and who had been their slaves. . . .

During the second week of May [1837] was held the first General Convention of Women that was ever assembled. Modest as were its pretensions, and quietly as it was conducted, it will stand as a great event in history—from the nature of the fact itself, and probably from the importance of its consequences. "This," says the Report, reasonably enough, "was the beginning of an examination of the claims and character of their clergy, which will end only with a reformation, hardly less startling or less needed than that of Luther."

The Convention met at New York, and consisted of one hundred and seventy-four delegates, from all parts of the Union. Lucretia Mott, an eminent Quaker preacher of Philadelphia—a woman of an intellect as sound and comprehensive as her heart is noble—presided. The Convention sat for three successive days; and, by means of wise preparation, and the appointment of sub-committees, transacted a great deal of business. Some fine addresses, to different classes interested in the question, were prepared by the sub-committees, and a plan of political action and other operations fixed on for the year. One resolution was passed to the effect that it was immoral to separate persons of colour from the rest of society, and especially in churches; and that the members of the Convention pledged themselves to procure for the coloured people, if possible, an equal choice with themselves of sittings in churches; and, where this was not possible, to take their seats with the despised class. Another resolution was to this effect, "that whereas our fathers, husbands, and brothers have devoted themselves to the rescue of the enslaved, at the risk of ease, reputation, and life, we, their daughters, wives, and sisters, honouring their conduct, hereby pledge ourselves to uphold them by our sympathy, to share their sacrifices, and vindicate their characters." After having discharged their function, and gained some strength of heart and enlightenment of mind by their agreement in feeling and differences of opinion, these women went home, to meet again the next year at Philadelphia.

On the 27th of June the orthodox clergy took up their position against the abolitionists. The occasion was the General Association of Massachusetts Clergymen. They had long shown themselves to be uneasy at the improvement in certain of their flocks in self-reliance; and their anger and fear blazed out at the meeting of this association. Their causes of complaint were two-fold: that there was a decay of deference to the pastoral office, and that an alteration was taking place in the female character. On the first point they alleged that discussion of moral questions was promoted among their people independently of the pastors, and that "topics of reform were presented within the parochial limits of settled pastors without their consent. . . ." The complaint regarding the women of the age urged that female influence should be employed in bringing minds to the pastor for instruction, instead of presuming to give it through any other medium. The movement begun by these Resolutions, worthy of the dark ages, was kept up by a set of sermons, in which this magnanimous clergy came out to war against women—the Misses Grimké in particular. It is wonderful how many of these sermons ended with a simile about a vine, a trellis and an elm.

It does not appear that the parties most interested would have thought of mixing up the question of the Rights of Woman with that of the Rights of Man in Slavery: but the clergy thus compelled the agitation of it. The women themselves merely looked into their own case, and went on doing what they found to be their duty. But men had more to do regarding it; more to learn upon it; and the result of the examination to which they have been driven is, that many newspapers,* and a large proportion of the Anti-Slavery body, have come out boldly and without reservation for the political rights of woman: the venerable [John Quincy] Adams has pertinaciously vindicated their right of petition on the floor of Congress, and the clergy are completely foiled. Long before all this took place, there was a clergyman who advocated the agency of woman in social questions, in words which are worthy of preservation. At a public meeting in 1836, Dr. Follen spoke [in favor of this idea]. He is not, like his clerical brethren, of the same mind with Rabbi Eliezur, who said, "Perish the Book of the Law rather than it should be expounded by a woman!" . . .

As no degree of violence directed to break up the meetings of Ladies' Society, was too strong for the consciences of certain of the gentlemen of Boston, so no device was clearly too low for their purpose of hindering utterance. When they found they could not stop the women's tongues by violence, they privily sprinkled cayenne-pepper on the stove of their place of meeting, thus compelling them to cough down their own speakers.

The next attempt of such of the orthodox clergy as had professed abolitionism, was to break up the Massachusetts Anti-Slavery Society, in which more freedom of thought was allowed than they considered suitable to the dignity of their body. They declared the society to be composed of materials so heretical and anti-christian, that they proposed to withdraw

*The prospectus of the 'Liberator,' January 1838, has the following paragraph:—"As our object is *Universal* Emancipation—to redeem woman as well as man from a servile to an equal condition—we shall go for the Rights of Woman to their fullest extent. W. L. Garrison, *Editor*. I. Knapp, *Publisher*."

from it, and form a new association with a uniform profession of faith. The attempt failed. The laity of all denominations protested with absolute unanimity against any new organization upon sectarian grounds, and the harmony of the body at large is more assured than ever. The clergy have for the present succumbed. If they adduce any further clerical claims, it is highly probable that the stir will, indeed, "end only with a reformation hardly less startling or less needed than that of Luther." It is evident to those who remember the conference between George Thompson and Mr. Breckinridge at Glasgow, that it would be unwise in the American clergy to provoke an inquiry into the conduct of their body during the great moral struggle of the age. . . .

If the orthodox clergy are wise, they will let matters rest where they are.* . . .

The second General Convention of Women was held, as appointed, at Philadelphia, in the spring of the present year [1838]. Once, again, has the intrepidity of these noble Christian women been put to the proof; the outrages in this "city of brotherly love" having been the most fearful to which they have yet been exposed. The cause of the extraordinary violences of this year is to be found in the old maxim that men hate those whom they have injured. The State Convention, which had been employed for many previous months in preparing a new constitution for Pennsylvania, had deprived the citizens of colour of the political rights which they had held (but rarely dared to exercise) under the old constitution. Having done this injury, the perpetrators, and those who assented to their act, were naturally on the watch against those whom they had oppressed, and were jealous of every movement.

---

*A resident of Boston was expressing to an European traveller one day, in the year 1836, his regret that strangers should be present in the country when its usual quiet and sobriety were disturbed. "I am glad," observed the traveller, "to have been in the country in its martyr age." "—Martyr age! martyr age!" cried a clergyman, remarkable for the assiduity of his parochial visiting. "What *do* you mean? We don't burn people in Smithfield here."— "No," replied the stranger, "because 'Boston refinement' will not bear the roasting of the bodies of men and women: but you come as near to this pass as you dare. You rack their consciences and wring their souls."—"Our martyr age! our martyr age!" the clergyman went on muttering to himself, in all the excitement of a new idea.

When the abolitionists began to gather to their Convention, when the liberal part of the Quaker population came abroad, and were seen greeting their fellow-emancipators in the city of Penn—when the doors of the fine new building, Pennsylvania Hall, were thrown open, and the people of colour were seen flocking thither, with hope in their faces, and with heads erect, in spite of the tyranny of the new laws, the hatred of their oppressors grew too violent for restraint. It was impossible to find reasonable and true causes of complaint against any of the parties concerned in the Convention, and falsehoods were therefore framed and circulated. Even these falsehoods were of a nature which makes it difficult for people on this side of the Atlantic to understand how they should be used as a pretext for such an excess of violence as succeeded. The charge against the abolitionists was, that they ostentatiously walked the streets arm-in-arm with people of colour. They did not do this, because the act was not necessary to the assertion of any principle, and would have been offensive; but if they had, it might have been asked what excuse this was for firing Pennsylvania Hall?

The delegates met and transacted their business, as in the preceding year, but this time with a yelling mob around the doors. The mild voice of Angelina Weld was heard above the hoarse roar; but it is said that the transient appearance of Maria Chapman was the most striking circumstance of the day. She was ill, and the heat of the weather was tremendous; but, scarcely able to sustain herself under an access of fever, she felt it her duty to appear on the platform, showing once more that where shame and peril are, there is she. Commenting upon the circumstances of the moment, the strain of her exhortation accorded well with the angelic beauty of her countenance, and with the melting tones of her voice, and with the summary of duty which she had elsewhere presented: "Our principles teach us how to avoid that spurious charity which would efface moral distinctions, and that our duty to the sinner is, not to palliate, but to pardon; not to excuse, but to forgive, freely, fully, as we hope to be forgiven." To these principles she has ever been faithful, whether she gathers her children about her knees at home, or bends over the pillow of a dying friend, or stands erect amidst the insults and outrages of a mob, to strengthen the souls of her fellow-sufferers. Her strain is ever the same—no compromise, but unbounded forgiveness.

If the authorities had done their duty, no worse mischief than threat and insult would have happened; but nothing effectual was done in answer to a demonstration on the part of the mob, repeated for three or four nights; so at last they broke into Pennsylvania Hall, heaped together the furniture and books in the middle of the floor, and burned them and the building together. The circumstance which most clearly indicates the source of the rage of the mob was their setting fire to the Orphan Asylum for coloured children; a charity wholly unconnected with abolitionism, and in no respect, but the complexion of its inmates, on a different footing from any other charitable institution in the Quaker city. . . .

It appears as if each State had to pass through riot to rectitude on this mighty question. Every State which has now an abolition legislature, and is officered by abolitionists, has, we believe, gone through this process. . . . Mrs. Child said long ago that this evil spirit having so long intimately possessed the nation, we cannot expect that it should be cast out without much rending and tearing. . . .

During the last year, several Halls of State Legislatures have been granted to the abolitionists for their meetings, while the churches have remained closed against them. The aspect of these assemblages has been very remarkable, from the union of religious and political action witnessed there. But the most extraordinary spectacle of all—a spectacle perhaps unrivalled in the history of the world—was the address of Angelina Grimké before a Committee of the Legislature of Massachusetts. Some have likened it to the appeal of Hortensia to the Roman Senate; but others have truly observed that the address of Angelina Grimké was far the nobler of the two, as she complained not as the voice of a party remonstrating against injuries done to itself, but as the advocate of a class too degraded and helpless to move or speak on its own behalf. The gentle dignity of the speaker's manner, and the power of statement and argument shown in her address, together with the righteousness of her cause, won the sympathies of as large an audience as the State House would contain, and bore down all ridicule, prejudice, and passion. Two emotions divided the vast assemblage of hearers;—sympathy in her cause, and veneration for herself. The only fear now entertained by the abolitionists with regard to the cause in the leading State of Massachusetts, is lest it should become too flourishing, and lose something of its rectitude in its prosperity.

The history of this struggle seems to yield a few inferences which must, we think, be evident to all impartial minds; and which are as important as they are clear.—One is, that this is a struggle which cannot subside till it has prevailed. If this be true, the consequence of yielding to it would be the saving of a world of guilt and woe.—Another is, that other sorts of freedom, besides emancipation from slavery, will come in with it;—that the aristocratic spirit in all its manifestations is being purged out of the community;—that with every black slave a white will be also freed. . . .

It is a wide world that we live in, as wonderful in the diversity of its moral as of its natural features. A just survey of the whole can leave little doubt that the abolitionists of the United States are the greatest people now living and moving in it. There is beauty in the devotedness of the domestic life of every land: there is beauty in the liberality of the philosophers of the earth, in the laboriousness of statesmen, in the beneficence of the wealthy, in the faith and charity of the poor. All these graces flourish among this martyr company, and others with them, which is melting to the very soul to contemplate. To appreciate them fully, one must be among them. One must hear their diversity of tongue,—from the quaint Scripture phraseology of the Pilgrims to the classical language of the scholar—to estimate their liberality. One must witness the eagerness with which each strives to bring down the storm upon his own head to save his neighbour, and to direct any transient sunshine into his friend's house rather than his own, to understand their generosity. One must see the manly father weeping over his son's blighted prospects, and the son vindicating his mother's insulted name, to appreciate their disinterestedness. One must experience something of the soul-sickness and misgiving caused by popular hatred, and of the awful pangs of an apprehended violent death, to enter fully into their heroism.

TO MRS. CHAPMAN

DEAR FRIEND,—I have seen Garrison; and among all the pleasures of this meeting I seem to have been brought nearer to you. If I were well, and had health, and if my mother's life were not so fast bound to mine as it is, I think I could not help coming to live beside you. Great *ifs*, and many of them. But I dream of a life devoted to you and your cause, and the very dream is cheering. I have not been out of these two rooms for months, and now I begin to doubt whether I shall ever again step across their threshold. I may go on just as I am, for years, and it may end any day; yet I am not worse than when I last wrote.

We had a happy day, we four, when Garrison was here. I am sure he was happy. How gay he is! He left us with a new life in us.

Garrison was quite right, I think, to sit in the gallery at Convention. I conclude you think so. It has done much for the woman question, I am persuaded. You will live to see a great enlargement of our scope, I trust; but, what with the vices of some women and the fears of others, it is hard work for us to assert our liberty. I will, however, till I die, and so will you; and so make it easier for some few to follow us than it was for poor Mary Wollstonecraft to begin.

I must not begin upon Convention subjects. I am so tired; and there would be no end. You know what I should say, no doubt. The information brought out will do good, but the obvious deficiencies of the members in the very principles they came to advocate will surely do more.

Garrison brings you £2 from me, which I have earned by my needle for your society, being fond of fancy-work, and fit only for it, in this my invalid state. I feel in my soul the hon-

---

Harriet Martineau, *Autobiography*, with Memorials by Maria Weston Chapman, 4th ed. (Boston: Houghton, Osgood and Co., 1879), vol. 2, pp. 350–351. Written in 1840.

our of the appointment of delegate. You know that I could not have discharged its duties, even if the others had been admitted. But there is in me no lack of willingness to serve our cause in any capacity.

Believe me ever your faithful and affectionate,
HARRIET MARTINEAU.

LETTER FROM MISS MARTINEAU TO THE EDITOR OF *MIND AMONGST THE SPINDLES*

Tynemouth, May 20, 1844

MY DEAR FRIEND,—Your interest in this Lowell book can scarcely equal mine; for I have seen the factory girls in their Lyceum, and have gone over the cotton-mills at Waltham, and made myself familiar on the spot with factory life in New England; so that in reading the 'Offering,' I saw again in my memory the street of houses built by the earnings of the girls, the church which is their property, and the girls themselves trooping to the mill, with their healthy countenances, and their neat dress and quiet manners, resembling those of the tradesman class of our country.

My visit to Lowell was merely for one day, in company with Mr. Emerson's party,—he (the pride and boast of New England as an author and philosopher) being engaged by the Lowell factory people to lecture to them, in a winter course of historical biography. Of course the lectures were delivered in the evening, after the mills were closed. The girls were then working seventy hours a-week, yet, as I looked at the large audience (and I attended more to them than to the lecture) I saw no sign of weariness among any of them. There they sat, row

—

Mind amongst the Spindles: A Selection from the Lowell Offering, edited by C. Knight (London: Charles Knight, 1844), pp. xvii–xxii.

behind row, in their own Lyceum—a large hall, wainscoted with mahogany, the platform carpeted, well lighted, provided with a handsome table, desk, and seat, and adorned with portraits of a few worthies; and as they thus sat listening to their lecturer, all wakeful and interested, all well-dressed and ladylike, I could not but feel my heart swell at the thought of what such a sign would be with us.

The difference is not in rank, for these young people were all daughters of parents who earn their bread with their own hands. It is not in the amount of wages, however usual that supposition is, for they were then earning from one to three dollars a-week, besides their food; the children one dollar (4s. 3d.), the second-rate workers two dollars, and the best three: the cost of their dress and necessary comforts being much above what the same class expend in this country. It is not in the amount of toil; for, as I have said, they worked seventy clear hours per week. The difference was in their superior culture. Their minds are kept fresh, and strong, and free by knowledge and power of thought; and this is the reason why they are not worn and depressed under their labours. They begin with a poorer chance for health than our people; for the health of the New England women generally is not good, owing to circumstances of climate and other influences; but among the 3800 women and girls in the Lowell mills when I was there, the average of health was not lower than elsewhere; and the disease which was most mischievous was the same that proves most fatal over the whole country—consumption; while there were no complaints peculiar to mill life.

At Waltham, where I saw the mills, and conversed with the people, I had an opportunity of observing the invigorating effects of MIND in a life of labour. Twice the wages and half the toil would not have made the girls I saw happy and healthy, without that cultivation of mind which afforded them perpetual support, entertainment, and motive for activity. They were not highly educated, but they had pleasure in books and lectures, in correspondence with home; and had their minds so open to fresh ideas, as to be drawn off from thoughts of themselves and their own concerns. When at work they were amused with thinking over the last book they had read, or with planning any account they should write home of the last Sunday's sermon, or with singing over to themselves the song they meant to practise in the evening; and when evening came, nothing was heard of tired limbs and eagerness for bed, but, if it was summer, they sallied out, the moment tea was over, for a walk, and, if it was winter, to the lecture-room or to the ball-room for a dance, or they got an hour's practice at the piano, or wrote home, or shut themselves up with a new book. It was during the hours of work in the mill that the papers in the 'Offering' were meditated, and it was after work in the evenings that they were penned.

There is, however, in the case of these girls, a stronger support, a more elastic spring of vigour and cheerfulness than even an active and cultivated understanding. The institution of factory labour has brought ease of heart to many; and to many occasion for noble and generous deeds. The ease of heart is given to those who were before suffering in silent poverty, from the deficiency of profitable employment for women, which is even greater in America than with us. It used to be understood there that all women were maintained by the men of their families; but the young men of New England are apt to troop off into the West, to settle in new lands, leaving sisters at home. Some few return to fetch a wife, but the greater number do not, and thus a vast over proportion of young women remains; and to a multitude of these the opening of factories was a most welcome event, affording means of honourable maintenance, in exchange for pining poverty at home.

As for the noble deeds, it makes one's heart glow to stand in these mills, and hear of the domestic history of some who are working before one's eyes, unconscious of being observed or of being the object of any admiration. If one of the sons of a New England farmer shows a love for books and thought, the ambition of an affectionate sister is roused, and she thinks of the glory and honour to the whole family, and the blessing to him, if he could have a college education. She ponders this till she tells her parents, some day, of her wish to go to Lowell, and earn the means of sending her brother to college. The desire is yet more urgent if the brother has a pious mind, and a wish to enter the ministry. Many a clergyman in America has been prepared for his function by the devoted industry of sisters; and many a scholar and professional man dates his elevation in social rank and usefulness from his sister's, or even some affectionate aunt's entrance upon mill life, for his sake. Many girls, perceiving anxiety in their fathers' faces, on account of the farm being incumbered, and age coming on without release from the debt, have gone to Lowell, and worked till the mortgage was paid off, and the little family property free. Such motives may well lighten and sweeten labour; and to such girls labour is light and sweet.

Some, who have no such calls, united the surplus of their earnings to build dwellings for their own residence, six, eight, or twelve living together with the widowed mother or elderly aunt of one of them to keep house for, and give countenance to the party. I saw a whole street of houses so built and owned, at Waltham; pretty frame houses, with the broad piazza, and the green Venetian blinds, that give such an air of coolness and pleasantness to American village and country abodes. There is the large airy eating-room, with a few prints hung up, the piano at one end, and the united libraries of the girls, forming a good-looking array of books, the rocking chairs universal in America, the stove adorned in summer with flowers, and the long dining-table in the middle. The chambers do not answer to our English ideas of confort. There is there a strange absence of the wish for privacy; and more girls are accommodated in one room than we should see any reason for in such comfortable and pretty houses.

In the mills the girls have quite the appearance of ladies. They sally forth in the morning with their umbrellas in threatening weather, their calashes to keep their hair neat, gowns of print or gingham, with a perfect fit, worked collars or pelerines, and waistbands of ribbon. For Sundays and social evenings they have their silk gowns, and neat gloves and shoes. Yet through proper economy,—the economy of educated and thoughtful people,—they are able to lay by for such purposes as I have mentioned above. The deposits in the Lowell Savings' Bank were, in 1834, upwards of 114,000 dollars, the number of operatives being 6000, of whom 3800 were women and girls.

I thank you for calling my attention back to this subject. It is one I have pleasure in recurring to. There is nothing in America which necessitates the prosperity of manufactures as of agriculture, and there is nothing of good in their factory

system which may not be emulated elsewhere—equalled elsewhere, when the people employed are so educated as to have
the command of themselves and of their lot in life, which is
always and everywhere controlled by mind, far more than by
outward circumstances.

I am very truly yours,
H. MARTINEAU

SARAH PELLATT, FLORENCE NIGHTINGALE, AND TEMPERANCE

The Sierra Nevada, in California, is considered one of the
most fearful regions in the world for travellers. Its deep ra-
vines, its solemn gorges, its glaring rocks, and its rushing tor-
rents make it an outlying district where men will not go if they
can find gold at an easier rate; and those who do go are always
armed to the teeth, expecting conflicts at any hour with roving
robbers, quarrelsome neighbours, or outlaws who have shed
too much blood to be tolerated in any organized society. In
that region, as well as over the exposed plains and the half-
barbaric towns of California, a woman—a delicately nurtured
lady—is making her way alone, bearing fatigue and hardship,
and encountering danger of every sort, in the hope of achiev-
ing a great social good. This lady's name is SARAH PELLATT.
She is, we believe, a native of New England. . . . Multitudes
of Americans grieve over the spirit and habits which, in California, as nearer home, convert the finest opportunity of establishing civilisation into a dissemination of barbarism: but
this lady is not satisfied with grieving. Convinced, as our British magistrates are throughout the land, that nearly the whole
amount of violent crime proceeds from intemperance, she has
gone, alone and single-hearted, to try what she can do among
the Californian gold-diggers, to wean them from spirit drink-

---

Daily News (London), November 22, 1855.

ing, and raise them out of their gross habits and savage passions. Few of the most robust men in the colony have undergone such toil as this self-appointed missionary; and few of the bravest have had to encounter such risks from accident and violence. Yet, at the last accounts, she was safe and well, and busy, and obtaining great success in her object. She drops into a mining hamlet, talks to the men when their work is done, or calls them together to a familiar lecture; shows them how they waste their gains, their health, their respectability, their life, by their indulgence in spirit drinking; and is so wholly engrossed by her object as to drive from other minds, as completely as from her own, all notion of misconstruction, or of personal danger from human hands. Every hut and tent is open to her, and the entrance is guarded by men who keep sober for her sake. The roughest voices are tamed, the profanest speech is purified where she appears; and tears run in streams from eyes which have not wept since the innocent days of childhood. Such is her present success, guaranteed as she and her disciples believe, by the springing up of temperance societies wherever she has been. Those who, like ourselves, are outside of the atmosphere of enthusiasm in which she and her disciples live, must, of course, have doubts about the permanence of her influence and the durability of her work, unless better securities than mere associations for moral objects can be instituted. Meantime, there she is, purifying and redeeming wherever she goes. Everywhere she is revered as a saint, and guarded as a sister. "In all her wanderings among the men of the hills," says an eye-witness, "her ear has never been insulted by a libertine remark, nor pained by an unkind word."

Now, what would be thought of any person, or number of persons, who should follow this lady's steps, introducing typhus fever or any other infectious disease among the groups and households whom she has retrieved from vice and moral destruction? If society in the Sierra Nevada were organised from Washington, and affairs were so managed at headquarters as to encourage the introduction and spread of the plague, so that there should be scarcely a tent or a hut from which the dead should not be carried forth, who would not fling back in the face of Government all its professions of admiration for the missionary and of interest for the people under her charge? Who would not join in the cry to the administrative powers to hold their tongues and do their business—to leave off spreading the plague, and try to give the people some chance of living, in order to use and enjoy the new life proposed to them by their benefactress?

The application of this parable is probably by this time clear to our readers. The mission of SARAH PELLATT will have at once recalled that of FLORENCE NIGHTINGALE. Where the one has cured moral disease, the other has wrestled with physical suffering; and now, to permit a wide devastation of moral disease, in the shape of drunkenness, among those whom FLORENCE NIGHTINGALE and her companions have saved, is about as atrocious a guilt as it would be for the American Government to foster the plague among those whom SARAH PELLATT has retrieved from intemperance. Yet who that reads the accounts of the drunkenness among our soldiers in the Crimea can deny that the guilt lies at the door of the authorities who put the poison, and the seduction, and the opportunity in the soldier's way, while withholding every inducement which could win him from the fatal indulgence?

Most of us have by this time had means of knowing how FLORENCE NIGHTINGALE is regarded by the soldiers among whom her work has lain. One here and there is stirred to compose a ballad in her praise, which is sung to a listening group—

On a dark lonely night on Crimea's dread shore.

One poor fellow writes: "Before she came it was a horrid place—such cursin' and swearin'; now it's as holy as a church. She got everything for us we wanted. If we wanted a book from the library, she'd get it and bring it herself, if it took her an hour to find it." Another says: "She spoke to as many as she could, and nodded and smiled to many more; but she could not notice us all, you know, for we lay there by hundreds; but we could kiss her shadow as it fell, and lay our heads down on the pillow quite content." One who has seen the whole, and who is qualified to pronounce dispassionately on the achievement, says: "What I conceive Miss NIGHTINGALE to have done is this: The world considered the army to consist of gentlemen and brutes; and the soldiers were always treated as such. She has taught the officials and the officers to treat them with respect as Christian men." We do not subscribe to the statement that our private soldiers have been regarded and treated as brutes, at least since the measures adopted of late years, for the education and innocent amusement of our soldier at home; but that Miss NIGHTINGALE has caused them to be considered, on the spot, as Christian men, we have no doubt. The thing which remains to be done is to consider and treat them so from head-quarters.

How far otherwise it is every one who reads about the Crimea knows but too well.

V

PORTRAYALS OF WOMEN

All that can be done with contemporary history is to collect and methodize the greatest amount of reliable facts and distinct impressions, to amass sound material for the veritable historian of a future day,—

—Harriet Martineau
self-obituary

Miss Nightingale with her tame owl, Athena, c. 1850
F. Holl, after a drawing by Parthenope Lady Verney
National Portrait Gallery, London

S ketches of individual people occur frequently in Martineau's works. Her portrayals of famous Americans are a strong feature of *Retrospect of Western Travel*, and accounts of individual English political leaders are found in *The History of England during the Thirty Years' Peace, 1816–1846*. Her *Autobiography* offers a rich vein of contemporary opinion about personalities she knew. Above all, she published numerous obituaries in the London *Daily News*, remarkable evaluations of her peers' lives. At times, she also wrote composite pictures of groups of people, the most enduring being, of course, *Society in America*. Another such composition, less full and less celebrated, was her *Letters from Ireland*, first published as separate pieces in the *Daily News* and in 1852 issued as a book. To some extent, also, her other travel book, *Eastern Life, Present and Past*, though thematically on the religions originating in the Middle East, was centrally about people in groups. Through all this writing is the core assumption of the need to understand people in society, whether writing of them as individuals or as groups. In her biographical or current history writings, she anticipated the purposes of future sociologists and historians.

About women she wrote liberally. Some of her biographical pieces about women are wonderfully revealing of the priorities of the age and of the tangle of intellectual and emotional judgments women holding similar or different world views would make of each other. Some of them are public tributes; some are gossip.

Included here are two pieces about women in groups— "The Hareem" from *Eastern Life* and the ninth letter, "The Women," from *Letters from Ireland*—and three pieces about individuals—Charlotte Brontë, Margaret Fuller, and Florence Nightingale.

Martineau's respect for Charlotte Brontë was not unalloyed. The two women were temperamentally a contrast. They differed philosophically, and close understanding between them was not likely. Martineau was practical, theoretical, worldly; Brontë was romantic, sheltered, devoutly religious. At first they were eager to know each other. Before it was known that "Currer Bell" was a pseudonym for Charlotte Brontë, Martineau had speculated from textual evidence that *Jane Eyre* had been written by a woman. The selection from her *Autobiography* reprinted here describes her sense of their relationship after it developed. Martineau wrote in a criticism of *Villette* that Brontë was too sensitive to love, that she allowed too large an emotional play in the novel. Brontë was deeply hurt. She in turn was horrified at Martineau's abandonment of religion in *Letters on the Laws of Man's Nature and Development*. They did not become totally estranged during Brontë's lifetime, but Martineau became more and more distressed with Brontë after the publication of Mrs. Gaskell's *Life of Charlotte Brontë*, which she felt had represented her disparagingly. In a letter written after Brontë's death, Martineau accused her of double-dealing by writing to a publisher while a guest in Martineau's home attempting to discourage him from publishing the "Atkinson Letters." In the same letter she said she had "long ceased to consider C. Brontë truthful."[1] Martineau also published an obituary of Brontë that was a less personal rendering of the theme that Brontë was too much driven by emotions.

Margaret Fuller, like Charlotte Brontë, got Martineau's dander up. At first meeting they liked each other and seemed to have much in common as female writers. But Fuller's transcendentalist philosophy included exactly the kinds of cosmic speculations that Martineau became bent on straining out of philosophy as she came to prefer a positivistic logic of natural laws. Also, Fuller's manner was emotive and flamboyant. They, too, got into trouble about who wrote what about whom. Fuller wrote a biting criticism of Martineau's *Society in America* for its abolitionist focus. Martineau got even by calling Fuller a "'gorgeous' pedant" and ill-mannered to boot. Her redemption, Martineau claims in the piece from her *Autobiography* reprinted here, occurred in her Italian period when she fought for Mazzini and the Italian revolution. Presumably, this made up for her lack of commitment to abolition in her own country.

On Florence Nightingale's death in August 1910 one front-page story carried a headline reading "Graphic Story of Early Life by Miss Harriet Martineau." Since Martineau had

---

[1] "'Severe to the Point of Injustice,' Two Letters by Harriet Martineau Purchased," *Brontë Society Transactions* 16 (Keighley: The Keighley Printers, 1973), pp. 199–202. Also, see [H. A. Hammelmann], "Charlotte Brontë and Harriet Martineau," *Times Literary Supplement*, June 9, 1950, p. 364.

died in 1876, it may have seemed somewhat incredible that the account of Nightingale's life published in the *Daily News* came largely from Martineau's pen.[2] It is wonderfully appropriate, however, since the two invalids had corresponded voluminously in Martineau's later years. They were great friends, and staunch supporters of one another, both expecting to die imminently but accomplishing an enormous amount of public work under protection of their invalidism. Martineau wrote frequently about Nightingale's achievement during the Crimean War and in support of her school of nursing at St. Thomas' Hospital in London. In Martineau's later years she wrote, at Nightingale's behest, about issues relating to reform of the War Office. The two women seem to have shared a genuine collegiality and a warm professional friendship, largely carried on long distance via letters. Like Martineau, Nightingale was very businesslike. They understood each other.

THE HAREEM

I saw two Hareems in the east; and it would be wrong to pass them over in an account of my travels; though the subject is as little agreeable as any I can have to treat. I cannot now think of the two mornings thus employed without a heaviness of heart greater than I have ever brought away from Deaf and Dumb Schools, Lunatic Asylums, or even Prisons. As such are my impressions of hareems, of course I shall not say whose they

---

Harriet Martineau, *Eastern Life, Present and Past* (Philadelphia: Lea and Blanchard, 1848), pp. 259–270.

[2] The Fawcett Library in London has Martineau's manuscript with the editing marks made by the newspaper. The editorial comment on the obituary labels Martineau as "one of the most intellectual of her sex." "Earl Spencer and Miss Florence Nightingale," *Daily News* (London), August 15, 1910, p. 4.

were that I visited. Suffice it that one was at Cairo and the other at Damascus.

The royal hareems were not accessible while I was in Egypt. . . . —The one which I saw was that of a gentleman of high rank; and as good a specimen as could be seen. . . .

Before I went abroad, more than one sensible friend had warned me to leave behind as many prejudices as possible; and especially on this subject, on which the prejudices of Europeans are the strongest. I was reminded of the wide extent, both of time and space, in which Polygamy had existed; and that openness of mind was as necessary to the accurate observation of this institution as of every other. . . . I learned a very great deal about the working of the institution; and I believe I apprehend the thoughts and feelings of the persons concerned in it: and I declare that if we are to look for a hell on earth, it is where polygamy exists: and that as polygamy runs riot in Egypt, Egypt is the lowest depth of this hell. I always before believed that every arrangement and prevalent practice had some one fair side,—some one redeeming quality: and diligently did I look for this fair side in regard to polygamy: but there is none. The longer one studies the subject, and the deeper one penetrates into it,—the more is one's mind confounded with the intricacy of its iniquity, and the more does one's heart feel as if it would break. . . .

At ten o'clock, one morning, Mrs. Y. and I were home from our early ride, and dressed for our visit to a hareem of a high order. The lady to whose kindness we mainly owed this opportunity, accompanied us, with her daughter. We had a disagreeable drive in the carriage belonging to the hotel, knocking against asses, horses and people all the way. We alighted at the entrance of a paved passage leading to a court which we crossed: and then, in a second court, we were before the entrance of the hareem.

A party of eunuchs stood before a faded curtain, which they held aside when the gentlemen of our party and the dragoman had gone forward. Retired some way behind the curtain stood, in a half circle, eight or ten slave girls, in an attitude of deep obeisance. Two of them then took charge of each of us; holding us by the arms above the elbows, to help us up stairs.—After crossing a lobby at the top of the stairs, we entered a handsome apartment, where lay the chief wife,—at that time an invalid.—The ceiling was gayly painted; and so were the walls,—the latter with curiously bad attempts at domestic perspective. There were four handsome mirrors; and the curtains in the doorway were of a beautiful shawl fabric, fringed and tasseled. A Turkey carpet not only covered the whole floor, but was turned up at the corners. Deewans extended round nearly the whole room,—a lower one for ordinary use, and a high one for the seat of honor. The windows, which had a sufficient fence of blinds, looked upon a pretty garden, where I saw orange trees and many others, and the fences were hung with rich creepers.

On cushions on the floor lay the chief lady, ill and miserable-looking. She rose as we entered; but we made her lie down again: and she was then covered with a silk counterpane. Her dress was, as we saw when she rose, loose trowsers of blue striped cotton under her black silk jacket; and the same blue cotton appeared at the wrists, under her black sleeves. Her head-dress was of black net, bunched out curiously behind. Her hair was braided down the sides of this head-dress behind, and the ends were pinned over her forehead. Some of the black net was brought round her face, and under the chin, showing the outline of a face which had no beauty in it, nor traces of former beauty, but which was interesting to-day from her manifest illness and unhappiness. There was a strong expression of waywardness and peevishness about the mouth, however. She wore two handsome diamond rings; and she and one other lady had watches and gold chains. She complained of her head; and her left hand was bound up: she made signs by pressing her bosom, and imitating the dandling of a baby, which, with her occasional tears, persuaded my companions that she had met with some accident and had lost her infant. On leaving the hareem, we found that it was not a child of her own that she was mourning, but that of a white girl in the hareem: and the wife's illness was wholly from grief for the loss of this baby;—a curious illustration of the feelings and manners of the place! The children born in large hareems are extremely few: and they are usually idolized, and sometimes murdered. It is known that in the houses at home which morally most resemble these hareems (though little enough externally) when the rare event of the birth of a child happens, a passionate joy extends over the wretched household: . . . This natural outbreak of feminine instinct takes place in the too populous hareem, when a child is given to any one of the many who are longing for the gift: and if it dies naturally, it is mourned as we saw, through a wonderful conquest of personal jealousy by this general instinct. . . .

A sensible looking old lady, who had lost an eye, sat at the head of the invalid: and a nun-like elderly woman, whose head and throat were wrapped in unstarched muslin, sat behind for a time, and then went away, after an affectionate salutation to the invalid.—Towards the end of the visit, the husband's mother came in,—looking like a little old man in her coat trimmed with fur. Her countenance was cheerful and pleasant. We saw, I think, about twenty more women,—some slaves,—most or all young—some good-looking, but none handsome. Some few were black; and the rest very light:—Nubians or Abyssinians and Circassians, no doubt. One of the best figures, as a picture, in the hareem, was a Nubian girl, in an amber-colored watered silk, embroidered with black, looped up in festoons, and finished with a black boddice. The richness of the gay printed cotton skirts and sleeves surprised us: the finest shawls could hardly have looked better. One graceful girl had her pretty figure well shown by a tight-fitting black dress. Their heads were dressed much like the chief lady's. Two, who must have been sisters, if not twins, had patches between the eyes. One handmaid was barefoot, and several were without shoes. Though there were none of the whole large number who could be called particularly pretty individually, the scene was, on the whole, exceedingly striking, as the realization of what one knew before, but as in a dream. The girls went out and came in, but, for the most part, stood in a half circle. Two sat on their heels for a time: and some went to play in the neighboring apartments.

Coffee was handed to us twice, with all the well-known apparatus of jeweled cups, embroidered tray cover, and gold-flowered napkins. There were chibouques, of course: and sherbets in cut glass cups. . . .

The mourning worn by the lady who went with us was the subject of much speculation: and many questions were asked about her home and family. To appease the curiosity about her home, she gave her card. As I anticipated, this did not answer. It was the great puzzle of the whole interview. At first the poor lady thought it was to do her head good: then, she fidgeted about it, in the evident fear of omitting some observance; but at last, she understood that she was to keep it. When we had taken our departure, however, an eunuch was sent after us to inquire of the dragoman what "the letter" was which our companion had given to the lady.

The difficulty is to get away, when one is visiting a hareem. The poor ladies cannot conceive of one's having anything to do; and the only reason they can understand for the interview coming to an end is the arrival of sunset, after which it would, they think, be improper for any woman to be abroad. And the amusement to them of such a visit is so great that they protract it to the utmost, even in such a case as ours to-day, when all intercourse was conducted by dumb show. It is certainly very tiresome; and the only wonder is that the hostesses can like it. To sit hour after hour on the deewan, without any exchange of ideas, having our clothes examined, and being plied with successive cups of coffee and sherbet, and pipes, and being gazed at by a half-circle of girls in brocade and shawls, and made to sit down again as soon as one attempts to rise, is as wearisome an experience as one meets with in foreign lands.—The weariness of heart is, however, the worst part of it. I noted all the faces well during our constrained stay; and I saw no trace of mind in any one except in the homely one-eyed old lady. All the younger ones were dull, soulless, brutish, or peevish. How should it be otherwise, when the only idea of their whole lives is that which, with all our interests and engagements, we consider too prominent with us? There cannot be a woman of them all who is not dwarfed and withered in mind and soul by being kept wholly engrossed with that one interest,—detained at that stage in existence which, though most important in its place, is so as a means to ulterior ends. The ignorance is fearful enough; but the grossness is revolting.

At the third move, and when it was by some means understood that we were waited for, we were permitted to go,—after a visit of above two hours. The sick lady rose from her cushions, notwithstanding our opposition, and we were conducted forth with much observance. On each side of the curtain which overhung the outer entrance, stood a girl with a bottle of rose water, some of which was splashed in our faces as we passed out.

We had reached the carriage when we were called back: —his excellency was waiting for us. So we visited him in a pretty apartment, paved with variegated marbles, and with a fountain in the centre. His excellency was a sensible-looking man, with gay, easy and graceful manners. He lamented the mistake about the interpreter, and said we must go again, when we might have conversation. He insisted upon attending us to the carriage, actually passing between the files of beggars which lined the outer passage. The dragoman was so excessively shocked by this degree of condescension, that we felt obliged to be so too, and remonstrated; but in vain. He stood till the door was shut, and the whip was cracked. He is a liberal-minded man; and his hareem is nearly as favorable a specimen as could be selected for a visit; but what is this best specimen? I find these words written down on the same day, in my journal: written, as I well remember, in heaviness of heart. "I am glad of the opportunity of seeing a hareem: but it leaves an impression of discontent and uneasiness which I shall be glad to sleep off. And I am not conscious that there is prejudice in this. I feel that a visit to the worst room in the Rookery in St. Giles' would have affected me less painfully. There are there at least the elements of a rational life, however perverted; while here humanity is wholly and hopelessly baulked. It will never do to look on this as a case for cosmopolitan philosophy to regard complacently, and require a good construction for. It is not a phase of natural early manners. It is as pure a conventionalism as our representative monarchy, or German heraldry, or Hindoo caste; and the most atrocious in the world."

And of this atrocious system, Egypt is the most atrocious example. It has unequaled facilities for the importation of black and white slaves; and these facilities are used to the utmost; yet the population is incessantly on the decline. But for the importation of slaves, the upper classes, where polygamy runs riot, must soon die out,—so few are the children born, and so fatal to health are the arrangements of society. The finest children are those born of Circassian or Georgian mothers; and but for these, we should soon hear little more of an upper class in Egypt.—Large numbers are brought from

the south,—the girls to be made attendants or concubines in
the hareem, and the boys to be made, in a vast proportion,
those guards to the female part of the establishment whose
mere presence is a perpetual insult and shame to humanity.
The business of keeping up the supply of these miserable
wretches,—of whom the Pasha's eldest daughter has fifty for
her exclusive service,—is in the hands of the Christians of
Asyoot. It is these Christians who provide a sufficient supply,
and cause a sufficient mortality to keep the number of the
sexes pretty equal: in consideration of which we cannot much
wonder that Christianity does not appear very venerable in
the eyes of Mohammedans.

These eunuchs are indulged in regard to dress, personal
liberty, and often the possession of office, domestic, military,
or political. When retained as guards of the hareem, they are
in their master's confidence,—acting as his spies, and indispensable to the ladies, as a medium of communication with
the world, and as furnishing their amusement,—being at once
playmates and servants. It is no unusual thing for the eunuchs
to whip the ladies away from a window, whence they had
hoped for amusement; or to call them opprobrious names; or
to inform against them to their owner: and it is also no unusual
thing for them to romp with the ladies, to obtain their confidence, and to try their dispositions. Cases have been known of
one of them becoming the friend of some poor girl of higher
nature and tendencies than her companions; and even of a
closer attachment, which is not objected to by the proprietor
of both. It is a case too high for his jealousy, so long as he
knows that the cage is secure. It has become rather the fashion
to extenuate the lot of the captive of either sex: to point out
how the Nubian girl, who would have ground corn and woven
garments, and nursed her infants in comparative poverty all
her days, is now surrounded by luxury, and provided for for
life: and how the Circassian girl may become a wife of the son
of her proprietor, and hold a high rank in the hareem: and how
the wretched brothers of these slaves may rise to posts of military command or political confidence; but it is enough to see
them to be disabused of all impressions of their good fortune.
It is enough to see the dull and gross face of the handmaid of
the hareem, and to remember at the moment the cheerful,
modest countenance of the Nubian girl busy about her house-

hold tasks, or of the Nubian mother, with her infants hanging about her as she looks, with face open to the sky, for her husband's return from the field, or meets him on the river bank. It is enough to observe the wretched health and abject, or worn, or insolent look of the guard of the hareem, and to remember that he ought to have been the head of a household of his own, however humble: and in this contrast of what is with what ought to have been, slavery is seen to be fully as detestable here as anywhere else. These two hellish practices, slavery and polygamy, which, as practices, can clearly never be separated, are here avowedly connected: and in that connection, are exalted into a double institution, whose working is such as to make one almost wish that the Nile would rise to cover the tops of the hills, and sweep away the whole abomination. . . .

The youngest wife I ever saw (except the swathed and veiled brides we encountered in the streets of Egyptian cities) was in a Turkish hareem which Mrs. Y. and I visited at Damascus. I will tell that story now, that I may dismiss the subject of this chapter. I heartily dreaded this second visit to a hareem, and braced myself up to it as one does to an hour at the dentist's, or to an expedition into the city to prove a debt. We had the comfort of a good and pleasant interpreter: and there was more mirth and nonsense than in the Cairo hareem; and, therefore, somewhat less disgust and constraint: but still it was painful enough. We saw the seven wives of three gentlemen, and a crowd of attendants and visitors. Of the seven, two had been wives of the head of the household, who was dead: three were the wives of his eldest son, aged twenty-two; and the remaining two were the wives of his second son, aged fifteen. The youngest son, aged thirteen, was not yet married; but he would be thinking about it soon. The pair of widows were elderly women, as merry as girls, and quite at their ease. Of the other five, three were sisters:—that is, we conclude, half-sisters;—children of different mothers in the same hareem. It is evident at a glance what a tragedy lies under this; what the horrors of jealousy must be among sisters thus connected for life;—three of them between two husbands in the same house! And we were told that the jealousy had begun, young as they were, and the third having been married only a week. This young creature, aged twelve, was the bride of the husband of fifteen. She was the most conspicuous person in the place, not only for the splendor of her dress, but because she sat on the deewan, while the others sat or lounged on cushions on the raised floor. The moment we took our seats, I was struck with compassion for this child—she looked so grave, and sad and timid. While the others romped and giggled, pushing and pulling one another about, and laughing at jokes among themselves, she never smiled, but looked on listlessly. I was determined to make her laugh before we went away; and at last she relaxed somewhat—smiling, and growing grave again in a moment: but at length she really and truly laughed; and when we were shown the whole hareem, she also slipped her bare and dyed feet into her pattens inlaid with mother-of-pearl, and went into the courts with us, nestling to us, and seeming to lose the sense of her new position for the time: but there was far less of the gayety of a child about her than in the elderly widows. Her dress was superb;—a full skirt and bodice of geranium-colored brocade, embossed with gold flowers and leaves; and her frill and ruffles were of geranium-colored gauze. Her eyebrows were frightful—joined and prolonged by black paint. Her head was covered with a silk net, in almost every mesh of which were stuck jewels or natural flowers: so that her head was like a bouquet sprinkled with diamonds. Her nails were dyed black; and her feet were dyed black in checkers. Her complexion, called white, was of an unhealthy yellow: and, indeed, we did not see a healthy complexion among the whole company; nor anywhere among women who were secluded from exercise, while pampered with all the luxuries of eastern living.

Besides the seven wives, a number of attendants came in to look at us, and serve the pipes and sherbet; and a few ladies from a neighboring hareem; and a party of Jewesses, with whom we had some previous acquaintance. Mrs. Y. was compelled to withdraw her lace veil, and then to take off her bonnet: and she was instructed that the street was the place for her to wear her veil down, and that they expected to see her face. Then her bonnet went round, and was tried on many heads— one merry girl wearing it long enough to surprise many new comers with the joke. My gloves were stretched and pulled in all manner of ways, in their attempts to thrust their large, broad brown hands into them, one after another. But the great amusement was my trumpet. The eldest widow, who sat next

me, asked for it, and put it to her ear; when I said "Bo!" When
she had done laughing, she put it into her next neighbor's ear,
and said "Bo!" and in this way it came round to me again. But
in two minutes, it was asked for again, and went round a
second time—everybody laughing as loud as ever at each
"Bo!"—and then a third time! Could one have conceived it!
The next joke was on behalf of the Jewesses, four or five of
whom sat in a row on the deewan. Almost everybody else was
puffing away at a chibouque or a nargeeleh, and the place was
one cloud of smoke. The poor Jewesses were obliged to decline joining us; for it happened to be Saturday: they must not
smoke on the Sabbath. They were naturally much pitied: and
some of the young wives did what was possible for them.
Drawing in a long breath of smoke, they puffed it forth in the
faces of the Jewesses, who opened mouth and nostrils eagerly
to receive it. Thus was the Sabbath observed, to shouts of
laughter.

A pretty little blue-eyed girl of seven was the only child we
saw. She nestled against her mother; and the mother clasped
her closely, lest we should carry her off to London. She begged
we would not wish to take her child to London, and said she
"would not sell her for much money." One of the wives was
pointed out to us as particularly happy in the prospect of becoming a mother: and we were taken to see the room in which
she was to lie in, which was all in readiness, though the event
was not looked for for more than half a year. She was in the
gayest spirits, and sang and danced. While she was lounging
on her cushions, I thought her the handsomest and most
graceful, as well as the happiest, of the party: but when she
rose to dance, the charm was destroyed for ever. The dancing
is utterly disgusting. A pretty Jewess of twelve years old
danced, much in the same way; but with downcast eyes and
an air of modesty. While the dancing went on, and the smoking, and drinking coffee and sherbet, and the singing, to the
accompaniment of a tambourine, some hideous old hags came
in successively, looked and laughed, and went away again.
Some negresses made a good background to this thoroughly
Eastern picture. All the while, romping, kissing and scream-
ing, went on among the ladies, old and young. At first, I
thought them a perfect rabble; but when I recovered myself a

little, I saw that there was some sense in the faces of the elderly women. In the midst of all this fun, the interpretess assured us that "there is much jealousy every day;" jealousy of the favored wife; that is, in this case, of the one who was pointed out to us by her companions as so eminently happy, and with whom they were romping and kissing, as with the rest. Poor thing! even the happiness of these her best days is hollow: for she cannot have, at the same time, peace in the hareem and her husband's love.

They were so free in their questions about us, and so evidently pleased when we used a similar impertinence about them, that we took the opportunity of learning a good deal of their way of life. Mrs. Y. and I were consulting about noticing the bride's dress, when we found we had put off too long: we were asked how we liked her dress, and encouraged to handle the silk. So I went on to examine the bundles of false hair that some of them wore; the pearl bracelets on their tattooed arms, and their jeweled and inlaid patterns.—In answer to our question of what they did in the way of occupation, they said "nothing;" but when we inquired whether they never made clothes or sweetmeats, they replied "yes."—They earnestly wished us to stay always; and they could not understand why we should not. My case puzzled them particularly. I believe they took me for a servant; and they certainly pitied me extremely for having to go about without being taken care of. They asked what I did: and Mrs. Y., being anxious to do me all honor, told them I had written many books: but the information was thrown away, because they did not know what a book was. Then we informed them that I lived in a field among mountains, where I had built a house; and that I had plenty to do; and we told them in what way: but still they could make nothing of it but that I had brought the stones with my own hands, and built the house myself. There is nothing about which the inmates of hareems seem to be so utterly stupid as about women having anything to do. That time should be valuable to a woman, and that she should have any business on her hands, and any engagements to observe, are things quite beyond their comprehension.

The pattens I have mentioned are worn to keep the feet and flowing dress from the marble pavement, which is often wetted for coolness. I think all the ladies here had bare feet. When they left the raised floor on which they sat, they slipped their feet into their high pattens, and went stumping about, rather awkwardly. I asked Dr. Thompson, who has admission as a physician into more houses than any other man could familiarly visit, whether he could not introduce skipping-ropes upon these spacious marble floors. I see no other chance of the women being induced to take exercise. They suffer cruelly from indigestion,—gorging themselves with sweet things, smoking intemperately, and passing through life with more than half the brain almost unawakened, and with scarcely any exercise of the limbs. Poor things! our going was a great amusement to them, they said: and they showed this by their entreaties to the last moment that we would not leave them yet, and that we would stay always.—"And these," as my journal says, "were human beings, such as those of whom Christ made friends!"—The chief lady gave me roses as a farewell token.—The Jewish ladies, who took their leave with us, wanted us to visit at another house: but we happily had not time.—I am thankful to have seen a hareem under favorable circumstances; and I earnestly hope I may never see another."

I kept those roses, however. I shall need no reminding of the most injured human beings I have ever seen,—the most studiously depressed and corrupted women whose condition I have witnessed: but I could not throw away the flowers which so found their way into my hand as to bespeak for the wrongs of the giver the mournful remembrance of my heart.

WOMEN IN IRELAND

Considering that women's labour is universally underpaid, in comparison with that of men, there is something very impressive to the traveller in Ireland in the conviction which grows upon him, from stage to stage, that it is the industry of women which is in great part sustaining the country. Though, in one view, there is moral beauty in the case, the symptom is a bad one. First, the men's wages are reduced to the lowest point; and then, capital turns to a lower-paid class, to the exclusion of the men, wherever the women can be employed in their stead. We should be sorry to draw any hasty conclusions on a matter of so much importance; but, recalling what we have seen since we landed, we cannot but declare that we have observed women not only diligently at work on their own branches of industry, but sharing the labours of the men in almost every employment that we happen to have witnessed. As an economical symptom, the employment of the least in the place of the most able-bodied is one of the peculiarities which marks the anomalous condition of Ireland. The famine time was, to be sure, an exception to all rules; but the same tendency was witnessed before, and is witnessed still. At that time, one of the London Companies sent directions to their agent to expend money to a certain amount, and on no account to allow anybody on their estates to starve. The agent determined to have a great piece of "slob" land dug,—employing for this purpose one boy out of every family of a certain number, with a staff of aged men for overseers, to superintend and measure the work. Spades, from a moderate to a very small size, were ordered; and a mighty provision of wheaten cakes was carried down to the place every day at noon. The boys were earnest

Harriet Martineau, *Letters from Ireland* (London: John Chapman, 1852), pp. 65–72.

185

and eager and conscientious about their engagement. They were paid by the piece, and they worked well. Some little fellows, who were so small that they had to be lifted up to take their wages, earned 5s. a week. They grew fat upon their wheaten food, and their families were able to live on their earnings; and if the Company did not gain, they did not lose. But it must have been a piteous sight to see households supported by their children and grannies, instead of by the strong arm of him who stood between. The women were at work at the same time. The women of Ireland so learned to work then that it will be very long indeed before they get a holiday, or find their natural place as housewives.

We do not say recover their place as housewives; for there is abundance of evidence that they have not sunk from that position, but rather risen from a lower one than they now fill. Some years ago, the great authority on Irish peasant life was Mrs. Leadbeater, whose 'Cottage Dialogues' was the most popular of Irish books till O'Connell's power rose to its height. In the suspicion and hatred which he excited towards the landlords, and the aristocracy generally, works like Mrs. Leadbeater's, which proceed on the supposition of a sort of feudal relation between the aristocracy and the peasantry, went out of favour, and have been little heard of since. Elderly people have them on their shelves however, and we know, through them, what was the life of the Irish peasant woman in the early part of the century. We know how, too often, the family lived in a mud hovel, without a chimney, all grovelling on the same straw at night, and perhaps with the pig among them; and at meals tearing their food with their fingers, and so forth. We know how the women were in the field or the bog, while the children were tumbling about in the manure at home. Those who have been to Stradbally, Queen's County, where Mrs. Leadbeater lived, are aware of the amelioration in cottage life produced by the efforts of her daughter-in-law, by the introduction of domestic industry in the place of field labour. The younger Mrs. Leadbeater taught fancy knitting to a bedridden woman and her daughters, many years ago, for their support. The example spread. Women came in from the reaping and binding,—girls staid at home from haymaking, and setting and digging potatoes. They kept their clothes dry, their manners womanly, and their cabins somewhat more decent. The quality of the work grew finer and finer, till now we see issuing from the cabins of Stradbally the famed "Spider Mitts," "Impalpable Mitts," "Cobweb Mitts," or whatever else English and American ladies like to call them. Upwards of two hundred women and girls are employed in this knitting; and people who knew Stradbally thirty years ago are so struck with the improvement in the appearance of the place, that they declare that the lowest order of cabins appears to them to be actually swept away.

Stradbally is only one of many such places. In every house of the gentry one now sees sofas, chairs, screens, and fancy tables spread with covers of crochet-work—all done by the hands of peasant women. In the south and west, where the famine was sorest, terrible distress was caused, we are told, by the sudden abolition of the domestic manufactures on which a former generation was largely dependent. The people used to spin and weave linen, flannel, and frieze, which were carried to market, as were the knitted stockings of Connaught. In the famine, the looms and spinning-wheels disappeared, with all other cabin property. It is very well that, when this had once happened, the same manufactures should not be restored, because they are of a kind surely destined to destruction before the manufacturing system. The knitting goes on; and it may long go on, so superior as knitted stockings are to woven ones in point of wear. And a variety of fine works are going on, in wild western districts, where the workwomen who produce such beautiful things never saw a shrub more than four feet high. In the south-west, lace of a really fine quality is made in cabins where formerly hard-handed women did the dirtiest work about the potato-patch and piggery. Of the "hand-sewing," some mention has been made before. We are assured at Belfast —and it only confirmed what we heard in Scotland—that no less than 400,000 women and girls are employed, chiefly by the Glasgow merchants, in "hand-sewing" in the Irish cabins. Their wages are low, individually; but it is a striking fact that these women and girls earn from £80,000 to £90,000 per week. It is a regular branch of industry, requiring the labour of many men at Glasgow and Belfast, to stamp the patterns on the muslin for the women to work, and, again, to bleach it when it comes in "green" (that is, dirty—so dirty!) from the hands of the needlewomen. They earn but 6d. a-day, poor things! in a general way, though at rare times—such as the Exhibition season—their pay amounts to 1s.; but it must be considered that their wear and tear of clothes is less than formerly, and that there must, one would think, be better order preserved at home.

So much for proper "women's work." But we observe women working almost everywhere. In the flax-fields there are more women than men pulling and steeping. In the potato-fields it is often the women who are saving the remnant of the crop. In the harvest-fields there are as many women as men reaping and binding. In the bog, it is the women who, at half wages, set up, and turn, and help to stack the peat,—not only for household use, but for sale, and in the service of the Irish Peat Company. In Belfast, the warehouses we saw were more than half peopled with women, engaged about the linens and muslins. And at the flax-works, near the city, not only were women employed in the spreading and drying, but in the rolling, roughing, and finishing, which had always till now been done by men. The men had struck for wages; and their work was given to girls, at 8d. per day.

Amidst facts like these, which accumulate as we go, one cannot but speculate on what is to be the end; or whether the men are to turn nurses and cooks, and to abide beside the hearth, while the women are earning the family bread. Perhaps the most consolatory way of viewing the case is that which we are quite willing to adopt,—that, practically, the condition of women, and therefore of their households, is rising. If there is something painful in seeing so undue a share of the burdens of life thrown upon the weaker sex; and if we cannot but remember that such a distribution of labour is an adopted symptom of barbarism; still, if the cabins *are* more decent, and the women more womanlike, it seems as if the process of change must be, on the whole, an advance. As to the way out of such a state of things, it seems as if it must be by that path to so many other benefits—agricultural improvement. The need of masculine labour, and the due regard of it, must both arise out of an improved cultivation of the soil; and it is not easy to see how they can arise in any other way.

CHARLOTTE BRONTË

On the last evening of my stay at Mr. Knight's a parcel arrived for me, enclosing a book, and a note which was examined as few notes ever are. The book was "Shirley;" and the note was from "Currer Bell." Here it is.

"Currer Bell offers a copy of "Shirley" to Miss Martineau's acceptance, in acknowledgment of the pleasure and profit ~~she~~ [sic] he has derived from her works. When C. B. first read "Deerbrook" he tasted a new and keen pleasure, and experienced a genuine benefit. In his mind, "Deerbrook" ranks with the writings that have really done him good, added to his stock of ideas, and rectified his views of life."

"November 7th, 1849"

We examined this note to make out whether it was written by a man or a woman. The hand was a cramped and nervous one, which might belong to any body who had written too much, or was in bad health, or who had been badly taught. The erased "she" seemed at first to settle the matter; but somebody suggested that the "she" might refer to me under a form of sentence which might easily have been changed in the penning. I had made up my mind, as I had repeatedly said, that a certain passage in "Jane Eyre," about sewing on brass rings, could have been written only by a woman or an upholsterer. I now addressed my reply externally to "Currer Bell, Esq.," and began it "Madam."—I had more reason for interest than even the deeply-interested public in knowing who wrote "Jane Eyre;" for, when it appeared, I was taxed with the authorship by more than one personal friend, and charged by others, and even by relatives, with knowing the author, and having sup-

---

Harriet Martineau, *Autobiography*, with Memorials by Maria Weston Chapman, 4th ed. (Boston: Houghton, Osgood and Co., 1879), vol. 2, pp. 21–25. Written in 1855.

plied some of the facts of the first volume from my own childhood. When I read it, I was convinced that it was by some
friend of my own, who had portions of my childish experience
in his or her mind. "Currer Bell" told me, long after, that she
had read with astonishment those parts of "Household Education" which relate my own experience. It was like meeting her
own fetch,—so precisely were the fears and miseries there described the same as her own, told or not told in "Jane Eyre."

A month after my receipt of "Shirley," I removed, on a
certain Saturday, from the house of a friend in Hyde Park
Street to that of a cousin in Westbourne Street, in time for a
dinner party. Meanwhile, a messenger was running about to
find me, and reached my cousin's when we were at dessert,
bringing the following note.

December 8th, 1849

"MY DEAR MADAM,—I happen to be staying in London for
a few days; and having just heard that you are likewise in
town, I could not help feeling a very strong wish to see you. If
you will permit me to call upon you, have the goodness to tell
me when to come. Should you prefer calling on me, my address is ... ...

"Do not think this request springs from mere curiosity.
I hope it has its origin in a better feeling. It would grieve me to
lose this chance of seeing one whose works have so often made
her the subject of my thoughts.

"I am, my dear Madam,
"Yours sincerely,
"CURRER BELL"

My host and hostess desired me to ask the favour of
C. B.'s company the next day, or any subsequent one. According to the old dissenting custom of early hours on Sundays,
we should have tea at six the next evening:—on any other day
dinner at a somewhat later hour. The servant was sent with
this invitation on Sunday morning, and brought back the following reply.

"MY DEAR MADAM,—I hope to have the pleasure of seeing

you at six o'clock today:—and I shall try now to be patient till six o'clock comes."

"I AM, &C., &C."

"That is a woman's note," we agreed. We were in a certain state of excitement all day, and especially towards evening. The footman would certainly announce this mysterious personage by his or her right name; and, as I could not hear the announcement, I charged my cousins to take care that I was duly informed of it. A little before six, there was a thundering rap:—the drawing-room door was thrown open, and in stalked a gentleman six feet high. It was not "Currer," but a philanthropist, who had an errand about a model lodging-house. Minute by minute I, for one, wished him away; and he did go before any body else came. Precisely as the time-piece struck six, a carriage stopped at the door; and after a minute of suspense, the footman announced "Miss Brogden;" whereupon, my cousin informed me that it was Miss Brontë; for we had heard the name before, among others, in the way of conjecture.—I thought her the smallest creature I had ever seen (except at a fair) and her eyes blazed, as it seemed to me. She glanced quickly round; and my trumpet pointing me out, she held out her hand frankly and pleasantly. I introduced her, of course, to the family; and then came a moment which I had not anticipated. When she was seated by me on the sofa, she cast up at me such a look,—so loving, so appealing,—that, in connection with her deep mourning dress, and the knowledge that she was the sole survivor of her family, I could with the utmost difficulty return her smile, or keep my composure. I should have been heartily glad to cry. We soon got on very well; and she appeared more at her ease that evening than I ever saw her afterwards, except when we were alone. My hostess was so considerate as to leave us together after tea, in case of C. B. desiring to have private conversation with me. She was glad of the opportunity to consult me about certain strictures of the reviewers which she did not understand, and had every desire to profit by. I did not approve the spirit of those strictures; but I thought them not entirely groundless. She besought me then, and repeatedly afterwards, to tell her,

at whatever cost of pain to herself, if I saw her afford any justification of them. I believed her, (and I now believe her to have
been) perfectly sincere: but when the time came (on the publication of "Villette," in regard to which she had expressly
claimed my promise a week before the book arrived) she could
not bear it. There was never any quarrel, or even misunder-
standing between us. She thanked me for my sincere fulfilment of my engagement; but she could not, she said, come "at
present" to see me, as she had promised: and the present was
alas! all that she had to dispose of. She is dead, before another
book of hers could (as I hoped it would) enable her to see what
I meant, and me to re-establish a fuller sympathy between us.
—Between the appearance of "Shirley" and that of "Villette,"
she came to me;—in December, 1850. Our intercourse then
confirmed my deep impression of her integrity, her noble con-
scientiousness about her vocation, and her consequent self-
reliance in the moral conduct of her life. I saw at the same time
tokens of a morbid condition of mind, in one or two directions;—much less than might have been expected, or would
have been seen in almost any one else under circumstances so
unfavourable to health of body and mind as those in which she
lived; and the one fault which I pointed out to her in "Villette"
was so clearly traceable to these unwholesome influences that
I would fain have been spared a task of criticism which could
hardly be of much use while the circumstances remained un-
changed. But she had exacted first the promise, and then the
performance in this particular instance; and I had no choice.
"I know," she wrote (January 21st, 1853) "that you will give
me your thoughts upon my book,—as frankly as if you spoke
to some near relative whose good you preferred to her grati-
fication. I wince under the pain of condemnation—like any
other weak structure of flesh and blood; but I love, I honour, I
kneel to Truth. Let her smite me on one cheek—good! the
tears may spring to the eyes; but courage! There is the other
side—hit again—right sharply!" This was the genuine spirit
of the woman. She might be weak for once; but her permanent
temper was one of humility, candour, integrity and conscien-
tiousness. She was not only unspoiled by her sudden and prodigious fame, but obviously unspoilable. She was somewhat
amused by her fame, but oftener annoyed;—at least, when
obliged to come out into the world to meet it, instead of its

reaching her in her secluded home, in the wilds of Yorkshire. There was little hope that she, the frail survivor of a whole family cut off in childhood or youth, could live to old age; but, now that she is gone, under the age of forty, the feeling is that society has sustained an unexpected, as well as irreparable loss.

MARGARET FULLER

In Margaret Fuller's Memoirs there is a letter which she declared she sent to me, after copying it into her common-place book. It is a condemnatory criticism of my 'Society in America;' and her condemnation is grounded on its being what she called 'an abolition book.' I remember having a letter from her; and one which I considered unworthy of her and of the occasion, from her regarding the anti-slavery subject as simply a low and disagreeable one, which should be left to unrefined persons to manage while others were occupied with higher things: but I do not think that the letter I received was the one which stands in her common-place book. I wish that she had mentioned it to me when my guest some years afterwards, or that my reply had appeared with her criticism. However, her letter, taken as it stands, shows exactly the difference between us. She who witnessed and aided the struggles of the oppressed in Italy must have become before her death better aware than when she wrote that letter that the struggle for the personal liberty of millions in her native republic ought to have had more of her sympathy, and none of the discouragement which she haughtily and complacently cast upon the cause. The difference between us was that while she was living and moving in an ideal world, talking in private and dis-

—

Harriet Martineau, *Autobiography*, with Memorials by Maria Weston Chapman, 4th ed. (Boston: Houghton, Osgood and Co., 1879), vol. 2, pp. 70–74. Written in 1855.

coursing in public about the most fanciful and shallow con-
ceits which the transcendentalists of Boston took for philosophy, she looked down upon persons who acted instead of
talking finely, and devoted their fortunes, their peace, their repose, and their very lives to the preservation of the principles
of the republic. While Margaret Fuller and her adult pupils sat
'gorgeously dressed,' talking about Mars and Venus, Plato and
Göthe, and fancying themselves the elect of the earth in intellect and refinement, the liberties of the republic were running
out as fast as they could go, at a breach which another sort
of elect persons were devoting themselves to repair: and my
complaint against the 'gorgeous' pedants was that they regarded their preservers as hewers of wood and drawers of
water, and their work as a less vital one than the pedantic ora-
tions which were spoiling a set of well-meaning women in a
pitiable way. All that is settled now. It was over years before
Margaret died. I mention it now to show, by an example already made public by Margaret herself, what the difference
was between me and her, and those who followed her lead.
This difference grew up mainly after my return from America. We were there intimate friends; and I am disposed to consider that period the best of her life, except the short one
which intervened between her finding her real self and her
death. She told me what danger she had been in from the
training her father had given her, and the encouragement to
pedantry and rudeness which she derived from the circumstances of her youth. She told me that she was at nineteen the
most intolerable girl that ever took a seat in a drawing-room.
Her admirable candour, the philosophical way in which she
took herself in hand, her genuine heart, her practical insight,
and, no doubt, the natural influence of her attachment to myself, endeared her to me, while her powers, and her confidence in the use of them, led me to expect great things from
her. We both hoped that she might go to Europe when I returned, with some friends of hers who would have been happy
to take her: but her father's death, and the family circumstances rendered her going out of the question. I introduced
her to the special care of R. Waldo Emerson and his wife: and
I remember what Emerson said in wise and gentle rebuke of
my lamentations for Margaret that she could not go to Europe,
as she was chafing to do, for purposes of self-improvement.

'Does Margaret Fuller,—supposing her to be what you say,—believe her progress to be dependent on whether she is here or there?' I accepted the lesson, and hoped the best. How it might have been with her if she had come to Europe in 1836, I have often speculated. As it was, her life in Boston was little short of destructive. I need but refer to the memoir of her. In the most pedantic age of society in her own country, and in its most pedantic city, she who was just beginning to rise out of pedantic habits of thought and speech relapsed most grievously. She was not only completely spoiled in conversation and manners: she made false estimates of the objects and interests of human life. She was not content with pursuing, and inducing others to pursue, a metaphysical idealism destructive of all genuine feeling and sound activity: she mocked at objects and efforts of a higher order than her own, and despised those who, like myself, could not adopt her scale of valuation. All this might have been spared, a world of mischief saved, and a world of good effected, if she had found her heart a dozen years sooner, and in America instead of Italy. It is the most grievous loss I have almost ever known in private history,—the deferring of Margaret Fuller's married life so long. The noble last period of her life is, happily, on record as well as the earlier. My friendship with her was in the interval between her first and second stages of pedantry and forwardness: and I saw her again under all the disadvantages of the confirmed bad manners and self-delusions which she brought from home. The ensuing period redeemed all; and I regard her American life as a reflexion, more useful than agreeable, of the prevalent social spirit of her time and place; and the Italian life as the true revelation of the tender and high-souled woman, who had till then been as curiously concealed from herself as from others.

If eccentricities like Margaret Fuller's, essentially sound as she was in heart and mind, could arise in American society, and not impair her influence or be a spectacle to the community, it will be inferred that eccentricity is probably rife in the United States.

FLORENCE NIGHTINGALE

For many years no such grief has been felt at the loss of any woman in this country as at this moment. England never before had such a woman to lose as Florence Nightingale. There may have been heroines as calm, wise, and devoted, there may have been nurses as skilful and as inexhaustible in perseverence and disinterestedness; but none has ever before held such a position as hers, or done such deeds.

Florence Nightingale had perhaps the highest lot ever fulfilled by woman, except women Sovereigns who have not merely reigned but ruled. She had the highest lot that the remedial function admits of. The loftier creative or institutive function is so rare, and so few human beings have as yet been adequate to it, that it is no wonder if there is no female exemplification of it in the history of the world. It is no small distinction to our time that it produced a woman who effected two great things: a mighty reform in the care of the sick and an opening for her sex into the region of serious business, in proportion to their ability to maintain a place in it.

This is all true; and it is very important truth; but it is not what can satisfy us at such a moment as this. We shall grieve too bitterly at such a loss to care for any estimate of the position held by her whom the nation mourns. We think of her today as the nurse and the dispenser of comfort and relief, and we care little for her greatness, while conscious that her gentle voice will never more rouse the sufferer to courage, nor her skilful hand administer ease.

THE LADY WITH THE LAMP

We think of her dressing wounds, bringing wine and food, carrying her lamp through miles of sick soldiers in the middle of the night, noting every face and answering the appeal of

—

"Earl Spencer and Miss Florence Nightingale," *Daily News* (London), August 15, 1910, pp. 1–2.

every eye as she passed. We think of her spending precious hours in selecting books to please the men's individual wish or want, and stocking her coffee-house with luxuries and innocent pleasures to draw the soldiers away from poisonous drinks and mischief. We think now of the poor fellow who said that he looked for her coming in hospital, for he could at least kiss her shadow on his pillow as she passed.

We think to-day of the little Russian prisoner, the poor boy who could not speak or be spoken to till she had taken him in and had him taught and made useful; and how he answered when at length he could understand a question. When asked if he knew where he would go when he was dead, he confidently said: "I shall go to Miss Nightingale."

She is gone from us now; and there may be thousands older and less simple than that forlorn child who may be saying in their hearts, though they would not utter it so artlessly, that they hope, when they die, they shall go to her who was so much to them here.

In early childhood Florence Nightingale heard a good deal of a different class of sufferings from that to which she devoted herself at last. She was the granddaughter of William Smith, the well-known member for Norwich, who for a long course of years sustained the interests of the Dissenters in Parliament, and was a prominent member of the anti-slavery party there. She was not near enough to the daily life of the abolition clique to incur the danger expressed in the maxim that the children of philanthropists are usually heartless; and the spectacle of eminent men taking a world of trouble to get slavery abolished, as they had already put an end to the legal slave trade, may, naturally, have disposed the grandchildren of the abolitionists to consider, at least, the case of any suffering class.

It was William Smith's daughter Frances who married Mr. Nightingale—born Shore, of the Yorkshire family of Shores, and assuming the name of Nightingale, with the estates which made him a wealthy man. The marriage was an early one, and the young people went abroad, to spend two or three years—a proceeding less common then than it is now. Their first child (afterwards Lady Verney) was born at Naples, and was called Parthenope. The next, and only other, was born on May 15th, 1820, at Florence, and named accordingly.

EARLY EDUCATION

The two little girls had every educational advantage that could be afforded to them by their father's scholarship, by the literary tastes of the whole large and cultivated family connection, and by the most earnest solicitude of both parents.

One fortunate circumstance was the choice of a governess at an important period of the children's lives. Miss Christie, afterwards Mrs. Collman, was a woman of rare character and influence, and her discipline, and the affection she inspired, were hallowed only too soon by her death, a few months after her marriage. She succeeded completely in obviating the danger which besets such cases—of children growing up with the knowledge that grown people are living for them, shaping their lives by children's conditions.

The sisters grew up unspoiled, and thoroughly exercised in the best parts of middle-class education, while living in an atmosphere of accomplishment, such as belongs to a station and a family connection like theirs. Their grandmother refused a peerage; their father refused a peerage; yet, as we have all seen, Florence had as familiar an acquaintance with the world's daily work as any farmer's or shopkeeper's daughter. She was never quite happy, in fact, till she had escaped from the region of factitious interests and superficial pursuits and devoted herself to stern, practical toil, appropriated to a benevolent end.

All around her were fond of art, and practised it to considerable purpose; but Florence's heart was never in it. She knew all Italy and much of France, Germany and Switzerland, and just before her final adoption of her special career she went with her friends, the Bracebridges, up the Nile and to their estate near Athens. She was a travelled lady, with the best accomplishments of travel, a great provision of languages, and the enlightenment and liberality which follow upon a wide observation of mankind. But art could never have been her life's pursuit, nor any considerable solace.

Nor was there enough in the benevolence of country gentry, bountiful as they were, in the shape of schools and other care of the poor around her father's estates of Lea Hurst, in Derbyshire, and Embley, in Hampshire. As little girls Miss Christie's pupils had spent a winter with her in a plain Norfolk farmhouse where a friend of hers lived and moved among the poor. At such places they left luxury behind them and learned much of actual life, and they put it in practice round their various homes. But still Florence's nature craved more.

HER FIRST "CASE"

The earliest incident that her family can recall, revealing her peculiar tendencies, occurred in childhood, when some boy cousins were at play, and their sport ended in a dreadful cut on the hand of one of them. The others turned away from the sight, but Florence bound up the hand. She found that, as she said, she "liked it"; and the simplicity of her character secured the "liking" from being extinguished, or even hidden, through false shame or fear of singularity.

Her mind being once revealed to herself, her career followed as of course—not as foreseen by her or others, but because she had the virtue to commit herself to her own forces, and her family the yet greater virtue not to interfere. It was no small sacrifice to some of them, but they made it nobly, not merely submitting to it, but helping Florence to go forth to her work when their judgment and inclination would have alike urged her to remain at home. They duly respected her decisions in regard to her personal duties, and for this all the world will for ever respect them.

She studied in various schools of charitable ministration —not merely visiting the inmates for the sake of those inmates of the hour, as many before her have visited prisons and workhouses and hospitals; but undertaking study and undergoing training such as few physicians have gone through, and as only Sisters of Charity ever put themselves in the way of. She lived some time in the Kaiserwerth institution on the Rhine, practising the hardest duties of the nurse.

The first step which fixed the attention of the world was her undertaking the management of the sanatorium for sick ladies in Harley-street. It is instructive, though humiliating, to recall the hubbub that arose in London society when Florence Nightingale became matron of that institution. It was related at the time by persons who appreciated the act that if she had forged a bill, or eloped, or betted her father's fortune away at Newmarket, she could not have provoked a more virulent hue and cry than she did by settling herself to a useful work in a quiet way, in mature age, and without either seeking or deprecating the world's opinion. Her object was to retrieve the institution, which was in debt and disorder. She stipulated for power, and she achieved the work. She set about it like an accountant; looked into things like a housekeeper; organized the establishment like a born administrator, as she was; nursed the inmates like a Sister of Charity; and cheered the sufferers by the indescribable graces of the thoroughly developed and high-bred woman.

At one time there was not one inmate who could possibly recover. "How can she bear it?" asked some. She knew the fact as well as any physician who came to the house, but she had something else to think of than her own feelings, and she had cheerfulness enough for them all.

UNGENEROUS OPPOSITION

The next call made upon her was the well-known appeal of Mr. Sidney Herbert in that letter which was treacherously stolen and made public by an officious person who subjected the friends to ungenerous criticism, and to imputations of vanity and self-seeking, purely absurd to all who had any knowledge whatever of Florence and her friends. All that matters little now; but it should be simply recorded, because no picture of her career can be complete which omits the oppositions she had to encounter.

From the formalists at home who were shocked at her handling keys and keeping accounts to the jealous and quizzing doctors abroad who would have suppressed her altogether, and the vulgar among the nurses who whispered that she ate the jams and jellies in a corner which were meant for the sick, she had all the hostility to encounter which the great may always expect from those who are too small to apprehend their minds and ways.

She had a strong will and a clear purpose in every act of her life, and she was not troubled with a too acute self-consciousness, nor with any anxiety about the popular judgment on her course. To her it was "a small thing to be judged by man's judgment" while the sick were suffering before her eyes; and nothing but her freedom and egotism could have left her mind clear and open for the study how to extend the benefits of good nursing to the greatest number. So she went on her own way, and the critics and maligners were left far behind, where they never found any considerable number to listen to them.

In October, 1854, Florence Nightingale set out for the seat of war in the East, accompanied by her friends, Mr. and Mrs. Bracebridge, and leading a company of thirty-seven nurses. We all remember how they were received in France, from the landing, when the Boulogne fish women insisted on carrying their luggage, and the innkeeper on feasting them without pay, to the generous farewells at Marseilles. We remember, only too painfully, the difficulties to be got over at Scutari, and the horrors to be witnessed and the delays to be endured. The two pictures —of Scutari hospital before the reforms, and the same place afterwards—were burnt in upon the brain of the passing generation; and Florence Nightingale was throughout the prominent figure.

A WOMAN OF STRONG WILL

Before she was believed in on the spot, we see her using her strong will—pointing to a locked door, and ordering, on her own responsibility, that it should be broken open, to get at the bedding within. We see her obtaining a gift of five refused "cases" after a battle—soldiers hopelessly wounded, on whom it would be wrong to spend the surgeon's time—feeding them by spoonfuls all night, so that they were in a condition next day to be operated upon, and were saved. We see her silent under aggressive inquiries into her religious opinions, obedient to medical orders, and constraining others to the same obedience, and gradually obtaining the ascendency she deserved, till not only were the hospitals in a state of unhoped-for order and efficiency, but the medical and military officers were almost as vehement in their admiration of her as her patients.

We see again the rising up of the kitchen, "Miss Nightingale's kitchen," which was to save more lives than any amount of medicine and surgery could do without it; and some of us foresaw at the moment a reform of soldiers' food, and therein of their health and morals, throughout the Empire, and through coming generations, beginning from the saving of life at Scutari—from the punctuality and nourishing and palatable quality of the meals sent out from that kitchen. Success carried all before it; in a short time all good people were helping; and before the close of the war the British soldiery in the East were in a condition of health and vigour excelling that of any class of men at home.

Many of the wisest of men and women have said that talk about the powers and position of women is nearly useless, because all human beings take rank, in the long run, according to their capability. But it is true, and will remain true, that what women are able to do they will do, with or without leave obtained from men. Florence Nightingale encountered opposition—from her own sex as much as the other; and she achieved, as the most natural thing in the world, and without the smallest sacrifice of her womanly quality, what would beforehand have been declared a deed for a future age.

She was no declaimer, but a housewifely woman; she talked little, and did great things. When other women see that there are things for them to do, and train themselves to the work, they will get it done easily enough. There can never be a more unthought-of and marvellous career before any working woman than Florence Nightingale has achieved; and her success has opened a way to all others easier than anyone had prepared for her.

Though dozens of portraits were put forth as hers during the Crimean War which were spurious, or were wholly unlike, her general appearance was well known—the tall, slender figure, the intelligent, agreeable countenance, and the remarkable mixture of reserve and simplicity in her expression and manner, with the occasional sparkle of fun on the one hand and the general gravity, never degenerating into sentimentality, on the other.

She was the most quiet and natural of all ladylike women; presenting no points for special observation, but good sense and cultivation as to mind, and correctness in demeanour and manners. One would fain linger on these particulars; for this is the only way now left to retaining their very traces. She is gone, and we can only dwell on what has been.

VI

ON ECONOMIC, SOCIAL, AND POLITICAL ISSUES

The question has been asked, from time to time, in more countries than one, how obedience to the laws can be required of women, when no woman has, either actually or virtually, given any assent to any law.

—*Harriet Martineau*
SOCIETY IN AMERICA

Harriet Martineau c. 1834
From the portrait by Sir R. Evans
National Portrait Gallery, London

Just as the social position of women changed over her lifetime, so Martineau herself changed from writing about women as incidental to some other purpose to writing deliberately and definitely on women's behalf. This section tries to indicate something of that progression. It opens with the ending pages of the birth control tale from the *Illustrations of Political Economy*, chosen to represent her early work in which the objective was to promote the ideas of political economy and the benefit to women was only implicit. Later pieces in this section are more consciously in aid of feminist causes.

The *Illustrations of Political Economy*, which established Martineau's fame as a writer in England, used fiction as a means of popular instruction. The tales were published monthly during 1832–1833, and the first one was an immediate success. Cabinet ministers read them, common people read them, royalty at home and abroad read them, and Martineau became the literary rage of London. Because of them, crowned heads both adored and abhorred her (the czar banned her from ever entering Russia). Because we no longer find them readable as economics, morality, or fiction, it is hard for us to understand the extent of their popularity when they were published.

In the tale "Weal and Woe in Garveloch" Martineau set out to illustrate the economic principle of population control. She was promoting simple Malthusian concepts: that resources would fall below the level necessary to maintain subsistence in an area experiencing a marked increase of workers; thus, limits on population should be voluntarily adhered to. The means of birth control advocated—"the mild preventive check"—were late marriage and sexual abstinence.

Martineau was always matter-of-fact about her writing, and one imagines her purposefully sitting down to begin her rapid composition without taking a second thought, but this tale caused her much anxiety. In the short piece from her *Autobiography* reprinted here after the tale she tells of the perspiration streaming down her face as she wrote about the controversial topic.

The tale is set on Garveloch, an island off Scotland where fishing brings prosperity. Ella and Fergus live there happily with their ten children until the Fishing Company comes, bringing many more workers to the island and squeezing its resources. One son of Ella of Garveloch, Ronald, loves the widow Katie, who makes fishing nets; but though Ronald is flourishing economically and is a handsome and virile man, he chooses not to marry Katie and thus not to create more people and thereby harm society. Ella of Garveloch interprets the moral of the story for Katie. She and Fergus had believed that there would be plenty for their ten children, but there is not. Ronald is wise to forgo having children; it is not that he does not love Katie, but that he does not want to see children in need and knows that people must consider the needs of society before marrying.

Although there was nothing intentionally feminist about this story—it was the economic lesson Martineau was concerned with—to the feminist analyst today the tale can be seen as feminist both because of its recognition of the importance of birth control to women's freedom and because, in the choice of the character Ella as the intelligent articulator of the lesson, of its recognition of women's intelligence. Both points are important for contemporary feminism: the particular need of women for birth control in order to achieve social and biological liberty from a norm of childbearing, and the need for respect for women as wise teachers with or without regard to prevailing male or social opinion. The excerpt from the tale includes the concluding portrait of Katie and her family, after the vital decisions have been made, and the summary of principles illustrated by the tale.

After the passage from the *Autobiography* come two newspaper editorials Martineau had written two years earlier in support of an overt feminist campaign of the 1850s, the attempt to get a Married Women's Property Bill through Parliament. This was compromised, some would say subverted, by a related and successful, though more conservative, effort to make divorce more accessible for women. What finally passed was a modified Divorce and Matrimonial Causes Act in 1857.[1]

In editorials for the *Daily News* Martineau argued tren-

---

[1] See Constance Rover, *Love, Morals and the Feminists* (London: Routledge and Kegan Paul), pp. 71–85. See also Margaret K. Woodhouse, "The Marriage and Divorce Bill of 1857," *American Journal of Legal History* 3 (1959): 260–275.

chantly on the need to change the laws governing divorce. She made a very clearheaded statement about the "confusion among us as to what marriage is," citing the mix of ecclesiastical, parliamentary, and genealogical authority held over marriage. The burden, almost universally, however, was woman's. She pointed out that "it is assumed as a matter of course in our Legislature that the sin of conjugal infidelity is immeasurably greater in the wife than the husband; and a murmur of applause follows when a legislator asks whether any father would not infinitely rather see his son fall into vice than his daughter; whereas, the farmer or tradesman, reading the debate next day, mutters that the peer or the gentleman forgets that for the son's sin somebody's daughter must fall."[2]

Further, Martineau argued that the Commission on the Law of Divorce of 1853 had brought in a report on divorce favorable to the husbands, who were the lawmakers, the wives being unrepresented. She provided several illustrations of injured wives who had no recourse to the law or to divorce, such as the case of a wife whose earnings supported an adulterous husband who took all her earnings and threatened to take her whole property. She took issue with another point of the report suggesting that divorce should only be allowed on grounds of adultery. Surely, this should be broadened, for "conjugal hatred is even more terrible to the poor than to the rich."

Her position was that divorce should be allowed in the event of willful desertion, conjugal infidelity, and gross cruelty, that divorce should be taken into the realm of common law (and thus out of the jurisdiction of Parliament and the Church), and that the new divorce courts should admit pauper suits (giving poor women equal access to divorce).

She reiterated her themes in subsequent editorials, hammering home with additional illustrations the need of women, and especially poor women, for access to divorce. She left nothing to the imagination in her accounts of brutality to women and sided with the women determinedly. In one of the editorials included here, she appealed to the Catholic clergy, for she said many of the men guilty of brutality to wives were

[2] More from this editorial appears as the third selection in this section.

Irish and Catholic. Since the Catholics think marriage is indissoluble, the parish priests should take responsibility for inducing better conduct from the men for whom they had performed the sacrament of marriage.

The fifth selection deals with women's work and economic security. During the 1850s and 1860s, Martineau wrote over a dozen leaders in the *Daily News* on women's work. Although at times she singled out the reforming work of an individual such as Florence Nightingale (army nursing), Sarah Pellatt (temperance in California), or Catherine Sinclair ("female beneficense"), more often she wrote about occupational opportunity for women in general, standards of health for women at work, and adequate pay.[3] In both *Once a Week* and the *Daily News*, she wrote strong condemnations of the generally appalling requirements and unhealthy environment of women's work, and the low pay in the occupational groups in which the largest numbers of employed women were found: needlewomen, maids of all work, governesses, and women in agriculture.[4] From Ireland in 1852, she wrote that, though women in Irish agricultural labor were underpaid, as women universally were in relation to men, it was the Irish women workers who maintained the agricultural economy.[5] She also wrote powerful statements urging women to enter the new profession of nursing. Until Florence Nightingale reformed nursing practice and nursing education, nursing was considered a disreputable job, often carried out in ignorance with

---

[3] Leader 1 beginning "Among the exhilerating," *Daily News* (London), June 2, 1855, p. 4; Leader 2 beginning "The Sierra Nevada," ibid., November 22, 1855, p. 4; Leader 2 beginning "The death," ibid., August 16, 1864, p. 4; Leader 3 beginning "For a good," ibid., November 17, 1859, p. 4; Leader 3 beginning "As soon as," ibid., November 23, 1859, p. 4; Leader 3 beginning "The surgery," ibid., November 25, 1859, p. 4; Leader 3 beginning "We have taken," ibid., November 2, 1860, p. 4.

[4] Leader 3 beginning "The Christmas," *Daily News* (London), January 13, 1857, p. 4; and Harriet Martineau, "The Needlewoman," *Health, Husbandry and Handicraft*, a book reprinting articles first published in *Once a Week* (London: Bradbury and Evans, 1861), pp. 226–237; Martineau, "The Maid of All Work," ibid., pp. 158–165; Martineau, "The Governess," ibid., pp. 188–201; Leader 2 beginning, "Two and twenty," *Daily News* (London), May 20, 1865, p. 4.

[5] Most of this letter is reprinted as the second selection in Section V.

hazard to both nurse and patient. Martineau publicized the need for respectable middle-class students to attend Nightingale's St. Thomas' Hospital Nursing School.[6] Martineau also became an advocate of women physicians, the female practice of medicine having been brought to London from the United States by Elizabeth Blackwell. Martineau made the still valid point that many women would prefer to be treated by a woman doctor.[7]

Martineau paid attention to women in factories, though her account in 1844 of the beauties of the lives of Lowell "factory girls" in America was a bit unrealistically glowing. Still, she instigated the publication in England of a volume of creative literature by those factory operatives, *Mind amongst the Spindles*. The volume, to which Martineau wrote a letter of introduction, was derived from *The Lowell Offering*.[8]

She also paid special attention to women in what she called "the criminal class." She recognized that women who participated in criminal actions often did so in concert with men and were frequently subjects of sexual exploitation, and she recommended rehabilitation by education and worthwhile work for both women and men released from prison.[9]

The most comprehensive summation of her views on women's work is contained in the article entitled "Female Industry," published in the *Edinburgh Review* in 1859.[10] Lee Holcombe in *Victorian Ladies at Work* says this article was "widely read and very influential" and "was frequently credited with having first shocked the public into an awareness of the problem of 'redundant women,' that is, the unmarried."[11] Martineau began the article: "Wearied as some of us are with the incessant repetition of the dreary stories of spirit-broken governesses and starving needlewomen, we rarely obtain a

---

[6] Martineau, "Women's Battle-field-Nurses," *Health, Husbandry and Handicraft*, pp. 82–98.

[7] Leader 3 beginning "It is quite true," *Daily News* (London), March 25, 1859, p. 4.

[8] Martineau's letter appears as the fourth selection in Section IV.

[9] "Life in the Criminal Class," *Edinburgh Review* 122 (October 1865): 337–371.

[10] See note 19, Introduction.

[11] Lee Holcombe, *Victorian Ladies at Work* (Newton Abbot, Devon: David and Charles, 1973), p. 10.

glimpse of the full breadth of the area of female labour in Great Britain."

Combined with her intention of showing the whole economic and social spectrum of women's work in "Female Industry" is the thesis she presented in another context, writing in support of the Married Women's Property Bill, that "in the old days, men worked as money getters, women as governors of households. Leaving aside the question of the Rights of Woman, [for] nineteen-twentieths of women from the Queen . . . down to the maid of all work the rule for English women in our time is—work; . . . Thus, property and responsibility should not be vested in a male head of household."[12]

Martineau showed that women *were* working at a vast array of occupations. Drawing on the census of 1851, she provided statistics and revealing illustrations of women at work in a great many jobs—making cheese and driving ploughs, separating out ore in the mines, serving middle-class families as cooks or housekeepers or maids of all work, overseeing households, teaching as governesses, bookkeeping, selling, and even manufacturing in shops with their husbands or fathers. The detail of her picture is dramatically colorful as well as rationally documented. She begins "Female Industry" with a succinct history of the rise of the middle class and with it the need for people "to earn their bread." This had been recognized for men, she said, but no less so should it be for women.

Twice in the *Daily News* in 1856, Martineau wrote on the themes of "the fashionable follies of women" and "female dress and despotism."[13] A longer piece in *Once a Week*, reprinted here, she titled "Dress and Its Victims." In each of these articles she pointed out how the extravagance of women's fashions exhausts, blinds, drives to insanity, and sometimes kills the needlewomen who make them. She argued against the current fashions on grounds of economy, morality, nationalism, and the health of the women who wore the clothing. Dresses made with nineteen to twenty yards of fabric were frivolous and expensive. They were dictated by foreign, that

[12] Leader 3 beginning "At the annual, *Daily News* (London), February 29, 1856, p. 4.

[13] Leader 2 beginning "In a secluded," *Daily News* (London), June 17, 1856, p. 4; Leader 3 beginning "When we read," ibid., July 17, 1856, p. 4.

is, French, despots of fashion and were economically unsound as well as silly. The clothes were cumbersome, deforming, and ugly; but the women adopted them because they came from Paris.

In the *Once a Week* piece, she singled out several characteristic female garments for criticism. The hoop skirt she particularly ridiculed as detrimental to health. Hats, too, and shoes should be sensible and English, not flimsy and French. Hats should shelter the eyes and the head from sun and wind. "A chimney-pot hat with a tall upright plume may possibly suit a volunteer rifle corps or a regiment of Amazons rehearsing for the opera, but it is not very English in taste." Similarly, the popular gutta-percha and thin patent leather shoes were a menace to health in not keeping the feet dry and warm, and their designs threw the body into an unnatural posture. The opposite peril of being too warm and confined was brought on by wearing the fashionable boa around one's neck. (It is amusing to discover that the younger Martineau was not immune to such fashionable follies as we can see from the portrait at the beginning of this section.)

Worst of all, female dress did not fit the female form naturally. Excessive, heavy material, tight-lacing corsets, and cumbersome crinoline petticoats were all harmful to female vigor and well-being. In 1859, Martineau proposed criteria for good dress that were contrary to the petticoats, stays, and extravagance of material in vogue at the time.

Unlike her writing on women's work in the same year, Martineau's proposal for dress reform (like the Bloomer clothes she advocated from the United States) failed to catch on with the general public in England, and a full-scale dress reform did not come about. Indeed, the English did not pay nearly the attention to dress reform as a women's issue that the Americans did. This is another of the several areas in which Martineau's thought in general and feminism in particular were closely linked with the United States.

WEAL AND WOE
IN GARVELOCH

Nobody had time to lose this season in the island, but those who were willing to run the risk of future scarcity. Labour was in great request, and, of course, well paid. Angus found ample employment for his crane, and received very good interest for the capital laid out upon it. His younger sons worked it with as much zeal as Kenneth had shown in its construction; but their father, proud as he was of them, thought in his inmost heart that no other of his flourishing tribe equalled the eldest, or could make up for his loss; and the haunting dream of the night, the favourite vision of the day, was of Kenneth's return to leave his native land no more. This was Angus's meditation while plying the oar, and this his theme in his own chimney corner. It was much to hear of Kenneth's honour and welfare, but while no hope of peace came with the tidings, they were not perfectly satisfying.

The only person to whom the improvement in the times brought any trouble was the widow Cuthbert. Her former lovers—not Ronald, but those who had broken off acquaintance with her when her young family seemed a dead weight in the scale against her own charms—now returned, and were more earnest than ever in their suit. Katie had discretion enough to be aware that the only respect in which she had become a more desirable match than before was in the growth of her boys, whose labour might soon be a little fortune to her, if she chose to employ it. She was therefore far from being flattered at becoming so much in request, and honoured and valued the disinterested friendship of Ronald more than ever.

The present time, even with the drawback of Kenneth's absence, was the happiest period of Ronald's life. He made his little home at the station sociable and comfortable, by gath-

—

Harriet Martineau, *Illustrations of Political Economy* (London: Charles Fox, 1832), no. 6, pp. 138–140.

ering his nephews and nieces about him; and his visits to Garveloch became more frequent and more welcome continually when his prosperous business allowed him leisure for the trip. Fergus, weighed down with care, had grown old before his time, and to Ronald's assistance it was owing that his family preserved their respectability till the lads were able to take on themselves a part of the charge which had been too heavy for their father.

Ella was the last of the family to show the marks of change. Her mind and heart were as remarkable for their freshness in age as they had been for their dignity in youth. Inured to early exertion and hardship, she was equal to all calls upon her energies of body and spirit. She was still seen, as occasion required, among the rocks, or on the sea, or administering her affairs at home. She was never known to plead infirmity, or to need forbearance, or to disappoint expectation. She had all she wanted in her husband's devotion to her and to his home, and she distributed benefits untold from the rich treasury of her warm affections. She had, from childhood, filled a station of authority, and had never abused her power, but made it the means of living for others. Her power increased with every year of her life, and with it grew her scrupulous watchfulness over its exercise, till the same open heart, penetrating eye, and ready hand, which had once made her the sufficient dependence of her orphan brothers, gave her an extensive influence over the weal and woe of Garveloch.

SUMMARY OF PRINCIPLES ILLUSTRATED
IN THIS VOLUME

The increase of population is necessarily limited by the means of subsistence.

Since successive portions of capital yield a less and less return, and the human species produce at a constantly accelerated rate, there is a perpetual tendency in population to press upon the means of subsistence.

The ultimate checks by which population is kept down to the level of the means of subsistence are vice and misery.

Since the ends of life are virtue and happiness, these checks ought to be superseded by the milder methods which exist within man's reach.

These evils may be delayed by promoting the increase of capital, and superseded by restraining the increase of population.

Towards the one object, a part of society may do a little: towards the other, all may do much.

By rendering property secure, expenditure frugal, and production easy, society may promote the growth of capital.

By bringing no more children into the world than there is a subsistence provided for, society may preserve itself from the miseries of want. In other words, the timely use of the mild preventive check may avert the horrors of any positive check.

The preventive check becomes more, and the positive checks less powerful, as society advances.

The positive checks, having performed their office in stimulating the human faculties and originating social institutions, must be wholly superseded by the preventive check before society can attain its ultimate aim—the greatest happiness of the greatest number.

ON THE POPULATION TALE

When the course of my exposition brought me to the Population subject, I, with my youthful and provincial mode of thought and feeling,—brought up too amidst the prudery which is found in its great force in our middle class,—could not but be sensible that I risked much in writing and publishing on a subject which was not universally treated in the pure, benevolent, and scientific spirit of Malthus himself. I felt that the subject was one of science, and therefore perfectly easy to

---

Harriet Martineau, *Autobiography*, with Memorials by Maria Weston Chapman, 4th ed. (Boston: Houghton, Osgood and Co., 1879), vol. 1, pp. 200–201. Written in 1855.

treat in itself; but I was aware that some evil associations had gathered about it,—though I did not know what they were. While writing 'Weal and Woe in Garveloch,' the perspiration many a time streamed down my face, though I knew there was not a line in it which might not be read aloud in any family. The misery arose from my seeing how the simplest statements and reasonings might and probably would be perverted. I said nothing to any body; and, when the number was finished, I read it aloud to my mother and aunt. If there had been any opening whatever for doubt or dread, I was sure that these two ladies would have given me abundant warning and exhortation,—both from their very keen sense of propriety and their anxious affection for me. But they were as complacent and easy as they had been interested and attentive. I saw that all ought to be safe. But it was evidently very doubtful whether all would be safe. A few words in a letter from Mr. Fox put me on my guard. In the course of some remarks on the sequence of my topics, he wrote, 'As for the Population question, let no one interfere with you. Go straight through it, *or you'll catch it.*' I did go straight through it; and happily I had nearly done when a letter arrived from a literary woman, who had the impertinence to write to me now that I was growing famous, after having scarcely noticed me before, and (of all subjects) on this, though she tried to make her letter decent by putting in a few little matters besides. I will call her Mrs. Z. as I have no desire to point out to notice one for whom I never had any respect or regard. She expressed, on the part of herself and others, an anxious desire to know how I should deal with the Population question; said that they did not know what to wish about my treating or omitting it;—desiring it for the sake of society, but dreading it for me; and she finished by informing me that a Member of Parliament, who was a perfect stranger to me, had assured her that I already felt my difficulty; and that he and she awaited my decision with anxiety. Without seeing at the moment the whole drift of this letter, I was abundantly disgusted by it, and fully sensible of the importance of its being answered immediately, and in a way which should admit of no mistake. I knew my reply was wanted for show; and I sent one by return of post which was shown to some purpose. It stopped speculation in one dangerous quarter. I showed my letter to my mother and brother;

and they emphatically approved it, though it was rather sharp. They thought, as I did, that some sharpness was well directed towards a lady who professed to have talked over difficulties of this nature, on my behalf, with an unknown Member of Parliament by her own fireside.

ON THE MARRIED WOMEN'S PROPERTY BILL

London, Friday, March 25 [1853]

The Commissioners appointed to inquire into the Law of Divorce have issued their Report, and it is understood that this Report is to be the ground of legislation during the present session. The existence of the Commission and the Report is evidence enough that no time should be lost, and that Government and the Legislature are of that opinion; for the difficulties of the case are so many, and so extremely serious, that everybody has been willing to put off to the last possible moment all action upon the subject. The necessity for some sort of action, amending the present state of the law, has been admitted, almost universally, since 1839, when a small instalment of relief to certain sufferers under unhappy marriages [was] granted in the passage of the Infants' . . . Custody Bill. This bill passed by large majorities in the Commons in 1838, was then thrown out in the Lords, when Lord BROUGHAM gave as his reason for opposing it the thorough badness of the marriage laws of this country, which were so cruel and indefensible that, if any part was touched, the whole mass must come down. Such a reason for keeping things as they were was a clear prophecy of change. The passage of the Infants' Custody Bill the next year began it; and during the succeeding years, opinion in favour of great changes in the Law of Divorce has strengthened into an irresistible demand, and the

---

Daily News (London), March 25, 1853, p. 4.

first result is the report before us. The merest glance at the subject, whether in the records of the House of Lords, or in every man's observation of society, or in the pages of this report, shows that the evils of our present system must be intolerable indeed to have driven us into the thicket of difficulties that we must struggle through to attain a better state. . . . One of the Commissioners appends to the report before us his dissent from its chief recommendation, and the grounds of it. On scriptural, as well as other grounds, he concludes that not only should marriage remain, as now, indissoluble under the law of England, but that divorce should no longer be attainable from the Legislature in any case. Some people think that Scripture wants divorce in case of adultery, and would have it for that cause alone, as now, but by some more attainable and impartial method than a special law passed for each case. Others, again, seeing that cruelty is admitted as a second cause for legal separation, do not see why it should not procure the more complete relief of divorce; and these are regarding, not the theological, but the moral view of the subject. This moral view occasions and justifies a great variety of opinion as to the limits of divorce: but then comes in the political view, and considerations of genealogy intervene, to alter again the whole character of the argument. Nothing, indeed, is so fatal to the moral view as the political, in this particular matter. It is from this regard to genealogical considerations ruling the descent of property that proceeds that extraordinary morality about the comparative guilt of the two parties to a marriage, in case of infidelity, which was uttered in the House of Lords twenty years ago, and has been presented occasionally since, and which strikes with amazement the lower orders in this country, and all orders in some other countries. It is assumed as a matter of course in our Legislature that the sin of conjugal infidelity is immeasurably greater in the wife than the husband; and a murmur of applause follows when a legislator asks whether any father would not infinitely rather see his son fall into vice than his daughter; whereas, the farmer or tradesman, reading the debate next day, mutters that the peer or the gentleman forgets that for the son's sin somebody's daughter must fall. This confusion of religious, moral and political considerations would be enough to make the question difficult to deal with. But there are other embarrassments at the very outset.

The common law of England "deems so highly, and with such mysterious reverence, of the nuptial tie," that it has not always maintained that clearness and consistency which would have saved much toil in past times, and afforded some welcome guidance now. The doctrine of indissolubility was sometimes given up, and then resumed, among the fluctuations of opinion which followed the Reformation; so that opposite judgments were given in the course of the reign of ELIZABETH; and any effect on opinion and moral views that might have been produced since by marriage being indissoluble by the laws of England, has been broken up by the Parliamentary faculty of granting divorce. Then again, there is the different state of the law in Scotland compelling the observation that either the English law must be very cruel, or the Scotch very profligate. In Scotland, there were ninety-five cases in the five years from 1836 to 1841, while in England there have been 110 from the first day of this century till now. Of the ninety-five Scotch divorces, one-third were at the suit of the wife; whereas in England the wife cannot seek a divorce at all, except in cases of unnatural atrocity; so that only four successful suits are on record. In Scotland, the parties in the ninety-five cases were almost all of the labouring classes, the expense being from 15£. to 30£., whereas in England divorce is wholly out of the reach of all but the rich—the expense rising from 500£. to several thousands. Wide limits these for the right and wrong to lie between! Again, there is the consideration that one of the two parties in the case is wholly unrepresented, and that the other party is the law maker. It is not merely that only one party can plead in a case of opposing interests; but that the pleading party decides as well as argues the case. It has hitherto been decided by husbands that husbands alone shall be able to obtain the relief; and it is now recommended by the Commissioners that while the facilities for divorce shall be increased, husbands shall still be the only party to benefit by them. In order to justify this, a necessary confusion is introduced as to whether the practicability of divorce is a good or an evil. The power of being divorced is shown to be good in the case of the husband, but the impossibility of divorce is asserted to be favourable to the happiness of the wife. And this, side by side with the narrative of a case related by Lord BROUGHAM, of which he says that he "cannot conceive of a harder case," but which is yet far from uncommon—the case of a lady maintaining by her ability and industry an adulterous husband, who claims all her earnings, and threatens the seizure of her whole property. Such a liability is to remain, by the recommendation of the Commissioners; and, no doubt, will remain under the new Law of Divorce, against which wives have no power of appeal.

The other suggestions are, that adultery shall be still the only ground of complete divorce; that wilful desertion shall be another ground of legal separation, in addition to the two, conjugal infidelity and gross cruelty—which are admitted now—both parties being able to obtain a separation for these causes; that the verdict at law, and ecclesiastical sentence, which must now be obtained as a title to divorce, shall no longer be necessary, and that divorce shall be legally obtainable without the intervention of Parliament; that a special tribunal shall have charge of all questions of marriage and divorce (thus, by the way, facilitating the abolition of the ecclesiastical courts), and that the three branches of the law, equity, common law, and ecclesiastical jurisdiction, shall be united in this tribunal, which shall consist of a vice-chancellor, a common-law judge, and a judge of the Ecclesiastical Courts; and that the methods shall be those of the improved Chancery proceedings, with some modifications from the existing procedure in such cases; that a large discretion be vested in the court, for providing for the interests of the parties and their children; and that the sole appeal shall be to the House of Lords.

These are very important changes—likely to occasion, if adopted, much good, though not of a very radical sort, and some evil. The grand feature is the transference of such a matter as this from exceptional legislation to the domain of common law—the making divorce obtainable by the laws of the country, which now interdict it. Few, we suppose, will object to this. If divorce is obtainable by Act of Parliament, it cannot be an objectionable license; and if not an objectionable license, it ought to be obtainable by all who have an equal need of it, without distinction of rank or wealth. It must follow from this that the new court, like our other courts, must admit pauper suits. Conjugal hatred is even more terrible to the poor than to the rich, because they cannot so easily part. It is cheering to think what may be the effect on the brutal husbands and wives, of whom we read in police reports with unavailing disgust or pity, of this new proposed power of obtaining a legal separation as a shelter from insult and cruelty. The doubt that is said to hang about the matter is lest the popular notions of marriage should become unsettled by increased means of relief, and by that want of uniformity of decision which is the attendant peril of all administration of law. On the other hand, there is the hope that, by the opening of means of relief, much of the profligacy which arises from despair may be obviated, and that the effect upon morality of an improvement in justice may be good rather than bad. It must be pretty safe to assume this. The carelessness with which marriages are formed, the mercenary motives which enter into them, the levity with which they are undertaken, and the selfishness and audacity with which they are brutalised under the present system of practical indissolubility, afford ground for very much more hope than fear from a change. If present evils were not too great for longer endurance, we should not be offered a change; and those who, under such circumstances, advise and prepare for the change, are not likely to propose a move in the wrong direction. The question is rather, whether the relief should not have been extended so as to include more cases of the oppression of the wife, and whether the facilities in England should not be at least equalised with those of Scotland. These are points for consideration; and we can only hope that all the wise and good men among us *will* consider, and give to our public and social morals the benefit of their wisdom when the discussion comes on.

BRUTALITY TO WOMEN

One domestic subject is again exciting universal remark and must surely lead to action of one kind or another. Everybody is talking about the continued revelation of the brutality with which women of the working classes are treated, as disclosed by the reports of the police courts. Not a week passes without a report of some dreadful case of husbands, drunk or sober, ill-using their wives to a degree which, if practised upon brutes, would be followed up by the Society for the Prevention of Cruelty to Animals. One fellow cooks his steak and eats it in the presence of wife and children who are famishing for bread. One, two, three, half a dozen, drag their wives about by the hair, knock their heads against the floor—and, even when pregnant, kick them about the body till they are insensible. Here a woman rushes into the street in the middle of the night, followed by her scared and naked children. Another is thrown down stairs, and is found by fellow lodgers half dead at the bottom. It is painful to write these things; but they are constantly being written by police reporters: and they engaged, as we know, so much notice from Parliament, whilst it was sitting, as to cause the passage of a new law for the punishment of brutality to women. This law, however, seems to avail little or nothing. It is observable that the culprits are often "amazed," "astounded," and so forth, at the severity of the sentences: but such a law can scarcely suffice to keep in check men who *can* be so amazed, and who thereby show how insensible they are to the seriousness of their crime.

To the thoughtful observer, a most painful, and by far the most pathetic, part of the business is the unwillingness of the wives to prosecute. The avowal of "who did it," which is the first natural impulse, is retracted when public justice takes up the sinner. The reason of the reluctance is only too mournfully

—

Daily News (London), September 8, 1853, p. 4.

obvious. One poor creature recently exclaimed, when her husband was committed to prison, "Thank God! I shall have quietness for two months!" But for one such there are a dozen who know not how their children are to be fed in the interval, and who look forward with evident horror to the day which shall bring their husbands home again, exasperated by vengeance, full of the hatred which men feel towards those whom they have injured, to inflict a slower and more concealed torture—penalties which the law cannot take hold of—a gradual murder, which can never be brought home. We need not enlarge on this. What such a home must be, every one can imagine for himself.

One obvious feature of this class of cases amongst the lowest ranks of society is that the mistress is in a better condition than the wife. The mistress can free herself from her tyrant at any moment, while the wife has no escape. What say our moralists to this? Could human wit devise a more effectual way of discouraging marriage amongst certain classes, and countenancing illicit connexion? And what is the actual effect, at this moment, in our moral and Christian England? If what we have to tell shocks the moral reader, and strikes alarm into the hearts of all who truly and wisely believe that the institution of the Family is the only basis of public and private morality, it can only be said that it is time such men were shocked and grieved, for it is truth which strikes the blow to their feelings. All such should be called upon, by all their veneration for the institution of the Family, by all their interest in the national morality, by all the principles and prepossessions which fortify and endear their interest in Home, to take heed of a sign of the times.

What must be done?

We may turn first to the Commission on the Law of Divorce, whose Report was presented to Parliament early in the late session. From that report we learn, first, that it is proposed to refuse divorce to women (in England) altogether, except in cases of such rare atrocity as to constitute, practically, no exception at all; and next, that in Scotland, there were 95 cases of successful suit for a divorce in five years,—the parties being almost all of the labouring classes, under favour of the smallness of the cost; one-third of these divorces were at the suit of the wife. Such is the state of the law beyond the

Tweed, while, on this side of it, the expense of a divorce rises from 500£. to several thousands, and, as we said, the wife is, practically speaking, excluded from release altogether. The Commissioners propose various and considerable relaxations; but all in favour of the husband; and their strange doctrine is that such facilities are good for the husband, while yet the impossibility of divorce is good for the wife. Such a view will not be sanctioned by the sense and feeling of the English people, if fairly brought before their judgment; and the present disclosures of the liabilities of wives will infuse new animation into that sense and feeling on behalf of the weaker party. It had need be so; for in this case only one party is represented. The husbands are the law makers; and the wife is dumb before the law, and Parliament, and the Commission which is to decide upon her interests. The case of divorce is proposed to be transferred from the jurisdiction of Parliament to that of a common law court, from being a matter of exceptional legislation to a position within the domain of common law. Divorce is to be obtainable by the laws of the country, which now interdict it. This is good, as far as it goes; that is, it is good for the husband. But the wife gains nothing by it. Another important benefit will be that pauper suits will be admissible in this, as in other cases, under the law of the land. But here again the wife gains nothing. Legal separation is to be made more attainable by both parties; and in this there is so much of good that we are anxious to obtain it without delay. But there will be no permanent settlement of the question till English and Scotch wives are placed on the same footing. Nobody pretends that the Scotch law is profligate: and if it is not, it follows that the English law is cruel. That cruelty must be abolished, and soon, or the cruelty of husbands, at which society now stands aghast, may, within a certain space of the social area, overbear marriage altogether.

One more appeal must be made—to the Catholic clergy, especially in London. It is observable that the great majority of brutal husbands sentenced in the police courts are Irishmen. We commend this fact to the notice of the priests of their religion. The Catholic doctrine is that marriage is indissoluble, and the more imperative is the obligation on the clergy of that faith to see that the institution is preserved from abuse. They have more influence over the conscience and conduct of the poor and ignorant than any other clergy; and it is unavoidable, therefore, that any class of offences which particularly distinguishes their flocks should be imputed to some imperfection in their discharge of their office. We appeal to them to look seriously into this matter, and to try whether they cannot preserve the sanctity of marriage by procuring better conduct among those whom they have admitted to that sacrament. In proportion to their dread and dislike of all relaxation of the bond should be their care to prevent its becoming unendurable. They can, if they will, restrain the brutality of men whom they hold in their spiritual charge; and they cannot be blind to the nature and extent of the consequences if they neglect the duty.

INDEPENDENT
INDUSTRY OF WOMEN

For a good many years now the subject of the independent industry of women in Great Britain has come up at shorter intervals, and with a more peremptory demand on the attention of society. From the day when the *Song of the Shirt* appeared there could be no doubt that the industrial condition of women would occupy attention as we see it doing now. The founding of the Governesses' Benevolent Institution, the controversies about factory employment for women, the movement in favour of women and watchwork, the opening of a few Schools of Design to women, and of an annual exhibition of pictures by them, and the successful footing they have established in various department of Art, have all pointed to the awakening of that wide interest in the subject which we witness now. The *Edinburgh Review* of last April contained a full narrative of the actual state of female industry in this country; and at the Social Science Meeting at Bradford, a paper read by Miss PARKES

Daily News (London), November 17, 1859, p. 4.

excited so much interest that the discussion has been kept up, and does not seem likely to drop at present.

Discussion about what? This is an important thing to know in a case in which so much sentiment is involved, and so much prejudice, and so much sense, and so much goodwill. What is the precise mischief to be taken in hand? and what is to be done to cure it?

Miss PARKES's paper was abundantly clear and definite. She tells us the truth that a multitude of the daughters of middle-class men are neither educated nor provided for like their brothers; and that if they do not marry, they must work (unprepared by education as they are) or starve. The terms demanded on behalf of women are that parents shall either educate their daughters so as to fit them for independent industry; or lay by a provision for them; or insure their own lives for the benefit of their daughters in the day which will make them fatherless. This is very simple and clear. It is also very interesting; and, as a natural consequence, we hear of sympathy, in the form of advice and suggestions, in all directions; and of various establishments, existing or proposed, with more or less of the charitable element involved for the relief and aid of industrial women of the middle class. Under such circumstances there must be a melancholy waste of effort, unless we ascertain betimes what it is that is wanted, and how the want may be met, with something like concert and business-like faculty. Looking at the matter from a practical point of view, the conditions of the case seem to be these.

It is supposed by persons whose attention has not been particularly called to the subject, that the women of Great Britain are maintained by their fathers, husbands, or brothers. It was once so; and careless people are unaware that we have long outgrown the fit of that theory of female maintenance. It has been out at elbows at least since the war which ended with Waterloo. From the last Census Report we learn how things were eight years ago—before the last war which has much increased the tendency of women to maintain themselves. In Great Britain, without Ireland, there were in 1851 six millions of women above twenty years of age. More than half of these work for their living. Does this surprise our readers? If it never occurred to them before, they will be still further impressed by the fact that two millions of women, out of the six millions, are independent in their industry—are self-supporting, like men. So far is the theory of women being maintained by their male relatives from being now true. But how do these women work? and how far do they succeed in maintaining themselves? for it is universally understood that women are paid less than men for the same kind and degree of work. Society has been a good deal surprised by the disclosures in the Divorce Court of the amount of effectual female industry, proved by applications for protection of earnings from bad husbands. That women should maintain themselves and their children seems a matter of course when they are unhappily married; and the revelation has caused a good many people to perceive that there is a good deal going on in middle-class life which they were unaware of. It may strike some observers that the matter has far outgrown the scope and powers of charitable societies, and that the independent industry of Englishwomen has become a fact which must be recognised by the law, and which must itself essentially modify middle-class education throughout the kingdom.

What, then, are these three millions and more of working women doing? and especially the two millions who are industrial in the same sense as men?

There were in 1851 nearly 130,000 employed in agriculture, without reckoning the farmers' wives and daughters, who usually have their hands full. This is also exclusive of the widow-farmers, who are numerous. Nearly half of the independent class of workers are dairymaids. The ores and clays of the mining districts afford occupation to 7,000, now that female labour has ceased (ostensibly) in coal-pits. It does not seem to be ascertained how many women are employed in the catching, curing, and itinerant sale of fish. Jersey oysters alone maintain 1,000 women, and this may give some notion of the scores of thousands so employed all round our coasts. The country districts, however, afford the greatest number of all in the department of domestic service. Nearly two-thirds of our maid-servants are country born; and there are considerably more than half-a-million of them altogether. They constitute a fourth part of the independent workers. We employ no fewer than 400,000 maids-of-all-work. Other female servants amount to above 180,000, without reckoning the large class (about 51,000) of charwomen.

There are many thousands of shopkeepers, but they are for the most part the widows of the men who had the business before them; and it is too common a thing to see them marry their assistants in the business, from their own inability to keep the books, and manage the financial part of their concerns. The Divorce Court and the police courts, all the year round, afford evidence of this weakness and ignorance among women who have had a good business as innkeepers or shopkeepers. There are 14,000 of this class, butchers and milk merchants; 8,000 waggon or hackney-coach proprietors; 10,000 beer-shop keepers or victuallers, besides 9,000 innkeepers. These are the independent proprietors, excluding the wives, who are yet the mainstay of the industry in houses of entertainment and many branches of retail trade. With all this shopkeeping by women, there are no more than 1,742 shopwomen. This is a fact eminently worthy of consideration. The function is one which occurs first to almost everybody's mind, when female industry is discussed, as one precisely fit for women. The failure may be partly owing to the jealousy of the men, who have hitherto engrossed it, and partly to the well-known prejudice of purchasers in favour of shopmen; but it is no doubt in part ascribable to the inferiority of women in the special training required; and especially in accounts and bookkeeping.

Manufactures maintain a million and a quarter of the women of Great Britain. More than half a million are employed on dress; that is, in millinery and laundry-work, exclusive of shoemakers' wives, who amount to nearly 100,000. Losing sight of the great field of female labour, because female industry is so completely established there, we are apt to say that there is no choice for a middle-class woman who must work but between the needle and tuition. The milliner's work-room and the school-room, we are wont to say, afford the only alternative. Yet we find in the Census returns "Teachers, Authors, and Artists," all lumped together, their collective number being under 65,000, exclusive of nearly 2,000 set down as "miscellaneous." Independent proprietors of lands, houses, or incomes are declared to be under 173,000.

Considering these figures in relation to each other, we strive at some sort of notion of what is wanted—first, to provide for a certain proportion of women now left helpless or miserable on the death of fathers, or under the accidents of fortune; and next, to improve the quality of existing female industry, so as to render it more effective for the support of the individual, and the benefit of society. We do not conceive that any appeal to fathers to provide better for their daughters, in comparison with their sons, will be of much practical use (however just and right) till the women have established the fact of their own capability, and their will to be independent. All sorts of people have to show what they can do before obtaining free scope to do it; and, antecedently unjust as this seems, it is a fact, and to be taken into the calculation. Women need not object to this, judging by what they have lately achieved for themselves under manifold disadvantages. They have won a good position in many departments of literature and art; and there is a good prospect of their soon occupying what we have repeatedly insisted on as their proper place in the medical profession. The thing would be done at once (as it is already in the United States), if the decision rested with our wisest physicians and most enlightened heads of households. We see women now entering in increasing numbers on new methods of industry, introduced by the progress of science and art. We see them in the telegraph offices and at railway stations, transmitting reports with remarkable accuracy, and selling railway tickets—if not yet in charge of the signals, like French women. The arts of design for manufactures are open to them; and this is a wide and profitable field of labour. As authors and artists there is no hindrance in their way when they can prove their capability. No doubt, the counting-house, the shop-counter, secretaryships, and indeed any trade, and the medical profession will afford them entrance, notwithstanding a good deal of jealousy and prejudice, if they can make themselves valuable enough to defy obstacles. The practical question is how to establish the fact of the capacity. The fitness which exists may be called out and put to use by such associations as those which we see proposing to register applicants for work and for workers, and to train young women to mechanical fitness for certain occupations. These efforts are good as far as they go; and we are always glad to hear of them. The educational preparation which is necessary to make effective workers of either men or women is a deeper and wider affair of which we must speak another day. Our present object is to show that it is mere waste of time to speak for or against the industrial independence of Englishwomen—above one-third of their whole number being already established in that destiny. A smaller number of women are passing miserable lives under the wreck of the old theory that women are not self-supporting. These sufferers are not supported: they cannot support themselves, and they form the most prominent of our "uneasy classes." The old theory can never be reinstated in practice, and the question is how best to obey the natural laws of society, which now compel women to work.

The first step is to perceive that the problem is now simply an educational one. This is the point which the facts of the last Census seem to us to establish. The next step will be to provide the education specially required.

DRESS AND ITS VICTIMS

There are a good many people who cannot possibly believe that dress can have any share in the deaths of the 100,000 persons who go needlessly to the grave every year in our happy England, where there are more means of comfort for everybody than in any other country in Europe.

How can people be killed by dress, now-a-days? they ask. We must be thinking of the old times when the ladies laced so tight that "salts and strong waters" seem to have been called for to some fainting fair one, as often as numbers were collected together, whether at church, or at Ranelagh,[14] or the theatres. Or perhaps we are thinking of the accidents that have happened during particular fashions of dress, as the burning of the Marchioness of Salisbury, from her high cap nodding

---

Harriet Martineau, *Health, Husbandry and Handicraft* (London: Bradbury and Evans, 1861), pp. 49–60. Published originally in *Once a Week* in 1859.

[14] A fashionable pleasure garden during the second half of the eighteenth century.

over the candle; or the deaths of the Ladies Bridgman two years since, from the skirts of one of them catching fire at the grate; or the number of inquests held during the fashion of gigot-sleeves, when a lady could scarcely dine in company, or play the piano at home, without peril of death by fire.

Perhaps it may be the heavy, towering head-dresses of the last century we may be thinking of, bringing in a crowd of bad symptoms, headaches, congestions, fits, palsies, with the fearful remedies of bleeding and reducing, which we read of in medical books, and in gossiping literature, like Horace Walpole's correspondence. Or we may even be thinking of the barbaric fashion of painting the face, neck, and hands, at one time carried on to the excess of enamelling the skin. That was not at so very remote a time; for I have heard from the lips of witnesses what it was like; and a friend of mine, yet living, can tell what she saw at a concert where a lady sat before her with a pair of broad shoulders which looked like tawny marble,—as smooth, as shining, and as little like anything human. These shoulders were once enamelled, and may have looked white in their day; but no life-long pains to renew their whiteness would serve after a certain lapse of time; and there they were, hopeless, tawny, and the quality of the skin destroyed. The poisonings by means of cosmetics that we read of in the history of past centuries, may have been sometimes intentional; but there was plenty of unconscious poisoning besides.

I do not, however, mean any of these things when I speak of dress, in connection with preventible mortality.

Perhaps I may be supposed to be referring to the notoriously afflicted and short-lived classes of milliners and shopworkers who are worn out and killed off in the cause of dress. No; I am not now going to bring forward their case, because it comes under a different head. At this moment I am not thinking of either the political economy or the general morality of the dress-question, or I should bring up the group of suicides who have perished, some from hopeless poverty, some from intolerable degradation, and some from the embarrassment of gambling debts incurred for the sake of dress.

If the secrets of the city were known, we might hear of more tragedies than the theatres show, from the spread of gambling among women, and especially among servant-girls and shop women, who have been carried beyond bounds by the extravagant fashion of the day. But I am not speaking of suicides, nor of the victims of the needle, whose case is too grave to be treated lightly, and whose day of deliverance, too, is at hand, if the sewing-machine is the reality it appears—and not a phantom, cheating the hopes of thousands. We may possibly look into that another time. Meanwhile our business is with the injurious and sometimes murderous effect of dress which we see worn every day.

It will not seem so wonderful that the familiar clothing of our neighbours and ourselves may be of such importance when we remember the explanations of physicians—that dress may, and usually does, affect the condition and action of almost every department of the human frame;—the brain and nervous system, the lungs, the stomach, and other organs of the trunk; the eyes, the skin, the muscles, the glandular system, the nutritive system, and even the bony frame, the skeleton on which all hangs. If dress can meddle mischievously with the action, or affect the condition of all these, it can be no marvel that it is responsible for a good many of the hundred thousand needless deaths which are happening around us this year.

Putting aside the ordinary associations, as far as we can, and trying for the moment to consider what is to be desired in the clothing of the human body,—what is requisite to make dress good and beautiful,—let us see what is essential.

Dress should be a covering to all the parts of the body which need warmth or coolness, as the case may be. It should be a shelter from the evils of the atmosphere, whether these be cold, or heat, or wet, or damp, or glare. This is the first requisite; for such shelter is the main purpose of clothing. In our own country the dress should easily admit of the necessary changes in degrees of warmth demanded by our changeable climate.

Dress should bear a close relation to the human form. No other principle can be permanent; no other can be durably sanctioned by sense and taste, because no other has reality in it. We may fancy that we admire the old Greek and Roman robes which look dignified in Julius Caesar on the stage, and in statues, and in our own imaginations of classical times; but we could not get through our daily business in such a costume; nor should we admire the appearance of our acquaintance in it. In fact, the wearers themselves were always tucking up or putting away their troublesome wrappers when they had anything to do: and the busy people of society appeared in their workshops and fields in garments which left their limbs free, and their whole body fit for action. On the whole, in a general way, with particular variations according to taste, the dress should follow the outline of the body. Any great deviation from this principle involves inconvenience on the one hand, and deformity on the other.

Where it follows the outline of the frame it should fit accurately enough to fulfil its intention, but so easily as not to embarrass action. It should neither compress the internal structure nor impede the external movement. An easy fit, in short, is the requisite. It is a part of this easy fit that the weight of the clothes should be properly hung and distributed.

After the peace of 1815 it was said that we gained two things from the French—gloves that would fit, and the shoulder-piece. It would make the difference of some lives out of the great number thrown away, if we made due use of the shoulder-piece, now. By the shoulder-piece, the weight of the garment is spread on the part best fitted to bear it, instead of being hung from the neck, as it was before we knew better or from the hips or the waist (in the case of women's dress) as now, when we ought to know better.

Next; dress ought to be agreeable to wear: and this includes something more than warmth and a good fit. It should be light, and subject to as few dangers and inconveniences as possible. . . .

[Women's] clothing does not protect them from cold, heat, damp, or glare. Some few uncover the chest and arms under trying circumstances of heat and draught: but they are few; and they must have heard all that can be said to them in the way of warning. The great body of Englishwomen—those of the middle and lower classes—have usually some sort of covering from the throat to the hands and feet, but it is too seldom judicious in degree or quality. The modern linsey petticoats are excellent as far as they go; but it is certain that the working-women of our country are too thoroughly weaned from the woollen clothing of their ancestors. At present, too, no woman who adopts the fashion of the hoop in any form is properly guarded against the climate. Any medical man in good practice can tell of the spread of rheumatism since women ceased to wear their clothing about their limbs, and stuck it off with frames and hoops, admitting damp and draught, with as little rationality as if they tried to make an umbrella serve the purpose of a bonnet.

Then observe the head and the feet. The eyes are unsheltered from sun and wind, and the most important region of the head is exposed by the bonnets which Englishwomen are so weak as to wear in imitation of the French. Again, the doctors have their painful tale to tell of neuralgic pains in the face and head, which abound beyond all prior experience, of complaints in the eyes, and all the consequences that might be anticipated from the practice of lodging the bonnet on the nape of the neck, and leaving all the fore part of the skull exposed.* Why the bonnet is worn at all is the mystery. A veil, white or black, would be considered an absurdity as a substitute for the bonnet in a climate like ours; but it would be actually more serviceable than the handful of flimsy decorations now usurping the place of the useful, cheap, and pretty straw bonnet, which suits all ages in its large variety. There are the hats, to be sure, which young ladies wear so becomingly. They are hardly simple enough in form for a permanence, but they are substantially unexceptionable for youthful wearers. Their advantages unfortunately tempt elderly ladies to put them on; but the class of mistaken wearers of hats is not a very large one, and we may let them pass. In praising the hat, however, I am thinking of the sort that has a brim. The new and brimless invention is nearly as bad as the bonnet for use, while more fantastic. A chimney-pot hat with a tall upright plume may possibly suit a volunteer rifle corps or a regiment of Amazons rehearsing for the opera, but it is not very English in taste.

The fearful spread of throat and chest diseases is ascribed, by those who should know best, mainly to the modern notion of muffling up the throat in furs and other heating substances. Before the boa came in, we heard little of any one of the tribe of throat diseases which we now meet at every turn. Some ladies carry a boa all through the summer, and many tie up their throats with a silk handkerchief whenever they go

*In 1859.

233

abroad, in all seasons; suffering their retribution in hoarse-nesses, bronchitis, sorethroat, and other ailments never endured by those who cultivate more hardy habits, reserving such wraps for very special occasions. People who use cold water in some form of bath every day of the year, and who give their faces and throats to the bracing air, under the safeguard of vigorous personal exercise, forget what colds and coughs are.

As for the other point—the feet—it is to be feared that some are still sent to the grave by thin shoes. The danger of gutta-percha and patent-leather shoes has been referred to. The Balmoral boots of the day would be admirable but for the military heels. Those heels throw the foot into an unnatural posture, by which a great strain is produced. If my readers happen to be acquainted with a respectable chiropodist, let them inquire the recent news of bunions—that severest of small maladies. They will learn that there has been an unheard-of increase and aggravation of bunions since the high-heeled boots came in. The danger of falls is also considerable: and those who have a dread of a long tumble down the stairs, had better put on their boots on the ground-floor.

If we consider the female dress of 1859 under any of the remaining conditions, what can we say of it? Does the costume, as a whole, follow the outline of the form? Does it fit accurately and easily? Is the weight made to hang from the shoulders? Are the garments of to-day convenient and agreeable in use? Is the mode modest and graceful? So far from it, that all these conditions are conspicuously violated by those who think they dress well. Here and there we may meet a sensible woman, or a girl who has no money to spend in new clothes, whose appearance is pleasing—in a straw bonnet that covers the head, in a neat gown which hangs gracefully and easily from the natural waist, and which does not sweep up the dirt: but the spectacle is now rare; for bad taste in the higher classes spreads very rapidly downwards, corrupting the morals as it goes.

The modern dress perverts the form very disagreeably. The evil still begins with the stays, in too many instances, though there is less tight-lacing than formerly. It is a pity that women do not know how little they gain by false pretences in regard to figure and complexion. Our grandmothers would not have worn paint if they had been aware that it is useless after forty to attempt to seem younger—the texture of the skin revealing at a glance the fact which paint and dyed hair cannot conceal; except perhaps in the parks, or across a theatre. In the same way, the round waist produced by tight-lacing is always distinguishable in a moment from the easy oval form of the genuine small waist. Compare the two extremes, and you will see it at once. Compare the figure of the Graces of Raffaelle, or the Venus de Medici, with the smallest and most praised waist in a factory, and observe the difference. Before the glass, the owner of the latter sees the smallness in front, and fancies it beautiful; but it is disgusting to others. It is as stiff as the stem of a tree, and spoils the form and movement more than the armour of ancient knights ever did; and we know what is going on within. The ribs are pressed out of their places, down upon the soft organs within, or overlapping one another: the heart is compressed, so that the circulation is irregular: the stomach and liver are compressed, so that they cannot act properly: and then parts which cannot be squeezed are thrust out of their places, and grave ailments are the consequence. At the very best, the complexion loses more than the figure can be supposed to gain. It is painful to see what is endured by some young women in shops and factories, as elsewhere. They cannot stoop for two minutes over their work without gasping and being blue, or red, or white in the face. They cannot go upstairs without stopping to take breath every few steps. Their arms are half numb, and their hands red or chilblained; and they must walk as if they were all-of-a-piece, without the benefit and grace of joints in the spine and limbs. A lady had the curiosity to feel what made a girl whom she knew so like a wooden figure, and found a complete palisade extending round the body. On her remonstrating, the girl pleaded that she had "only six-and-twenty whalebones!"

Any visitor of a range of factories will be sure to find that girls are dropping in fainting-fits, here and there, however pure the air and proper the temperature; and here and there may be seen a vexed and disgusted proprietor, seeking the warehouse-woman, or some matron, to whom he gives a pair of large scissors, with directions to cut open the stays of some silly woman who had fainted. Occasional inquests afford a direct warning of the fatal effects which may follow the practice of tight-lacing; but slow and painful disease is much more common; and the register exhibits, not the stays, but the malady created by the stays as the cause of death. That such cases are common, any physician who practises among the working-classes will testify.

Do the petticoats of our time serve as anything but a mask to the human form—a perversion of human proportions? A woman on a sofa looks like a child popping up from a haycock. A girl in the dance looks like the Dutch tumbler that was a favourite toy in my infancy. The fit is so the reverse of accurate as to be like a silly hoax—a masquerade without wit: while, at the same time, it is not an easy fit. The prodigious weight of the modern petticoat, and the difficulty of getting it all into the waistband, creates a necessity for compressing and loading the waist in a way most injurious to health. Under a rational method of dress the waist should suffer neither weight nor pressure—nothing more than the girdle which brings the garment into form and folds. As to the convenience of the hooped skirts, only ask the women themselves, who are always in danger from fire, or wind, or water, or carriage wheeles, or rails, or pails, or nails, or, in short, everything they encounter. Ask the husbands, fathers, or brothers, and hear how they like being cut with the steel frame when they enter a gate with a lady, or being driven into a corner of the pew at church, or to the outside of the coach, for want of room. As for the children—how many have been swept off pathways, or footbridges, or steamboat decks by the pitiless crinoline, or hoops of some unconscious walking balloon! More children have been killed, however, by the extension of the absurd petticoat fashion to them. For many months past, it has been a rare thing to see a child under the tunic age duly clothed. The petticoats are merely for show; and the actual clothing, from the waist downwards, is nothing more than thin cotton drawers and socks, leaving a bare space between. For older boys there is a great improvement in dress—the tunic and loose trousers being preferable in every way to the stiff mannish tailed coat and tight trousers of half a century ago. But the younger children are at present scarcely clothed at all, below the arms; and the blue legs of childhood are a painful sight, whether in a beggar boy or a citizen's son. Even in such a climate as Sierra Leone there is something forlorn in thinking of the lady's maid in a great house wearing (and possessing) nothing more in the way of clothing than a muslin gown and a blue bead-necklace (on an ebony throat, of course), but in winters like ours to see children's legs covered with nothing better than thin cotton (thin, because the ornamentation is the vanity), is in fact reading the sentence of death of many victims. Let it be remembered, too, that the neuralgic, rheumatic and heart diseases thus brought on are of a hereditary character. The wearer of crinoline and invisible bonnets, in incurring such diseases herself, renders her future children liable to them; and the children now bitten by the wintry winds, if they live to be parents, may see their offspring suffer from the ignorance and vanity of their own mothers. It is universally observed that certain diseases are becoming more common every year—neuralgia and heart disease, as well as the throat ailments of which we hear so much. It would be a great benefit if we could learn how much of the form and the increase of maladies is ascribable to our modes of dress.

What is to be done? Will anything ever be done? or is feminine wilfulness and slavishness to fashion to kill off hundreds and thousands of the race, as at present? I see, with much satisfaction, that the Messrs. Courtauld, the great silk manufacturers in Essex, have put up a notice in their factories, that a fine is imposed on the wearing of crinoline by their workwomen. The ground of the regulation is, that the work cannot be done with either decency or safety in that kind of dress. I hope this example will be followed in all mills and factories where the same reason can be assigned. There are whole societies in America who do not see the necessity for such mischief, and who hope to put an end to it—in their own country at least. The Dress-Reform Association of the United States was instituted some years since by women who refused the inconvenience of Paris fashions in American homesteads: and they have been aided, not only by physicians, but by other men, on the ground of the right of women to wear what suits their occupations and their taste, without molestation. The dress which was long ago agreed upon, after careful consideration—the so-called Bloomer costume (not as we see it in caricature, but in its near resemblance to the most rational English fashion of recent times)—is extensively worn, not only in rural districts, but in many towns. It seems to fulfil the various conditions of rational, modest, and graceful dress better than any other as yet devised for temperate climates; and if so, it will spread, in spite of all opposition.

What opposition it met with here is not forgotten at home or abroad, and never will be forgotten. Some of our highest philosophers and best-bred gentlemen were more indignant and ashamed than perhaps anybody else. They said that we constantly saw Englishmen angry and scornful because of the indignities cast by Mussulman bigotry on the dress of Europeans in Damascus and Jerusalem; but here were Englishmen doing the same thing, without equal excuse, when Englishwomen proposed to adapt their dress to their health, convenience, and notions of grace. The aggressors triumphed. They induced outcast women to adopt the dress, and stamped it with disrepute before it had a chance of a trial. It was an unmanly act; and if those who were concerned in it have since suffered from the extravagance of wife and daughters, or from sickness and death in their households, which might have been averted by a sensible method of clothing old and young, they have had their retribution. Some of our newspapers are rebuking others for meddling with the women's choice of fashions . . . but it is an affair which concerns both sexes and all ages. What hinders a simple obedience to common-sense in the matter? It is only for the women of those classes who really have business in life to refuse to encumber themselves with tight, or heavy, or long, or unserviceable dress, and to adhere to any mode which suits them; and then, whatever the idle and fanciful may choose to do, the useless mortality will be mainly stopped, and the general health prevented from sinking lower. It may be confidently avowed that in this way only can women win back some of the respect which they have forfeited by the culpable absurdity of their dress within the last few seasons. From the duchess to the maid-servant, the slaves of French taste have lost position; and it will require a permanent establishment of some leading points of the sense and morality of dress to restore their full dignity to the matronage and maidenhood of England.

VII

A WOMEN'S CAMPAIGN

"I am told," she said, "that this is discreditable work for woman, especially for an old woman. But it has always been esteemed our especial function as women, to mount guard over society and social life,—the spring of national existence,—and to keep them pure; and who so fit as an old woman?"

Being told that American ladies were shocked to think of such personal exposure, "English ladies think of the Lady Godiva!" was her reply.

*—Harriet Martineau as reported in
an interview with Maria Weston Chapman*

The Knoll, Ambleside, 1846
Reprinted from Martineau, *Autobiography*

In 1869 Harriet Martineau came out of retirement to write dozens of letters and pamphlets and posters on behalf of the organized effort to repeal the Contagious Diseases Acts. These two acts, passed by Parliament in 1866 and 1869, were intended to regulate prostitution; the first covered only garrison towns, the second extended jurisdiction to the areas around the towns. They gave police and medical officers authority to arrest and medically examine women suspected of prostitution. The acts included no such threat of arrest or examination for men. The laws were patterned after laws in Belgium and France, and had been in the making in England since 1859 when the press made a case for them. When the second act passed in 1869, eminently respectable women realized that a danger of mistreatment for all women was inherent in the laws, that women were treated unequally with men under the laws, and that the laws, rather than regulating prostitution, gave indiscriminate power to the police to arrest and humiliate women. They organized the Ladies' National Association for the Repeal of the Contagious Diseases Acts, led by Josephine Butler, and stormed England with their campaign.

Martineau had written in her Tynemouth journal in the early 1840s that she had a very strong desire to do service to "unhappy women," that is, prostitutes, and that she felt she would do something for them at some point later in her life.[1] She found that opportunity in the Contagious Diseases Acts campaign. Chapman wrote that

> no sooner had the American antislavery cause been merged in the national one, than the English cause of social virtue and national existence appealed to her [Martineau's] whole nature.
>
> "I am told," she said, "that this is discreditable work for woman, especially for an *old* woman. But it has always been esteemed our especial function as women, to mount guard over society and social life,—the spring of national existence,—and to keep them pure; and who so fit as an old woman?"
>
> Being told that American ladies were shocked

[1] *Autobiography*, vol. 2, p. 531.

to think of such personal exposure, "English ladies think of the Lady Godiva!" was her reply.[2]

She made good use in her campaign prose of the image of Lady Godiva, the legendary English noblewoman protesting her husband's treatment of the poor by riding naked through the town.

Martineau was ahead of her time even in this campaign. She did not merely join the protesters in 1869, she had foreseen the dangers of the proposed legislation as the public debate around it formed in the early 1860s. The issue figured in her correspondence with influential people even then, and she led the press debate with leaders in the *Daily News* opposing the passage of such laws. (The *Times* took the other side.) In a series of editorials published in 1863, she did not come down so strongly on the generalized incrimination of women inherent in the laws, which was to be her emphasis later when the laws were actually in effect. Rather, she argued against regulation of prostitution at all. She made a strong plea for treating "men as moral agents and not as animals," in fact emphasizing the dignity and responsibility denied soldiers and sailors by such laws.[3] She wrote,

> There is evidence, accessible to all, that the regulation system creates horrors worse than those which it is supposed to restrain. Vice once stimulated by such a system imagines and dares all unutterable things; and such things perplex with misery the lives of parents of missing children in continental cities, and daunt the courage of rulers, and madden the moral sense, and gnaw the conscience of whole orders of sinners and sufferers, of whom we can form no conception here. We shall have entered upon our national decline whenever we agree to the introduc-

[2] Ibid., p. 506.
[3] *The Contagious Diseases Acts as Applied to Garrison Towns and Naval Stations, Articles from the "Daily News" of 1863* (Liverpool: T. Brackell, 1870). Pamphlet in the collection of the Fawcett Library, City of London Polytechnic, London.

tion of such a system; and it is only necessary to bring the case fairly before the public conscience to secure us against any such fatal lapse.[4]

When the ladies' campaign began, Martineau's four editorials were reprinted as a pamphlet. She also lent her hand to writing petitions to form societies and hold meetings, and to writing speeches and letters to the electorate to persuade voters to oust members of Parliament who favored the acts. According to Chapman, Butler often mentioned Martineau's name in speeches to working people, and commented that "when I mentioned Harriet Martineau as sympathizing with them, a bright gleam passed over their faces, from town to town as I went."[5]

Martineau also contributed a chair cover of her own needlework to be sold by Butler to benefit the campaign—she was by this time again housebound as an invalid. She wrote numerous letters to public figures of her acquaintance. And, perhaps most important of all, she published three letters signed "An Englishwoman" in the *Daily News*, clearly setting out the arguments for repeal. Published in the last days of December 1869, these letters were followed on December 31, 1869, by a declaration Martineau drafted for The Ladies' National Association for the Repeal of the Contagious Diseases Acts, which was signed by a great many well known women. The names of Harriet Martineau and Florence Nightingale headed the list. These four items, preceded by excerpts from the *Autobiography* of letters and petitions written by Martineau, fittingly form the final selections in this volume.

In the first of the letters to the *Daily News* Martineau argued for women from women's point of view:

a second "Contagious Diseases Act"—was passed, by which the operation of the first is extended to many towns which are in no sense garrison towns. The system is now, in fact, applied to the civil population; and next session is to bring forward the crown-

[4] Ibid., p. 16.
[5] *Autobiography*, vol. 2, p. 534.

ing measure—the extension of the power of the police and the outrage and degradation of the new law over the whole womanhood of England. In our time, or any other, there never, perhaps, was a graver question than whether there are still time and means to rouse the country to the due sense and knowledge of what is doing, that is to be apprehended, and what is the duty of individuals in the crisis.

An example of her correspondence with a member of Parliament, however, shows her arguing for women from the point of view of men. Writing to the Right Honourable W. J. Forster, she contended:

The question is . . . how boldly he [Gladstone] will proceed to act on the plain fact of the unconstitutional character of the Acts, and in rebuke of the audacious sacrifice of virtue to passion, and of the defenceless to the strong and self-seeking half of society. . . . We are heartily sorry to think what he has to encounter in any case,—between the fierce passion of the men who believed they had gained their atrocious objects, and the strong determination of the fathers, brothers and husbands of Englishwomen to leave no rest or peace to their rulers till their wives, sisters, and daughters are securely sheltered under the law of the land, the best parts of which are no longer in existence for them.[6]

But in the association's petition in the newspaper, she again put the case squarely as it applied to women:

Unlike all other laws for the repression of contagious diseases, to which both men and women are liable, these two apply to women only, men being wholly exempt from their penalties. . . . Any woman can be dragged into court, and required to prove that she is not a common prostitute. The magistrate can

[6]Letter to W. J. Forster, Ambleside, July 16, 1871. Manuscript copy from the National Library of Scotland.

condemn her, if a policeman swears that he "has good cause to believe" her to be one. . . . When condemned, the sentence is as follows:—To have her person outraged by the periodical inspection of a surgeon, through a period of twelve months; or, resisting that, to be imprisoned, with or without hard labour. . . . Women arrested under false accusations have been so terrified at the idea of encountering the public trial necessary to prove their innocence, that they have, under the intimidation of the police, signed away their good name and their liberty by making what is called a "voluntary submission" to appear periodically for twelve months for surgical examination.

The petition goes on to protest the laws in strong civil libertarian terms; "so far as women are concerned, they remove every guarantee of personal security which the law has established and held sacred, and put their reputation, their freedom, and their persons absolutely in the power of the police."

Thus, in the last major surge of Harriet Martineau's long and distinguished public career, she was the driving force, second only to the organizing leader of the campaign, Josephine Butler, in a dramatic feminist coalescence of women's activity for women's good in England, the effort for the repeal of the Contagious Diseases Acts.

ON THE
CONTAGIOUS DISEASES ACTS

To this means the Reform Association had recourse; and this is a copy of their placard, written and first signed by Harriet Martineau:—[7]

TO THE WOMEN OF COLCHESTER

As Englishwomen loving your country, and proud of it, as many generations of women have been, listen to a word from three of your countrywomen.

The most endearing feature in our English life has been the reality of its *homes*. Married life is, with us, we have been accustomed to think, more natural and simple than in most other countries, youth and maidenhood at once more free and pure, and womanhood more unrestrained, more honoured and safe beyond comparison, in person and repute.

Are you aware that this eminent honour and security of our sex and our homes are at present exposed to urgent danger, and even undergoing violation? You women of Colchester ought to be aware of this fact, for the violation is going on within your own town. The story is short.

Some fifteen months ago a bill was carried through Parliament, by trick and under a misleading title, and without awakening the suspicions of the country, by which the personal violation of hundreds of thousands of Englishwomen is not only permitted, but rendered inevitable. And it is the aim and purpose of the authors of the law and its policy, to have

—

Harriet Martineau, *Autobiography*, with Memorials by Maria Weston Chapman, 4th ed. (Boston: Houghton, Osgood and Co., 1879), vol. 2, pp. 537–542. Written about 1869–1871.

[7] This introductory note and those preceding and following each of the letters and placards in this selection were written by Maria Weston Chapman and are published here exactly as Chapman presented them in the Memorials section of Martineau's *Autobiography*. The text of the letters, articles, and campaign literature is by Martineau.

the act extended over the whole country. It was asked for on account of our soldiers and sailors. It is now sought to be extended to the population of the whole kingdom. It was intended to mitigate the disease occasioned by debauchery; but it has aggravated it. It has not diminished the vice, but encouraged it by a false promise of impunity. It gives a distinct government sanction to profligacy, and is degrading to English society wherever it operates, to the fearful condition of health and morals existing on the continent wherever such legislation has been established long enough to show its effects.

Foremost among the promoters of this fearful system and fatal law is Sir Henry Storks, one of the candidates for the representation of Colchester. He was a candidate at the Newark election, some months since; but the Newark people knew what he had been doing, and they would not hear of him as a representative. He had no chance when the facts were understood, and he withdrew from certain defeat.

Do the people of Colchester know these facts? Let it be your work to take care that your husbands, fathers, and brothers hear of them. Sir Henry Storks's own words are to be found in the printed evidence offered to the Committee of the Lords on the Acts. At Newark he complained of false accusations and libels; but the following words written by his own hand, in a letter produced in that evidence, are full justification for any efforts you will make to drive him from Colchester:—

"I am of opinion that very little benefit will result from the best-devised means of prevention, until prostitution is recognized as a necessity!"

This is the professed "opinion" of a man who is regarded as a Christian gentleman, who cannot but be aware how fornication is denounced in the Scriptures.

Let his evidence be further studied in regard to the operation of the legal outrage which Sir Henry Storks is endeavouring to introduce wherever the sceptre of our virtuous queen bears sway, and there can be no doubt of his rejection at Colchester by every elector who values, as an Englishman should, the sanctity of his home, the purity of his sons, and the honour and safety of his daughters.

You surely will not sacrifice greater things to less by any indulgence of prudery. The subject is painful, even hateful to every one of us; but this is not our fault, and our country is not to be sacrificed to our feelings as women. We are not fine ladies, but true-hearted Englishwomen; and there are thousands at this hour who have proved that in this cause they can sacrifice whatever is necessary to save our country from the curse of these Acts.

It is your business to lift up your voices within your homes and neighbourhoods, against being ruled by lawmakers like the authors of these Acts; in other words, against Sir Henry Storks as candidate for Colchester.

HARRIET MARTINEAU
URSULA BRIGHT
JOSEPHINE BUTLER

Sir Henry Storks's election was defeated.

The same process of election-placards was repeated afterwards, abridged, as follows:—

OLD ENGLAND!
PURITY AND FREEDOM!

To the Electors of North Nottinghamshire

We, as Englishwomen, loving our country and our Old National Constitution, entreat you, the Electors of North Nottinghamshire, in the name of Religion, of Morality, and of our National Freedom, to vote for no man who will not pledge himself to vote for the total and unconditional Repeal of those un-English Laws, that Continental abomination stealthily smuggled into our Statute-Book, called the Contagious Diseases Acts, and to oppose any Future Legislation that involves their Principles.

HARRIET MARTINEAU
JOSEPHINE BUTLER
URSULA BRIGHT
LYDIA E. BECKER

Thus the kingdom was made aware of the earnestness of its women in the cause.

In 1871 a correspondent received the following words of rejoicing from Mrs. Martineau:—

"The conspiracy of silence is broken up, and the London papers have burst out. Our main point now is, to secure every variety of judgment inside and outside of the Commission. The 'Daily News' came out clearly and strongly on the right side before any other London paper broke the silence. The satisfaction to us all is immense, to see the paper uphold its high character—the very highest—in this hour of crisis. I feel unusually ill in consequence of heart-failure, but I must make you know something of what you shall know more of hereafter. . . ."

Again, in 1871:—

"I must tell you, though so feeble to-day, that our cause is, for this time, safe. The packed Commission, supplied with packed evidence, comes out thirteen to six in our favour! The conversions under every disadvantage are astonishing. Huxley's delights me. He and two others—Sir Walter James, military, and Admiral Collinson, naval—made speeches on the Commission, declaring that they had verily believed in the good of the C.D. Acts, but they have been compelled to see that they are thoroughly mischievous. We never could have dreamed of such a victory. *As* victory no matter. But what a prospect is opened for the whole sex in Old England! For the stronger and safer sort of women will be elevated in proportion as the helpless or exposed are protected."

At about this time Mrs. Butler received the following letter from Mrs. Martineau.

Letter from Harriet Martineau to Mrs. Butler
The Knoll, Ambleside
MY DEAR FRIEND,—I am truly grateful to you for taking charge of the chair which I have worked in hope of its bringing in some money—more money than I could offer in any other form—towards obtaining the repeal of the Contagious Diseases Acts. I assure you very earnestly that no one can be more thoroughly aware than I am that this is the very lowest method of assisting the movement. I can only say that I have adopted it simply because, in my state of health, no other is

open to me. While you and your brave sisters in the enterprise have been enduring exhausting toils, and facing the gravest risks that can appall the matronage and maidenhood of our country, I have been content to ply my needle when I could do no better, and thankful to witness the achievements of the younger and stronger who will live to rejoice in the retrieval of their dear nation.

It was no dream that I indulged in over my work. Nearly forty years ago I saw and felt the first stir,—saw the first steps taken in the wrong direction to suppress the evils of prostitution. After a long enforced pause the attempt was renewed eight years ago, and with a success which saddened a multitude of hearts besides my own. That triumph of wrong and ignorance has clouded the lives of some of the best men and women of England since 1864; but I have seen, for months past, from my easy-chair, as I looked abroad over your field of action, the foul vapours dispersed before the strong breeze of the popular opinion and will, and the clear light of our ancient domestic virtue spreading from roof to roof among the homes of our land. The few dark years that are past will be remembered as a warning when the Acts that disgraced them are repealed. Once understood, such legislation can never be renewed; and therefore is it reasonable for us to hope all things as we ply our task, whether our labours be as high and arduous as yours, or as humble as mine.

HARRIET MARTINEAU

Experience is the great teacher in the conduct of reforms. The first impulse of a mind deeply impressed with their necessity is to seek the most powerful influence for their promotion, whether from politics, pulpit, or press.

But there is a preparatory work to be done, before these, *as such*, can take the field. The devotedness of individuals must alone bear the burden and heat of the day, and so it was with this cause of national purity. . . .

Writing to Mrs. Chapman in America, Mrs. Martineau proceeds:—

. . . Day by day information reaches me which satisfies me that this question of national purity plunges us into the most fearful moral crisis the country was ever in, involving our primary personal liberties, and the very existence, except in name, of the home and the family. It struck me (and I was so cowardly as almost to wish that it had not) that some "letters" in the "Daily News," explaining the state of the case, and the grounds (eight) of the protest of the women of England against the Acts, would do more to rouse the country to inquire and act, than any amount of agitation by individuals. It was sickening to think of such a work; but who should do it if not an old woman, dying and in seclusion, &c., &c. I felt that I should have no more peace of mind if I did not obey "the inward witness." So I did it last week,—wrote four letters signed "An Englishwoman,"[7] and sent them to Mr. Walker, who still manages the editing of the "Daily News" till the proprietors decide how to fill the office for which he alone seems fit. He was ill in bed when the packet arrived, and his wife read the letters to him. He says, "At first she was horrified, but she ended by demanding the instant publication of every word of them." One of the proprietors was dead against the insertion of any part of them; but Mr. Walker writes that he approves them so strongly that he cannot but print them, but that he doubts being able to support them by any "leader." Still I shall not be surprised if he manages it when the opposing proprietor has seen the letters themselves. I could not have *undertaken* in my sick condition to write them; and, though done under impulse, they cost a dreadful effort. Happily I thought of Godiva; and that helped me through. Two have appeared, and I dare say to-morrow will finish them. Then the "Times" and the "Saturday Review" and the "Pall Mall Gazette" and others will open out against them. I do dread having to reply to the lies of opponents; perhaps Mrs. Butler and her colleagues may relieve me of this, when they know it was I; but Mr. Walker says he will not enter into any general controversy while it is possible to avoid it. I *know* it was a right thing to do, and that it is the fault of the other side, if modesty

[8]I assume that the four letters Martineau refers to here at the end of the letter of December 30, 1869, are the three letters and the petition published in the *Daily News* on the last four days of 1869. Although only the first three are literally letters signed "An Englishwoman," the petition from the Ladies' National Association for the Repeal of the Contagious Diseases Acts was clearly written by Martineau.

in others and myself is outraged; yet it turns me chill in the night to think what things I have written and put in print. The —— ——s are here at Fox How, and I have had a long conversation with him about these Acts. He and —— are my two friends in the Ministry. This subject belongs to the department of one of them, but it is uncertain which. Both, I believe, certainly are on the right side. —— —— instructs me how to proceed in Parliament, and in preparation for it, and I had to write it all to Mrs. Butler yesterday, instead of writing to you. I will say no more now on the subject, of which I am compelled to think too much day and night. . . .

Ever your loving
H.M.

THE CONTAGIOUS DISEASES
ACTS I

SIR,—It is not forgotten throughout the country that when, a few years ago, certain newspapers exerted their influence on behalf of a Bill in Parliament which will hereafter be considered one of the most conspicuous disgraces of our time, your journal advocated the side of morality and of the most sacred of personal liberties. The occasion was grave, and the *Daily News* understood it, and tried to make it understood by the public, who have a vital interest in the subject.

The occasion is graver now, and I trust you will permit me to explain, in a brief but careful way, what the danger is in which we find our country and everybody in it involved, through the ignorance of most of my countrywomen, the ignorance and carelessness of whole classes of our countrymen, whose duty it is to know better, the apathy of legislators who have permitted the destruction of our most distinctive liberties

Daily News (London), December 28, 1869, p. 4.

before their eyes, and the gross prejudices and coarse habits of thought of professional men who have been treated as oracles on a subject on which they are proved mistaken at every turn.

After occasional alarms, once or twice in a generation, about the supposed increase and aggravation of the loathsome disease which is the natural retribution of sexual vice, the case was thought to be so serious, towards the close of the last reign, that measures were privately taken by the Government to ascertain the facts, in regard to the metropolis, with a view to legislation, of which the police system of France was to be the example. Two eminent physicians, if I remember right, were commissioned to investigate and report upon the health of London, as affected directly and indirectly by the disease. The Report ultimately rendered was appalling. After years of more recent observation and inquiry, qualified persons are satisfied that there was much exaggeration at the time, and that the virulence of that class of diseases has since been moderated, as, indeed, it had then declined considerably from what it was in former centuries. The Report was, however, accepted; and the word of a very small number of physicians was taken without hesitation in regard to the course to be pursued. In order to check the ravage we must have a system like the French—of police and official medical examination, a registration of prostitutes, a licensing of brothels—an importation, in short, into our country, supreme in its privilege of personal liberty, of a system and method which a little patient observation would have shown to be as injurious to the health as it is fatal to the morals of every community which lies under the curse of it. For that time we were saved by the death of the old King, it being considered impossible for any minister to bring the subject to the notice of a young unmarried Queen. For that time we escaped; but the peril has come upon us now, and if we would avert the evils actually awaiting us—the utter loss of the sacredness of person—the corruption of the rising generation of citizens who will find the way of vice made easy, and the dens of vice thrown open to them—and the aggravation of disease attended by factitious horrors which cannot be described—we must exert ourselves to learn the precise position in which we stand, and to face the difficulty and endure the pain of entertaining the subject, and to stir up the legislature—every member of it—to undo the fearful mischief wrought by its carelessness and ignorance during the closing hours of last session.

The whole scheme was not proposed at first. In 1866 an Act was passed to apply the method to certain naval and military stations. It was accepted amidst the general ignorance as a beneficent measure, which would check and ameliorate disease, and protect our soldiers and sailors from the worst consequences of their own license, and amend the health, and possibly the morals and behaviour of the unhappy women who were the first of our countrywomen to undergo the outrage and heart-break (as it truly is to many of them) of personal violation under sanction of law and the agency of the police. After three years of strenuous and perverse laudation of the Act as a public benefit and blessing, so that a sufficient number of clergy and the benevolent classes should be won to tolerate it, the second great step has been taken. At the end of the last session, when only a handful of wearied members remained, and most of them were ignorant of its character, and insensible to its significance, another Bill—a second "Contagious Diseases Act"—was passed, by which the operation of the first is extended to many towns which are in no sense garrison towns. The system is now, in fact, applied to the civil population; and next session is to bring forward the crowning measure—the extension of the power of the police and the outrage and degradation of the new law over the whole womanhood of England. In our time, or any other, there never, perhaps, was a graver question than whether there are still time and means to rouse the country to the due sense and knowledge of what is doing, that is to be apprehended, and what is the duty of individuals in the crisis.

The physicians and military officers who are familiar with the subject as a special branch of professional practice or experience in command are highly complacent about the docility shown by the clergy, and the gratitude of persons in all classes who suppose the measure to have a philanthropic character. It is lamentable—many are saying it is disgraceful—that the clergy should understand the case no better than most of them do. I do not know that their heartiest friends could help them better than by referring them to the protest by the Bishop of Victoria against the Act recently passed in the colony. In the early part of this year Bishop Alford used the occasion of his charge to impress upon his clergy that such legislation promotes vice, while suppressing neither vice nor disease. Let his clerical brethren read and ponder his charge (parts of which are reprinted by the Ladies' National Association for the Repeal of the Contagious Diseases Acts). Let them read the report of Mr. Simon, the medical officer of the Privy Council. Let them read the analysis of the Act by Mr. Markby, of Cambridge, also issued by the Ladies' Association. Let them consult any Constitutional lawyer on the bearings of the Act on the rights and privileges hitherto the inheritance of the men and women of England, and they will see on what a precipice they stand, while more or less countenancing these new provisions of law.

As for the legislators who are most immediately responsible for the passage of the Act—we hear them on every hand confessing that they know nothing of the matter—that they supposed it was one of the Cattle Bills—that they have no wishes, and, in fact, no ideas, on the subject—and that they merely followed the lead of the managers, who ought to know what is right. Some members were absent from illness through overwork; some were assured that no measure of importance remained to be considered. But there are some who have never forgiven themselves for their absence at the critical moment. All of these ought to study the question in the short time that remains, that they may be qualified to deal intelligently with the question of further extension, and to support the effort that will be made for the repeal of the Acts.

But what of this Association of Ladies? some may ask. How can women speak or act on such a subject as this, while society supposes that the very existence of prostitutes, and of the horrors of their trade, is unknown to educated and modest women. What society supposes of the ignorance of many of our countrywomen is but too true; but, under the pressure of their present danger, women are awaking, day by day, to a sense of the realities about them. When the mind is awake all the rest follows of course. In this association we see some of the most honoured of the matronage of England, and the names of some of the most distinguished for intelligence and culture. Some are there as mothers of sons for whom they desire no new facilities for the practice of vice. Some are there as loyal Englishwomen, aghast at their loss of the most sacred personal liberties, and at being subjected, in the tenderest point of honour, to the caprices of the police and the oppression of the law. Some are there as rescuers of the lost,—friends of the outcast, whom they would save from the outrage which breaks or hardens the heart. All these are able and ready to undergo the sacrifice they incur by their position. It is the way of Englishwomen to give themselves to a good work, not without counting, but without too much heeding, the cost. That representative Englishwoman, Godiva of blessed memory, could not but have counted the cost of her deed; and so, no doubt, it has been with her countrywomen of every age between her and us. So it assuredly is with these honourable women who are now putting away the most sensitive of personal feelings, to help us out of the peril we have incurred, and to destroy the risk for all future time. Their deed is of a quality kindred to Godiva's, while its scope is wider and its import infinitely deeper. She pitied starvation in poor men's homes. These are striving to save home itself, and to preserve the most sacred of institutions, and one hitherto pre-eminently our own—the Family.

If you will allow me, I will show, in another letter or two, the nature of the protests offered by this Association. If its members succeed in proving that these Acts are as weak in reason as they are offensive to feeling, they must surely attain their object.—I am, &c.

AN ENGLISHWOMAN

THE CONTAGIOUS DISEASES ACTS II

SIR,—It is natural that the first shock given by these Acts to the women of England, and indeed to every good citizen, should be in the fact that legal safeguards of vital importance to their security and freedom have been set aside, and liabilities of the most fearful kind have been introduced, without any adequate warrant, without due warning, and actually without the knowledge of the people, or of any class among them, and even without any consciousness on the part of Parliament itself. Up to the date of the passage of these Bills every woman in the country had the same rights as men over her own person; and the law extended its protection over all alike—of both sexes, and altogether without regard to any question of character, manners, and calling. Prostitutes were as other women, and as men, in their claims upon the law. Now it is no longer. Any woman of whom a policeman swears that he has reason to believe that she is a prostitute is helpless in the hands of the administrators of the new law. She is subject to the extremity of outrage under the eyes, hands, and instruments of surgeons, for the protection of the sex which is the cause of the sin, which is to be protected in further indulgence in it, and which is passed over by the law, while the victim is punished. If a tithe of the stories were told which might be truly told of innocent women who have confessed, under the torture of the new peril, sin which they never dreamed of, or of real sinners so unable to endure what is now imposed upon them as to faint or to go mad, the people of the country would be heartbroken. Meanwhile, the men who have contrived this curse for their country and nation are always ready with their assurances that that sort of women get used to the new treatment. It is sad work at first, but they get used to it, and in time they leave off caring for anything. No doubt it will be new to

Daily News (London), December 29, 1869, p. 4.

257

many readers that the chance of retrieval has lately been cut off in this way from that class of women wherever the new Acts operate; it will be new to them that the legal position of women has been deprived of its most essential security. But the incredible part of the case will be that this has been effected in the dark and in silence. The press has not fulfilled its function and its trust in regard to the more recent Act. In Parliament no warning voice was raised. The most sacred liberties of half the people of England are gone, without being missed; and now it is the women, for the most part, who have to insist on their restoration. No one can wonder that when my countrywomen become conscious of their loss, and find on every hand that most men know nothing about it, that many care nothing about it, and there are professional men who say that honest women ought to be thankful for the institution of a test of their innocence, under the chance of false accusation— no one can wonder if, in such a posture of affairs, the first protest of honourable women should be against privation of sacred rights, wrought under cover of that ignorance of the country, and that negligence of the press and of Parliament, which have imposed upon women the painful task of agitation for the recovery of what they have lost and the vindication of what remains.

Again, it is a new and menacing fact that, in a country where civil liberty is professed, and for the most part enjoyed, penal consequences are imposed on an assumed offence which is not defined. A woman, chaste or unchaste, is charged by a policeman, rightly or wrongly, with being a prostitute. The law makes no distinctions of degrees or kinds, provides the accused with no means of trial or defence, but subjects her to legal violation. If she refuses submission, she is liable to imprisonment with hard labour for terms lengthened according to her persistence in refusal. If she had sense and courage to ask for a precise legal definition of her imputed offence, she would not get it. The loose description which stands in the Act, and is the substance of the policeman's charge, is the ground on which she, and she alone, is subject to judgment and punishment—to moral torture if unresisting, to imprisonment with hard labour—for life if she holds by her personal rights. This is contrary to all precedent, and to the whole spirit and method of British penal law.

And why is this innovation ventured upon? For whose sake are such encroachments on personal liberties perpetrated? Here, again, we see why it is that the Matronage of England is moved to avowal and action which it would have supposed impossible till these new perils became manifest.

The mothers of sons do not desire that the ways of vice should be made easy and safe to men; and further, they do not desire that the victims of the vice of men should bear the whole penalty of their common license. The extension of the recent Act to the whole civil population would cover with the protection of the law the brothel, *as* brothel, as expressly as the school or the church. Prostitutes, observing the provisions of the Act, are pursuing their trade under the sanction of Parliament. Young men, entering the world, find this kind of vice recognized as necessary by Parliament, the police, the magistracy, and the law; and with this discovery a host of scruples and shames and difficulties vanish. What is felt by mothers who find law and Government enlisted on the side of animal passion and against the old institutions of Marriage and the Home, may be conceived. To such mothers it is almost worse that the sex most guilty in regard to the sin should be protected from the natural retribution by the sacrifice of the victimised sex. The law lays hold of the woman for the purpose of preventing her injuring the man. It nowhere proposes to protect the woman from precisely the same injury by the man. Many thousands of girls, as innocent as any of their countrymen, have been courted down in the rural districts by a soldier, idling away his days, or a commercial traveller, appearing periodically, or a lawyer going the circuit, or some other heartless vagabond. Each of these many thousands has probably believed herself the favourite of Fortune—destined to marry a great man in the great town—London or other. After an agonising decline and a heart-breaking struggle, she finds herself an outcast in the streets of the great town—doomed to a fearful fate, from the earliest days of the existence of her calling: but now—What is it now under this new legislation? The mothers of sons, sinning sons as well as pure, shrink from any sort of countenance of a law which, on the one hand, proposes to render vice safe from its worst penalty, and, on the other, compels the wronged and deluded victim of man's guile and selfishness and grossness to bear the penal consequences, while all is arranged for the escape of the stronger and grosser sinner. The Matronage of England protest, as some of them are showing at this moment, against the selfishness and cowardness of men—whether sons or strangers—being made a shield against the retribution they have risked, and against the powerful influence of men—in army or navy, Parliament, hospital, or Council board—being brought to bear upon ruined women in their weakness, to place them where they may intercept the visitations of disease, and be made to endure sufferings inconceivable or incredible by men, in order to enable men to indulge in license with the least risk of incurring any suffering at all. This is a part which the mothers of England do not desire that their sons should enact, and therefore they rouse their courage to denounce the law which so arranges the *role* of both sexes in regard to their common sin.

But, we are told, what is there not which Government and Parliament, and doctors and lawyers, and the ignorant and the wise, and the Matronage of England itself would not do, to arrest, and perhaps to annihilate, the disease which threatens to destroy every nation in which it rages unchecked? This is the one remaining consideration—the question which is assumed to swallow up all others. It must be left for another letter. It must be treated as its prominence demands; and no true enemy of the new legislation has any desire to evade it.— I am, &c.

AN ENGLISHWOMAN

THE CONTAGIOUS DISEASES
ACTS III

SIR,—These Acts have been proposed, prepared, and administered on the ground, which cannot be sustained, that regulation and medical examination of prostitutes, and the virtual license of prostitution, are effectual in checking the spread and ameliorating the virulence of the disease. The evidence of the failure of such measures to answer the purpose is too ample to be fully treated in a letter like this, even if it were possible to present it in a form which could be offered to general readers; but a few facts, each of which might be the heading of a clear and satisfactory explanation, may occasion at least a pause in the procedure of those who are working for an extension of the law to the civil population of the kingdom.

The conditions of military and naval establishments are so unlike those of civil life, that to argue from the one to the other is to assume what requires very stringent proof. Bodies of men, for the most part unmarried, deprived of home, with large portions of their time unemployed professionally, and whose life is yet passed under external regulation which leaves no scope for personal interest and chosen pursuits, can never be any rule for men of other callings, whose life is their own, and whose tastes are free and natural. It is a striking comment on this difference that soldiers and sailors are assumed to be necessarily vicious in their propensities if they remain unmarried up to the age of thirty, while no such supposition exists in regard to men of other callings. Of working men generally it is not concluded that they cannot wait till they can marry with prudence, which is usually some years after their youth is passed. As a matter of fact, it is found that of the men in barrack and camp the idle are the most vicious, and the men of any degree of culture or of ingenuity and industry in useful pursuits are those who give the least trouble to the police and

—

Daily News (London), December 30, 1869, p. 4.

the doctors. Yet even in this peculiar case there is abundant and trustworthy evidence that the supervision and supposed protection of the laws relating to prostitution are ineffectual wherever tried for any length of time. No judgment can be formed from the reported working of the Act of 1866 in the military centres where it has been in operation. The men, as well as the women, have been under inspection; the women have gone elsewhere, or have been got rid of by the police, so that those who remained have been regarded as warranted harmless by the authorities. Moreover, the reporters are, to a man, committed to the advocacy of the system. The true test, if we resort to the military case at all, is the state of affairs which exists where the system has been at work for a course of years. There are establishments abroad where it has been found that only time was needed to breed such corruption, such a group of horrors, as have never been heard of at home. Evasion is found possible wherever it is desired. A provision of prostitutes has been made in places and under conditions which the law does not reach—as where the servants of re-freshment houses are always on hire, under the disguise of dear drink, payment for amusements, &c.; and the landlord's house is a brothel, unsuspected or impenetrable. It is but too true that there are instances on record of medical officers and the police being actually in the pay of the prostitutes, these wretched women being held at the mercy of the extortioners by threats of being informed against, or even by being sum-moned to judgment at moments when they could not deny their offences. Under such a system, the results upon the health of the soldiers could not be long in showing themselves, and the ravages of the disease have been greater than ever be-fore, and much worse than in places in a similar climate where no plan of supervision has ever been tried. A faithful study of the reports to the War-office, an honest inquiry into the evi-dence requisite to a real opinion on the subject, will be found to leave no doubt that, after a trial of the inspection system for a course of years—say eight or more—the proportion of sol-diers and sailors admitted to hospital under this disease is larger—in some cases very much larger—than at stations un-der the same conditions in other respects in which no such regulation has been attempted. Some statistical returns now before me show that in some foreign stations where rigid supervision and regulation have existed for a course of years, the proportion to strength (the number of cases under the disease) of admissions to hospital per thousand, is to "unprotected" stations, as twelve to nine.

If such is the working of the system in the military or naval case, what must it be when applied to the civil population! Any one who chooses to learn may look at the condition of society in France, Belgium, or wherever the Government undertakes to regulate the practice of sexual vice. We have the testimony of physicians in Paris who know more about the matter than anybody else that the system is a failure in regard to its main object, while there are other means of information by which it is fully understood, in their country and ours, that its results are in various ways thoroughly appalling. The condition of the streets at night in Paris and other foreign capitals is better than that of London as it is, though not better than that of London might be, and ought to be. But, under the veil of decency, there is a condition of health and morals which we have no reason to envy and which we should strain every nerve to avoid. The population of Paris is, we are told, less than two-thirds that of London; yet the estimate of the number of prostitutes mounts up to more than threefold. And not only does the supervision fail to diminish the proportion of offenders,—it fails also to mitigate the ravage of disease. Further, it directly and indirectly aggravates the ravage.

Men resort to the licensed houses and registered women, free from the dread which certainly deters many an Englishman under temptation. French citizens believe themselves guaranteed by the State against the perils of their indulgence. They find this a delusion, as their own special physicians inform us. They tell us that some of the most mischievous forms of that class of diseases escape observation, even when watched for, while some, comparatively harmless, engross the attention. They tell us that any effectual supervision would require an expenditure of money, time, sacrifice of every kind on the part of the community, utterly impracticable. Meantime, under the false confidence generated by the system, the sin spreads, sinners multiply, more women are heartbroken or hardened, and fewer can be reclaimed, while the diseases against which the whole machinery of law and police is directed, are more encouraged than checked. There is more, and worse, behind. While the many resort to the avowed homes of license, not a few—it is feared very many—shrinking from the conditions, tempt tradespeople, apparently above suspicion, to harbour them and their victims, or to find them victims, in children on their way to or from school, or other innocents who disappear as if through a trapdoor in the streets, or who are sold by vile parents, who take care that no notice shall reach the police. It is known to all whose business it is to inquire that wherever there is a regulation system to be evaded or defied, diseases fearful and monstrous, poison the lives of a large proportion of the middle and upper classes, and that the national vitality of France in particular is dwindling and sinking under a system of license of vice which breaks all its promises, and destroys the health and vigour which it engages to save.

Meanwhile, we seem to understand our own state no better than that of France. We are assured by some of the most experienced and enlightened physicians in the country, and by several members of our College of Surgeons, that the disease is continually assuming a milder character, as the science and art of their profession extend and improve, and that the estimates of its spread, proposed by special practitioners, and propagated by ignorant alarmists, are enormous exaggerations. It is the business of good citizens to examine into the truth of the opposing statements, in order to fulfil a duty incumbent upon us all in any case.

The misery, the danger, the sin, are fearful at best. What can be done to counteract, to avert, to prevent the risk, the woe, the offence—short of incurring greater risks, and even graver sin? We cannot, will not, must not, surrender any of the personal liberty which is our birthright; and we may be sure that that could be no true remedy for our grief which should demand such a sacrifice from us at the outset. There are resources within our reach; there are grounds of hope, if we will but take a firm stand upon them; there are means of prevention, if we will but apply them wisely and zealously, and without delay. What these are I may endeavour to point out in one more letter. There is the more reason for hopefulness in the endeavour that an association now exists to which my countrywomen may resort for companionship in effort, for information and guidance, and for strengthening in the determination to stand by the personal liberties of every one of us, as we would sustain the honour and the life of our country and people.

AN ENGLISHWOMAN

THE LADIES' NATIONAL ASSOCIATION FOR THE REPEAL OF THE CONTAGIOUS DISEASES ACTS

There are two Acts of Parliament—one passed in 1866, the other in 1869—called the Contagious Diseases Acts. These Acts are in force in some of our garrison towns, and in large districts around them. Unlike all other laws for the repression of contagious diseases, to which both men and women are liable, these two apply to women only, men being wholly exempt from their penalties. The law is ostensibly framed for a certain class of women, but in order to reach these, all the women residing within the districts where it is in force are brought under the provisions of the Acts. Any woman can be dragged into court, and required to prove that she is not a common prostitute. The magistrate can condemn her, if a policeman swears only that he "has good cause to believe" her to be one. The accused has to rebut, not positive evidence, but the state of mind of her accuser. When condemned, the sentence is as follows:—To have her person outraged by the periodical inspection of a surgeon, through a period of twelve months; or, resisting that, to be imprisoned, with or without hard labour—first for a month, next for three months—such imprisonment to be continuously renewed through her whole life unless she submit periodically to the brutal requirements of this law. Women arrested under false accusations have been so terrified at the idea of encountering the public trial neces-

---

Daily News (London), December 31, 1869, p. 5.

sary to prove their innocence, that they have, under the intimidation of the police, signed away their good name and their liberty by making what is called a "voluntary submission" to appear periodically for twelve months for surgical examination. Women who, through dread of imprisonment, have been induced to register themselves as common prostitutes, now pursue their traffic under the sanction of Parliament; and the houses where they congregate, so long as the government surgeons are satisfied with the health of their inmates, enjoy, practically, as complete a protection as a church or a school.

We, the undersigned, enter our solemn protest against these Acts—

1. Because, involving as they do such a momentous change in the legal safeguards hitherto enjoyed by women in common with men, they have been passed, not only without the knowledge of the country, but unknown to Parliament itself; and we hold that neither the representatives of the people nor the press fulfil the duties which are expected of them, when they allow such legislation to take place without the fullest discussion.

2. Because, so far as women are concerned, they remove every guarantee of personal security which the law has established and held sacred, and put their reputation, their freedom, and their persons absolutely in the power of the police.

3. Because the law is bound, in any country professing to give civil liberty to its subjects, to define clearly an offence which it punishes.

4. Because it is unjust to punish the sex who are the victims of a vice, and leave unpunished the sex who are the main cause, both of the vice and its dreaded consequences; and we consider that the liability to arrest, forced surgical examination, and where this is resisted, imprisonment with hard labour, to which these Acts subject women, are punishments of the most degrading kind.

5. Because, by such a system, the path of evil is made more easy to our sons, and to the whole of the youth of England; inasmuch as a moral restraint is withdrawn the moment the State recognises and provides convenience for the practice of a vice which it thereby declares to be necessary and venial.

6. Because these measures are cruel to the women who come under their action—violating the feelings of those whose sense of shame is not wholly lost, and further brutalising even the most abandoned.

7. Because the disease which these Acts seek to remove has never been removed by any such legislation. The advocates of the system have utterly failed to show, by statistics or otherwise, that these regulations have in any case, after several years' trial, and when applied to one sex only, diminished disease, reclaimed the fallen, or improved the general morality of the country. We have, on the contrary, the strongest evidence to show that in Paris and other continental cities, where women have long been outraged by this forced inspection, the public health and morals are worse than at home.

8. Because the conditions of this disease, in the first instance, are moral, not physical. The moral evil through which the disease make its way separates the case entirely from that of the plague or other scourges, which have been placed under police control or sanitary care. We hold that we are bound, before rushing into the experiment of legalising a revolting vice, to try to deal with the causes of the evil, and we dare to believe that with wiser teaching and more capable legislation those causes would not be beyond control.

HARRIET MARTINEAU
JOSEPHINE E. BUTLER
FLORENCE NIGHTINGALE
ELIZABETH C. WOLSTENHOLME
[followed by 124 other women's signatures]

BIBLIOGRAPHY

Those of Harriet Martineau's writings published as separate volumes are readily identifiable, but locating unsigned newspaper and periodical articles takes some detective work. The most helpful clues are in her *Autobiography*, and her biographers (a list of their works follows) have added to the identification of pieces she wrote. A large boost to scholars was given by R. K. Webb when he commissioned a record of the clippings of Martineau's London *Daily News* editorials from a near-complete collection then in the possession of Sir Wilfred Martineau, and made the handlist available to researchers. The *Wellesley Index* is helpful in identifying articles in the British journals it covers.

There is no single library repository of a large amount of Martineau manuscript material and letters, one reason being her request in 1843 to her correspondents that her letters be destroyed. Collections meriting the attention of the Martineau scholar can be found in the Boston Public Library, the British Museum Library, the University of Birmingham Library, and Manchester College, Oxford. The Manchester College collection includes a transcription of the shorthand copy Martineau's brother James made of her letters to him before honoring her request in 1843 to return her letters. Scholars are also indebted to R. K. Webb for that transcription. The single published bibliography of Martineau's works, Joseph B. Rivlin's *Harriet Martineau: A Bibliography* (New York: New York Public Library, 1947), covers only books.

I list below selected sources that have been useful in the making of this book, as well as ones that are by and about Martineau.

SELECTED WORKS BY HARRIET MARTINEAU

Autobiography. With Memorials by Maria Weston Chapman. 3 vols. London: Smith, Elder, and Co., 1877. Simultaneous publication in 2 vols. Boston: Houghton, Osgood and Co., 1877. Reprint (2 vols.). Farnborough: Gregg International, 1969, 1972. Reprint without Memorials (2 vols.). London: Virago Press, 1983.

Biographical Sketches. London: Macmillan & Co., 1869.

British Rule in India; A Historical Sketch. London: Smith, Elder & Co., 1857.

"Chicago in 1836. 'Strange Early Days,' by Harriet Martineau." In *The Present and Future Prospects of Chicago*, edited by H. Brown, pp. 33–48. Chicago: Fergus Printing Co., 1876.

Deerbrook. A Novel. 3 vols. London: E. Moxon, 1839. Reprint (3 vols. in one). London: Virago Press, 1983.

A Description of the English Lakes. Windemere: John Garnett, 1858. Reprint. Wakefield: E.P. Publishing, 1974.

Eastern Life, Present and Past. Philadelphia: Lea and Blanchard, 1848.

Endowed Schools of Ireland. London: Smith, Elder & Co., 1859.

The Factory Controversy: A Warning against Meddling Legislation. Issued by the National Association of Factory Occupiers. Manchester: A. Ireland and Co., Pall Mall, 1855. (Pamphlet.)

"Female Writers of Practical Divinity." *Monthly Repository* 17 (October 1822): 593–596.

Forest and Game-Law Tales. 3 vols. London: E. Moxon, 1845–1846.

The Guide to Service. London: Charles Knight, 1839.

Harriet Martineau's Letters to Fanny Wedgwood, edited by Elizabeth Sanders Arbuckle. Stanford: Stanford University Press, 1983.

Health, Husbandry and Handicraft. London: Bradbury and Evans, 1861.

A History of the American Compromises. London: Chapman, 1856.

A History of England during the Thirty Years' Peace: 1816–1846. 2 vols. London: Charles Knight, 1849–1850.

The Hour and the Man: A Historical Romance. 3 vols. London: E. Moxon, 1841.

Household Education. London: E. Moxon, 1848.

How to Observe Morals and Manners. London: Charles Knight, 1838.

Illustrations of Political Economy. 9 vols. London: Charles Fox, 1832–1833.

Illustrations of Taxation. 5 vols. London: Charles Fox, 1834.

Introduction to the History of the Peace: From 1800–1815. London: Charles Knight, 1851.

Letter to the editor. *Mind amongst the Spindles: A Selection from the Lowell Offering*, edited by C. Knight. London: Charles Knight, 1844.

Letters from Ireland. London: John Chapman, 1852.

Letters on the Laws of Man's Nature and Development. With Henry George Atkinson. Boston: Josiah P. Mandum, 1851.

Letters on Mesmerism. 2d ed. London: E. Moxon, 1845.

"Life in the Criminal Class." *Edinburgh Review* 122 (October 1865): 337–371.

Life in the Sick-Room. London: E. Moxon, 1844.

The "Manifest Destiny" of the American Union. New York: American Anti-Slavery Society, 1857.

"The Martyr Age of the United States." *London and Westminster Review* 32 (1839): pp. 1–59. Reprint in book form. Boston: Weeks, Jordan and Co., 1839. Reprint. New York: Arno Press, 1969.

Miscellanies. 2 vols. Boston: Hilliard, Gray & Co., 1836.

Norway and the Norwegians; or, Feats on the Fjord. A Tale. New York, 1842. Reprint. London: J.M. Dent and Sons; New York: E.P. Dutton and Co., 1915.

Our Farm of Two Acres. New York: Bunce and Huntington, 1865.

The Peasant and the Prince. London: George Routledge, n.d. Reprint. Boston and New York: Ginn and Co., 1917.

Poor Laws and Paupers. 4 vols. London: Charles Fox, 1833–1834.

The Positive Philosophy of Auguste Comte. Freely translated and condensed by Harriet Martineau. 2 vols. New York and London, 1853. Reprint. New York: AMS Press, 1974.

Retrospect of Western Travel. 3 vols. London: Saunders & Otley, 1838.

Society in America. 3 vols. London: Saunders & Otley, 1837. Reprint. New York: AMS Press, 1966. Reprint edited and abridged with introduction by Seymour Martin Lipset. Garden City, N.Y.: Doubleday, 1962. Reprint (Lipset ed.). Gloucester: Peter Smith, 1968.

Traditions of Palestine. 1830. 2d ed. London: Charles Fox, 1843.

SELECTED WORKS ABOUT HARRIET MARTINEAU

Bosanquet, Theodora. *Harriet Martineau: An Essay in Comprehension.* London: Frederick Etchells and Hugh Macdonald, 1927.

Calkins, Earnest Elmo. "Harriet Martineau: Deaf Blue-Stocking." *Colophon* 14 (May 1933): unpaginated.

Colson, Percy. "Virtue Is Its Own Reward [Harriet Martineau]." In *Victorian Portraits*, pp. 173–223. London: Rich and Cowan, 1932.

Courtney, Mrs. Janet E. (Hogarth). *Free Thinkers of the 19th Century (Seven Portraits).* London: Chapman & Hall, 1920.

Fay, C. R. Review of R. K. Webb, *Harriet Martineau: A Radical Victorian. Victorian Studies* 4 (1960): 74–75.

Greenhow, Thomas M. "Termination of the Case of Miss Harriet Martineau." *British Medical Journal* (April 14, 1877): 449–450.

[Hammelmann, H. A.] "Charlotte Brontë and Harriet Martineau." *Times Literary Supplement*, June 9, 1950, p. 364.

"Harriet Martineau." *Times Literary Supplement*, October 4, 1957.

Meyers, Mitzi. "*Harriet Martineau's Autobiography*: The Making of a Female Philosopher." In *Women's Autobiography*, edited by Estelle C. Jelinek, pp. 53–70. Bloomington and London: Indiana University Press, 1980.

Miller, Mrs. F. Fenwick. *Harriet Martineau*. 1884. Reprint. London and Port Washington, N.Y.: Kennikat Press, 1972.

Nevill, John Cranstoun. *Harriet Martineau*. London: Frederick Muller, 1943.

Pichanick, Valerie Kossew. *Harriet Martineau: The Woman and Her Work, 1802–76*. Ann Arbor: University of Michigan Press, 1980.

Pope-Hennessy, Una. *Three English Women in America*. London: Ernest Benn, 1929.

Rivenburg, Narola Elizabeth. *Harriet Martineau, An Example of Victorian Conflict*. Privately published Ph.D. dissertation, Columbia University, 1932.

Rossi, Alice S., ed. "The First Woman Sociologist: Harriet Martineau (1802–1876)." In *The Feminist Papers*, pp. 118–143. New York: Columbia University Press, 1973.

Seat, William R., Jr. "Harriet Martineau in America." *Notes and Queries* 204 (June 1959): 207–208.

S[tephen], L[eslie.] "Martineau, Harriet." *Dictionary of National Biography*.

Walford, L. B. *Twelve English Authoresses*. London: Longmans, Green and Co., 1892.

Webb, R. K. *Harriet Martineau: A Radical Victorian*. New York: Columbia University Press, 1960.

Wheatley, Vera. *The Life and Work of Harriet Martineau*. London: Secker and Warburg, 1957.

SELECTED BACKGROUND WORKS

Banks, J. A. and Olive Banks. *Feminism and Family Planning in Victorian England*. Liverpool: Liverpool University Press, 1964.

Cawelti, J. G. "Conformity and Democracy in America: Some Reflections Occasioned by the Republication of Martineau's *Society in America*." *Ethics* 73 (1963): 208–213.

Cazamian, Louis. *The Social Novel in England 1830–1850*. Translated from the French, with a foreword by Martin Fido. London: Routledge and Kegan Paul, 1973.

Courtney, Janet E. *The Adventurous Thirties: A Chapter in the Women's Movement*. London: Oxford University Press, Humphrey Milford, 1933.

DuBois, Ellen Carol. *Feminism and Suffrage*. Ithaca and London: Cornell University Press, 1978.

Fielding, K. J. and Anne Smith. "*Hard Times* and the Factory Controversy: Dickens vs. Harriet Martineau." *Nineteenth Century Fiction* 24 (1970). 404–427.

Flexner, Eleanor. *Century of Struggle*. Rev. ed. Cambridge, Mass. and London: Harvard University Press, 1975.

Gerin, Winifred. *Charlotte Brontë, The Evolution of Genius*. Oxford: Clarendon Press, 1967.

Hacker, Eugene A. *A Short History of Women's Rights*. New York and London: G. P. Putnam's Sons, 1911.

Holcombe, Lee. *Victorian Ladies at Work*. Newton Abbot, Devon: David and Charles, 1973.

Leach, William Riley. *True Love and Perfect Union*. New York: Basic Books, 1980.

Mill, John Stuart and Harriet Taylor Mill. *Essays on Sex Equality*. Edited and with an introductory essay by Alice S. Rossi. Chicago: University of Chicago Press, 1970. (Individual essays first published in 1832, 1851, and 1869.)

Miller, Perry, ed. *Margaret Fuller: American Romantic*. 1963. Gloucester, Mass.: Peter Smith, 1969.

Moers, Ellen. *Literary Women*. Garden City, N.Y.: Anchor Press/ Doubleday, 1977.

O'Neill, William. *The Woman Movement: Feminism in the United States and England*. London: George Allen and Unwin, 1969.

Petrie, Glen. *A Singular Iniquity: The Campaigns of Josephine Butler*. New York: Viking Press, 1971.

Rover, Constance. *Love, Morals and the Feminists*. London: Routledge and Kegan Paul, 1970.

Rubenius, Aina. *The Woman Question in Mrs. Gaskell's Life and Works*. Essays and Studies on English Language and Literature of the English Institute in the University of Upsala. Edited by S. G. Liljegren. Upsala: A.-B. Lundequistska Bokhandeln, 1950.

Stenton, Doris Mary. *The English Woman in History*. London: George Allen and Unwin, 1957.

Taylor, Clare. *British and American Abolitionists: An Episode in Trans-Atlantic Understanding*. Edinburgh: Edinburgh University Press, 1974.

Tocqueville, Alexis de. *Democracy in America*. 1835, 1840. Edited and abridged by Richard D. Heffner. New York: New American Library, 1956.

Tyler, Alice Felt. *Freedom's Ferment*. Minneapolis: University of Minnesota Press, 1944.

Vicinus, Martha, ed. *Suffer, and Be Still*. Bloomington: University of Indiana Press, 1972.

———, ed. "The Victorian Woman: A Special Issue." *Victorian Studies* 14 (September 1970).

Walkowitz, Judith R. "The Politics of Prostitution." *Signs* 6 (August 1980): 123–135.

———, *Prostitution and Victorian Society*. Cambridge: Cambridge University Press, 1980.

Walters, Ronald G. *The Antislavery Appeal: American Abolitionism after 1830*. Baltimore and London: Johns Hopkins University Press, 1976.

Woodham-Smith, Cecil. *Florence Nightingale, 1820–1910*. London: Constable and Co., 1950.

INDEX